Manhood Acts

Manhood Acts

Gender and the Practices of Domination

Michael Schwalbe

Paradigm Publishers
Boulder • London

Copyright © 2014 Paradigm Publishers

Published in the United States by Paradigm Publishers, 5589 Arapahoe Avenue, Boulder, CO 80303 USA.

Paradigm Publishers is the trade name of Birkenkamp & Company, LLC, Dean Birkenkamp, President and Publisher.

Library of Congress Cataloging-in-Publication Data

Schwalbe, Michael, 1956–
  Manhood acts : gender and the practices of domination / Michael Schwalbe.
      pages cm
  Includes bibliographical references and index.
  ISBN 978-1-61205-547-3 (pbk. : alk. paper)
  ISBN 978-1-61205-563-3 (consumer e-book)
  1. Sex role. 2. Male domination (Social structure) 3. Masculinity. I. Title.
  HQ1075.S377 2014
  155.3'32—dc23
                                                                    2013030690

Printed and bound in the United States of America on acid-free paper that meets the standards of the American National Standard for Permanence of Paper for Printed Library Materials.

Designed and Typeset by Straight Creek Bookmakers.

18 17 16 15 14   1 2 3 4 5

Contents

Chapter 1

Gender Theory after Auschwitz

I am haunted by Theodor Adorno's essay "Education after Auschwitz."[1] Adorno (1903–1969) was one of the major figures associated with the Frankfurt School of critical theory. The essay, first published in 1967, is both a cri de coeur and a somber exhortation. "The premier demand upon all education," Adorno begins, "is that Auschwitz not happen again.... Every debate about the ideals of education is trivial and inconsequential compared to this single ideal: never again Auschwitz." What education must do, Adorno argues, is to disrupt the conditions that enable holocausts to occur. Adorno feared that such conditions were still in place in the 1960s. I fear they are still in place today.

Adorno points to conditions that are both internal and external to individuals. One of the external conditions is aggressive nationalism. Another is a "netlike environment" of hierarchical administrative control—much like Max Weber's iron cage, albeit with real jailers at the ready. Cultural values that encourage the worship of action and efficiency, blind identification with the collective, and trust in authority are also enabling conditions. Adorno's main concern, however, is with what education must do to ensure that individuals cannot be mobilized to perpetrate mass horrors. What it must do, he says, is to reveal the social mechanisms that render people capable of horrific deeds. Education must also nurture capacities for critical self-reflection.

The goal of education, in Adorno's view, should be to create people who are sociologically mindful, self-reflective, and morally autonomous. Sociological mindfulness is an antidote to what Adorno calls reified consciousness—a consciousness "blinded to all historical past, all insight into one's own conditionedness, and posits as absolute what exists contingently." Sociological

1

mindfulness makes it possible to see that the social arrangements to which allegiance is demanded are neither divinely ordained nor immutable, but rather human creations reflecting the interests of the powerful.[2] Critical self-reflection is necessary to recognize and resist one's socially ingrained tendencies to obey, to identify with the collective, and to emotionally detach from the Other. The result, ideally, is an individual capable of making independent moral judgments and thus not being a willing or unwitting participant in the schemes of "desktop murderers."

In Adorno's essay, "Auschwitz" is a stand-in for the entire Nazi program of exterminating Jews, Romani ("Gypsies"), gays and lesbians, and communists. The scale, intentionality, and bureaucratic efficiency of this multifaceted genocide mark it as historically unique. Not so its enabling conditions. To see these conditions and counter the threat they pose, we must overcome investments in not seeing what is closest to us.

Although he does not speak of gender in the manner of contemporary sociologists, Adorno references it in several ways. He speaks of the "cult of action" that attracts those who desire to *do something*, to make things happen, and who vaunt "efficiency" even when it leads to irrational or inhumane results. He speaks of the "ideal of hardness" that encourages indifference to the pain of others. He speaks of virility construed as the ability to endure pain. He speaks of denigration heaped on the weak. He speaks of initiation rites that inflict pain as a condition of acceptance into the collective. Adorno has in mind the Nazi cult of masculinity.[3] But his description of the character that makes holocausts possible—hungry for action, eager to get the job done, tough, patriotic—fits the contemporary ideal of American manhood.

Adorno's essay haunts because it reminds me that the conditions that made Auschwitz and other Nazi crimes against humanity possible are not behind us. Aggressive US nationalism? Yes, see Afghanistan and Iraq. Hierarchical administrative control? Yes, in the workplace and, as the surveillance state has expanded post-9/11, ever more so in public life as well. Vaunting of action and efficiency, even if destructive in the long run? Yes, that's what market fundamentalism and privatization amount to. Indifference to the suffering of others? Yes, as evident in rationing health care on the basis of what is profitable to sell to whom. Indifference to the suffering of others is also evident in the use of bombs and drones that inevitably kill innocent civilians. Admirable manliness defined by power, toughness, and a capacity for violence? Yes, today still, as in Homer's day.

"All political instruction," Adorno concludes, "finally should be centered upon the idea that Auschwitz should never happen again. This would be possible only when it devotes itself openly, without fear of offending any authorities, to this most important of problems. To do this education must transform itself into sociology, that is, it must teach about the societal play of forces that operates beneath the surface of political forms." The requisite instruction, it seems to me, is that which equips us and compels us to critically examine the taken-for-granted systems of inequality that shape us as persons and within which we live our every-day lives.[4] Adorno believed, as do I, that the insights thereby possible can disrupt the processes that create humans with dangerous inclinations to dominate and to obey. What most needs to be disrupted, as Adorno implies but seems reluctant to say, is the making of particular kinds of men. To prevent another Auschwitz, what is thus necessary is a critical sociology of gender.

There is no shortage of sociologies of gender, as even a cursory perusal of textbook offerings and journals will make clear. More theorizing and research about gender goes on today than in Adorno's day; it has become a mainstream academic enterprise. But this mainstreaming has come at the cost of domestica-tion. It has entailed a loss, or sidelining, of the most critical perspectives—those that deconstruct gender at its roots, that treat gender itself as a system of inequal-ity, and that give central place to the exploitation and oppression of females and women by males and men. So while we have plenty of sociological studies of gender-related phenomena, we are not looking at gender in the ways necessary to satisfy Adorno's imperative. Until we do, as I argue in this book, we will remain poised to repeat the worst of human history, in between times of routine exploi-tation and smaller-scale violence. If there is a way out, finding it will require, as per Adorno's admonition, offending all manner of authorities.

*   *   *

All critical social theory is sociological in the sense of taking culture, social organi-zation, group interests, and interaction into account. Critical social theory is also particularly attentive to power and inequality, and to how power and inequality shape consciousness.[5] All *sociological* theory, however, is not critical social theory. Both aim to make sense of the social world, but conventional sociological theory embraces the positivist project of reducing the social world to "variables" and trying to explain patterns of covariation among those variables. The goal of this kind of theorizing, when it is intended for practical application, is knowledge that policy makers and managers can use to more effectively control others.[6] Conventional sociological theory thus seeks to emulate natural science theories that have yielded more control over the physical world. The aims of critical theory are different.

As noted, critical theory shares with mainstream sociological theory the purpose of making sense of the social world and how it works. I would add that both are concerned, or should be, with offering accounts and interpretations that are consistent with observation and experience. As hard as it can be to know what the facts are in some cases, theory must respect the best facts we have at the moment. If not—if theory is unmoored from observation and experience—it has little to make sense of. There must be, at some point, empirical referents for the sense-making work that we call "theorizing," or else this work will gain no traction in the real world. But to return to the purposes of critical theory: the point is not to generate knowledge for the sake of gaining more control over the social world in the way that science has given us more control over the physical world. The point, rather, is to gain insight into ourselves and the workings of society, such that we can more effectively pursue liberatory social change.[7]

To those steeped in the self-interested *Realpolitik* that has come to hold sway in the post-Reagan era, the phrase "liberatory social change" might seem like a woolly cliché from the 1960s or '70s. With a bit more historical perspective, however, the phrase can be understood to reference a project rooted in ancient Greek philosophy, Enlightenment rationalism, Marxist criticism of capitalism, and modern secular liberalism. The common thread is the expansion of human freedom and self-determination through rational thought and dialogue. This entails the questioning of superstition and tradition and overcoming ignorance imposed by those with greater social power. Critical theorizing is simply the disciplined intellectual effort to dissolve the bonds of superstition, tradition, and ignorance that hold exploitive social hierarchies in place.

I want to be more specific about the aims of critical theory, because these aims guide my efforts and will, I hope, serve as guides to others with similar interests. These aims also inform my critiques of mainstream sociological theorizing about gender. Much of that theorizing, in particular that which has to do with men and masculinity, is, when judged by the aims of critical theory, more a part of the problem than a part of the solution (see Chapter 2). Others might reject my critiques on the grounds that they do not share the liberatory aims of critical theory as I lay them out. Fair enough, provided that one puts one's own cards on the table.

One aim of critical theory is to give people analytic distance on their socialization. The Socratic injunction "know thyself" is given a sociological twist by critical theory. The point is not only to know oneself, but to know how that self came to be what it is—as a result of culture, social relationships, and multiple social locations. To sociologize oneself in this way is to try to see how one's values, attitudes, beliefs, identities, feelings, and desires are rooted in patterns of social experience. It is to try to fathom how one's individuality has been shaped by a particular social environment. The aim, more specifically, is to help us see how what we have become as individuals is a consequence of the power relations and inequalities in which we have been caught up since birth.

Sociological self-reflection, as fostered by critical theory, is undertaken for the sake of seeing how we are trapped by ideologies and practices that sustain domination and subordination. An example from American culture is what has been called the "achievement ideology."[8] This is the belief that everyone, regardless of class or social category, has an equal chance to get ahead; that all it takes is talent, hard work, and a willingness to play by the rules; and that anyone who displays these qualities will be fairly rewarded. The achievement ideology legitimates inequality by implying that the rich deserve to be rich, having won a fair contest. It also implies that the poor have only themselves to blame. This is an ideology that is congenial to those who benefit from current economic arrangements and would like to see these arrangements preserved. As a counter to the achievement ideology, sociological self-reflection might begin by asking, *How have I come to believe what is demonstrably false? How does the achievement ideology lead me to accept subordination or celebrate the powerful?* and *What does the achievement ideology lead me to do that helps to reproduce inequality?*

Another example of self-misunderstanding is the belief that we are in essence racial beings. This is the belief that one is biologically white, black, Latino/a, Asian, or whatever. As scientists have recognized for fifty years, these categories and labels are cultural, not biological.[9] They were invented, once upon a time, to construct some people as targets for exploitation, to impede solidarity among the exploited, and to legitimate the dominance of other groups. Racial ideologies still yield these results, and thus still help to preserve inequality. Sociological self-reflection can loosen the grip that fictions like "race" have on our beliefs about who and what we are. In this case, the questions might be, *How did I come to think of myself as raced? What does this mean about the kind of person I am and about who others are?* and *What consequences follow when people define themselves as belonging to racial groups?* A body of work that goes by the name of critical race theory provides resources for pursuing answers to these and other questions.[10]

It is a matter to which I will return later, but I want to note here what I consider a parallel self-misunderstanding when it comes to gender. The misunderstanding, as with race, is that we are biologically men or women. We are indeed biologically *male* or *female*, just as we carry genes that produce the phenotypical differences (e.g., skin color, hair texture, epicanthic folds, etc.) associated with race. But just as critical race theory deconstructs race and racial identities, helping us to see these things as divisive fictions, so, too, can critical gender theory help us to see how the belief that humans are fundamentally women or men is a fiction that upholds an exploitive social hierarchy. Given the deep investment most people have in their gender identities, I expect that critical gender theory will face a stronger ideological headwind than critical race theory. More about this later.

Self-reflection along the lines suggested above does not ensure that good answers will be found. Arriving at good answers depends on the conceptual framework employed and the facility with which it is used. The Frankfurt theorists used Marx and Freud. I, too, find Marx useful but prefer the American Pragmatist philosophers, second-wave radical feminists, and modern social psychologists to Freud.[11] But these are just possibilities; ideas useful for critical self-reflection can be found in many places. My concern here, however, is not with specific theories or lines of analysis. My concern is with the aims of critical theorizing. Self-reflection that can help us see how we are implicated and invested in systems of inequality is one such aim.

Another aim is to reveal the hidden workings of power. By "hidden workings" I don't mean the backstage machinations of political and economic elites. Such things should of course be revealed, but journalism and ethnography can do the job. What critical theory aims to reveal is how dominant cultural beliefs and practices—those that are hegemonic in the sense of being taken for granted as true and proper, those that are right in front of our noses—both reflect and reinforce inequality. The propagation of the achievement ideology and belief in competitive individualism is one example. Critical theory puts these propaganda efforts into relief by showing how they are built into the otherwise unremarkable socialization processes that occur in families, schools, sports activities, and workplaces, and via popular media.

Workings that are hidden in plain view can also include the exclusion of dissident values and voices from the mainstream. Serious critiques of capitalism and equally serious considerations of economic democracy are generally not found in basic school curricula in the United States. Nor are they found in mainstream media—news, films, television, literary fiction, and art. Such exclusions matter; people cannot consider critiques and alternatives to which they have never been exposed. Some critical theories—Marxism, for example—offer critiques and alternatives, but it is no less important to inspire dissident thought by posing questions: *What is the range of acceptable opinion here? What lies outside that range? What is being assumed about human nature or about how humans should organize themselves?* and (again) *Who benefits, how, if these definitions of reality are embraced and acted upon?* It is an aim of critical theorizing to foster these kinds of questions and thereby begin the process of ideology critique.

The aim of ideology critique is to "decolonize the mind," as it used to be said.[12] A closely related aim of critical theory is to reveal the unintended consequences of action. This is a matter of seeing how taken-for-granted practices, the typically unremarkable things we do in everyday life, have the consequence, often despite our intentions, of reproducing inequality. One of my favorite examples is Marilyn Frye's analysis of the male door-opening ritual.[13]

On the surface, the door-opening ritual appears to be a gesture of respect. Men say it is a matter of being polite, and many women (especially young women in college classrooms) say they like having doors opened for them. So what's the problem? As Frye points out, it is an unnecessary service, women being fully capable of opening doors for themselves, so its value is purely symbolic. Of what, then? If it were truly symbolic of greater respect accorded women in US society, one would expect to see women being paid more than men in every situation where all else was equal; one would expect to see men doing the bulk of the housework, especially the dirtiest jobs; and one would expect women to be free from sexual harassment, assault, and rape. But, alas, these things are not the case; just the opposite, in fact.

The claim that the door-opening ritual reflects the great respect men hold for women is thus belied by men's behavior in other situations, and inconsistent with every other indicator of women's status and power in US society. Men are willing to "show respect," in other words, when it doesn't matter and when it symbolizes women's weakness. If women like the gesture, it is because of its compensatory value. "We might get the short end of the stick everywhere else," the thinking goes, "but at least we get doors opened for us." But not all women receive even this form of compensation. As often comes out in classroom discussions, less conventionally attractive women report getting fewer doors opened for them than do conventionally attractive women.

Men who open doors for women intend no harm; and both parties to the ritual may come away feeling satisfied if the entry or exit is handled with aplomb. At the same time, however, two other things have happened: the reality of women's subordination in society at large has been masked, and a form of consciousness that sees women as weak and in need of men's strength has been reinforced. The latter makes it easier to believe that it is fitting for women to receive lesser rewards in other contexts, especially the workplace. Harm can thus be done—in the forms of reproducing sexism and gender inequality—by a seemingly innocuous practice.[14] Critical theorizing aims to reveal such harms by highlighting the unintended consequences of a social practice that differentiates men from women. The example of the door-opening ritual also suggests that critical answers to the question *What's really going on here?* are likely to make some well-meaning practitioners of those rituals uncomfortable.

Another example of critical analysis that can cause even more discomfort is exposing the sexism in everyday language. Forty years ago, second-wave feminists objected to sexist terms such as *mankind, chairman, mailman, policeman*; and to the use of masculine pronouns (*he, him, his*) to refer to persons of unspecified gender. Resistance to change was often fierce, but eventually most people got the point and adopted nonsexist or "inclusive" language: *humankind, chairperson* or *chair, mail carrier, police officer, he or she,* or *s/he*. Yet today it is still common to hear grown women referred to as "girls," groups of men and women, or even groups consisting entirely of women, referred to as "you guys," and first-year college students in the United States referred to as "freshmen." Even as some forms of sexist usage have been abandoned, others have become entrenched.[15] Women are still rendered invisible or subordinate in myriad symbolic ways that occur beneath conscious notice, though not without cumulative effect.

Trying to understand how commonplace linguistic practices grow out of and reinforce inequality is an exercise in critical theorizing. Explaining *resistance* to changing oppressive practices is part of the same intellectual project. In the case of sexist language, many people respond to the analysis defensively. The responses are predictable: "it's a trivial thing; it doesn't matter," or "if I don't intend to be sexist, then what I say can't be sexist," or "if no one is offended, no harm is done." As suggested earlier, critical theory must make sense of the social-psychological dynamics that underlie resistance to critical self-reflection and changes in practice. This resistance is part of the process whereby inequalities are reproduced, and it, too, must be subject to critical analysis. Ideally, this will happen as a matter of guided self-reflection, not authorial imposition.

To reiterate: an important aim of critical theory is to equip people to see the unintended, collective consequences of their actions. Sometimes this is described as "problematizing" practices that are otherwise taken for granted. Analyses can of course be disputed; what appears wrong from one perspective can appear desirable or harmless from another. Be this as it may, the dangerous condition—the condition that critical theorizing aims to overcome—is that in which there is no critical reflection on the values, beliefs, and practices that are hegemonic in a society fraught with inequalities. Critical theorizing aims to disrupt this complacency and obliviousness, and for this it is often disdained. Joy is rarely the first result of naming a problem.

Philosopher Brian Fay has argued that part of the project of critical theorizing is articulating felt dissatisfactions.[16] Unless there are genuine dissatisfactions to motivate analysis, Fay says, critical theory will have no uptake and no material force. The analysis, no matter how clever, will be dead on arrival. A first step in the process of liberation is thus to make clear that there exist felt needs for change, even if it's not clear what kind of change is needed. I think Fay is right, and that organic intellectuals—people who belong to, or are deeply connected to, oppressed and exploited groups—must play the crucial role of articulating what is felt, and felt to be wrong. This is necessary not only to motivate critical self-reflection and analysis, but also to evoke empathy and elicit support from allies.

More recently, however, under the influence of liberal multiculturalism, the value of "respecting the voices of the oppressed" has trumped the value of broader critical analysis. The new norm is to accept the articulation of dissatisfactions as a substitute for rigorous analysis that clarifies the social origins of these dissatisfactions. The aim of critical theory, as I construe it, is to do the latter, which can sometimes mean pointing out that members of oppressed groups do not necessarily have a good analysis of where the roots of their problems lie. "Insider analyses" can be as subject to distortion by self-interest and as limited by the analyst's resources as any other. Critical theorizing should not take insider analyses at face value, but should examine them for biases, illogic, incoherence, and factual error. If not, then there is little to distinguish critical social theorizing from propaganda.

Adorno refers to "reified consciousness" as blind to the past, unreflective about social conditioning, and unable to conceive of the current social world as just one possibility among many. De-reifying consciousness, as already noted with regard to self-reflection, is another aim of critical theory. This means, following Adorno, raising awareness that "things were not always this way"; guiding self-reflection into how our thoughts, feelings, and desires are shaped by systems of inequality; and revealing the constructedness of the social world. The goal, or perhaps the interim goal, is to encourage "refusal to surrender to the brute facticity of the world," to see the status quo as changeable in directions determined by rationality, democracy, and concerns for justice.

Another aspect of reified consciousness is attribution of agency to things or, to turn the point around, the inability to see human agency operating in the world. An example of this is the tendency to attribute change to "technology," as if it were a force in itself, with no human actors involved in deciding which technologies to develop and employ. The market is also often reified in the same way; it is credited with agency independent of the powerful economic actors who come together and make choices in search of profit, choices that can have far-reaching consequences for less-powerful others. A reified consciousness perceives these consequences as "just happening," as matters about which one can do nothing, because, as with the weather, no one is really responsible.[17] This way of perceiving the world benefits powerful actors who would prefer their agency to remain obscure.

Part of the process of de-reifying consciousness thus involves identifying actors, groups of actors, and the interests these actors pursue. Critical theorizing, in other words, aims to put human agency back in the picture, though not merely by rhetorically celebrating the capacity of the oppressed to fight back. What must be cultivated is the ability to penetrate abstractions such as "technology," "the market," "globalization," and "structural factors" and see who is doing what to whom, with whom, and how, based on what interests, such that certain consequences follow. This is necessary to make the world understandable as a place where powerful actors can, in principle, be called to account and their selfish behavior constrained, and where rational, democratic action can remake the world to better serve the interests of all. People in the grip of a reified consciousness see no such prospects for accountability or change.

In seeking to de-reify consciousness, critical theory threatens those whose interests lie in preserving exploitive social hierarchies. This threat and the potential for backlash are understood, if only intuitively, by mainstream sociologists who themselves are wont to attribute agency to abstract variables. It is common, for example, to see race and gender used to "predict" income (in this scheme, race and gender are called independent variables, and income the dependent variable). But what is missing when variations in income are attributed to race or gender are the *people* whose actions determine other people's incomes. What is missing, to put it bluntly, is the racist behavior of white people or the sexist behavior of men. By obscuring these actors and their behavior, conventional sociology contributes to reifying consciousness, despite the good intentions of its practitioners. Critical theory's project of de-reifying consciousness is thus likely to be resisted by those who prefer their agency to be obscured, *and* by those who fear the backlash that would come from naming those whose actions are oppressive and exploitive.

I inject the above point about conventional sociology to note a problem with much academic and popular thinking about gender inequality. The problem is that in reifying gender—turning it into a thing, a feature of nature, or a dichotomous variable—the agency of males and men, as groups actively seeking or passively accepting the benefits of domination, is obscured. It thus comes to seem sensible to say that *everyone* is "oppressed by gender" or by "gender roles." But in fact this is nonsense; no group can be oppressed unless there is a more powerful group able to do the oppressing. In the case of men, there is no such group. It makes as much sense to say that men are oppressed by gender roles as it does to say that white people are oppressed by race roles. Systems of racism and sexism are indeed *damaging* to the humanity of all, but the beneficiaries of these systems cannot claim to be oppressed by their own tools and methods.

Many men sometimes feel put upon and constrained for reasons they associate with being men, but these constraints can be traced back to the demands of more powerful men or audiences of men. To see this, it is necessary to de-reify consciousness so that the agency and actions involved in maintaining male supremacy become visible. Conventional theories that take gender categories for granted just reinforce the problem of reification. Critical theory seeks to overcome it.

Sociological self-reflection, understanding of cultural hegemony, awareness of the unintended consequences of action, and a de-reified consciousness are supposed to engender moral autonomy. The goal of critical education, as

Henry Giroux puts it in an essay commenting on Adorno, is to "create autonomous subjects capable of refusing to participate in unspeakable injustices."[18] To accomplish this it would seem that more than intellectual transformation is necessary. In Adorno's view, the inability to identify with others and thus to remain indifferent to their suffering was "the most important psychological condition" that enabled Auschwitz to occur. Somehow, then, critical theorizing must aim to change this condition.

Another way to put it is to say that critical theory must humanize those who are supposedly different. It must de-other the Other. Critical analysis of social categories is part of the process. Beliefs that there exist essentially different kinds of humans—essentially different based on gender, race, ethnicity, class, nationality, or sexuality—must be examined as ideological constructions; that is, as beliefs propagated to create and sustain exploitive social hierarchies. But ideological critique is not enough. De-othering also requires emotional connection. Here, critical theory must give way to literature, art, contact, and conversation.[19] What critical theory can do, however, is to identify the internal and external obstacles to empathy and to engender urgency about the need to find ways to overcome these obstacles and the indifference they permit.

It could be argued that for the purpose of creating people unwilling to cooperate in the butchering of others, extending the bounds of empathy is more important than theory and critique. I would agree that refusal to directly harm others depends more often on emotional identification than on moral philosophy. Yet, as argued above, harm can be perpetrated indirectly, at a distance, without intent. To see this—to see that there are seemingly innocuous practices in which one should not participate because they help make harms and injustices possible—requires analysis in addition to empathy. So even though analysis and critique are never enough, it is impossible to do without theory if we want to change the taken-for-granted social and economic conditions that make holocausts possible.

Theory is also important for educating the educators. If those who socialize the young understand the dangers of reinforcing the ideological categories and identities that limit empathy, they might be less inclined to do so. They might also be more inclined to teach that the social world is a constructed place that can be remade to operate more in accord with the laws of justice and mercy than with the laws of the jungle. Theory might not be a solution, but it is a needed attempt at intervention.

Conventional sociological theory tries to explain empirical regularities in the world as it exists. Critical theory aims to go beyond explanation and interpretation and become a catalyst for change. It does this by de-normalizing oppression, exposing the mechanisms of exploitation, and revealing the social world as constructed and thus potentially reconstructible. Critical theory can also help to overcome the self-blame and self-misunderstandings that lead people to accept subordination. This often means simultaneously putting the competence, morality, and deservingness of elites into question. It is no wonder, then, that members of dominant groups prefer conventional sociological theory to critical social theory. The former safely concerns itself with explaining what exists, whereas the latter inspires dissident imaginings about what can be made to exist.

In US culture, theorizing about the social world is often disparaged as *mere* theorizing, as the spewing of words that don't matter for how things actually happen. It seems to me that one source of this kind of anti-intellectualism is fear that the opposite is true: theory matters tremendously. Theory, understood in plain terms as consisting of the ideas we use to make sense of experience and guide action, has material force because it makes human bodies do what they do in social life. Old theories, often called "common sense" or "conventional wisdom," keep bodies acting in ways that sustain existing hierarchies. Getting minded bodies—*people*—to act in new ways thus requires ideas—*theories*—that challenge what passes for common sense. Critical theory, as I've construed it here, does this in a way that challenges dominant notions about how society works. Critical gender theory does it in a way that challenges dominant notions of who and what we are as social beings, and about the kind of beings we can become.

*   *   *

If there is to be any hope of preventing another Auschwitz, gender theory must be critical theory. The aims I have identified as defining of critical theory must also be the aims of theorizing about gender. I want to try to be more specific, however, about what it is that theorizing about gender needs to do if it is going to disrupt the conditions and processes that lead to holocausts. The first thing it must *not* do is take men for granted.

Much sociological discourse about gender presumes the existence of women and men. This picks up the story too late, taking for granted part of what needs to be explained. If "women" and "men" are indeed social constructions, then gender theorizing must explain how they come into being. Once upon a time, natural philosophers saw earth, air, fire, and water as the basic elements of the natural world. The sociological equivalent of this archaic view of the natural world sees women and men as basic constituent elements of the social world.

Most social scientists claim to see gender as socially constructed.[20] What is usually meant by this is that differences in how women and men think, feel, and behave are seen as resulting from social learning. This view counters the popular belief in gender essentialism—the notion that "gender differences" are genetically programmed and rooted in physiology, a notion that has been widely used to justify male dominance and excuse sexist behavior. Debunking this belief by showing how gender-related behavior is learned and is a response to circumstances is useful for resisting claims that male dominance is natural and immutable, for what is learned can be unlearned, and circumstances can be changed. Yet as the basis for a critical theory of gender, this version of social constructionism does not go far enough.

Critical gender theory begins with the recognition that "women" and "men" are social constructions in multiple ways: as categories, as objects to which cultural meanings are attached, and as conditioned social beings. Humans are of course sexually dimorphic; evolution has given us the differences in reproductive anatomy that we refer to by the shorthand terms *male* and *female*. But these differences are not gender any more than differences in skin tone are race. The construction of gender begins with the attachment of different meanings to male and female bodies and the concomitant imagining that these body types reflect essential internal differences. The construction of gender continues when these meanings are elaborated and when supposed differences are invoked to establish status differences, to assign unequal rights and privileges, and to legitimate exploitation. Gender, in other words, does not follow from anatomical difference, but from the use of anatomical difference to create exploitive hierarchies.

Critical gender theory thus does not take the existence of women and men for granted and ask how they enter into unequal relations with each other, as if gender could precede those relations. Nor does it take women and men as natural expressions of (or as equivalences of) femaleness or maleness. Rather, it sees women and men as categories that are defined into existence as unequal from the start, with the category "men" reserved for males who signify masculine selves and strive for dominance over others. Critical gender theory picks up the constructionist story earlier, so to speak, asking how it is that male supremacy has been achieved via the invention of gender, which includes creation of the categories "women" and "men," and the institutionalization of manhood as the preferred form of male existence. If we take these things for granted, if we do not radically deconstruct men and manhood, we cannot get at the root causes of holocausts, let alone put an end to those causes.

Sociologists of gender will insist that they have not taken men and manhood for granted, at least not since the emergence of profeminist men's studies in the 1980s.[21] It is true that this subfield has sought to study men as men, rather than as generic human beings. Manhood, too, has been studied, usually by way of examining different ways that men fashion themselves as men, or what are called "masculinities." The problem remains, however, that the field typically confuses males and men, treating them more or less synonymously, and typically presumes the existence of men, albeit with recognition that men "do manhood" differently depending on time, place, and culture. Invoking masculinities (about which more in Chapter 2) also tends to obscure the agency of males seeking advantages through membership in the privileged gender category. Moreover, the focus on masculinities implies that domination is a problem that arises only because some men practice a bad version of masculinity. This is like saying that white domination is caused by a bad version of whiteness that afflicts some people of European descent in North America.

Critical gender theory does not reify masculinity, turning it into a thing—either an internal quality or, as it is now often defined, a "form of practice"—that somehow impels men's behavior. In embracing a more radical constructionism, critical gender theory distinguishes body type from gender-category membership. This means looking at what *males* do to construct themselves as the social beings we call *men*—that is, as members of the privileged gender category—and how they then compete for status within the category. Critical gender theory thus does not equate males with men, nor females with women. Rather, it aims to reveal the processes through which males and females construct themselves and each other as members of dominant and subordinate gender categories. It also aims to show how male domination is achieved and maintained through situated action—especially the signification of masculine selves—and institutional arrangements. In this view, male domination no more "just happens" than capitalist domination just happens. It is an ongoing accomplishment by actors who can be identified and held accountable.

The contemporary view of gender as a form of enactment or performance—as a kind of doing rather than a form of being—would seem to provide grounding for a critical theory of gender.[22] Treating gender as a form of doing is indeed an essential part of the critical view I am sketching here; it is part of seeing gender *as* constructed and seeing *how* it is constructed. The emphasis on doing opens the door to analyzing who is doing what to whom and with whom, how, such that dominant and subordinate gender categories are created and maintained. In fact, it was precisely this kind of critical analysis that emerged in the late 1970s and early 1980s from the merger of second-wave feminism with the sociological approach to gender as a form of stylized and ritualized self-presentation.

Yet in recent years the analysis of gender as enactment has been de-radicalized, by which I mean it is has been detached from concerns with gender as a system of inequality. Gender is now more often seen as a kind of stylized self-presentation that people can "play with" to suit their desires to be accepted or seen as attractive in some community.[23] This view recognizes that gender identity is not dictated by anatomy—biological males and females can style themselves as women or men, masculine or feminine—and is thus usefully constructionist; it upsets the conventional gender binary that insists upon males being masculine men and females being feminine women. "Challenging the binary" is at least an abstract threat to the ideological notion that the privileges enjoyed by men rightfully derive from male superiority. But in treating gender as a matter of fun choices about how to express oneself, this view disconnects gender from domination.

A critical theory of gender incorporates the insights that gender depends on human imagining and doing and that human agency includes the possibility of imagining and doing gender differently, or not at all. But it does not let this insight displace the fact that historically and in the world today, males strive to control, and thereby derive disproportionate benefits from, the bodies, minds, and labor of females.[24] Gender is how this is accomplished, and it is a matter of life and death, not play. The Nazi bureaucratic machine, like the militaries of today, embraced a cult of masculinity, and this machine was not organized for fun. It was organized and operated as a means of achieving domination. Without the social creatures we call "men," it would have been inconceivable.

What the now popular (in academic circles) view of gender as situated performance lacks is a way to see what gender has to do with larger social arrangements. If gender is nothing more than a field of self-expression, it's hard to see what it has to do with authoritarianism, nationalism, militarism, imperialism, capitalism, or the ravaging of the planet. The view of gender as situated performance, which is a liberal view enamored of diversity in self-expression, leaves these dots unconnected. Critical gender theory, in contrast, links the situated doing of gender—especially competition for manhood status—to the larger structures within which these enactments occur. The aim is to understand the extra-situational forces that compel such enactments, as well as the larger political and economic relationships that they reproduce. An Auschwitz does not happen because a few odd males practice "military masculinity." An Auschwitz happens because the privileges of manhood can be used, systematically, to induce many thousands of males to put on uniforms, pick up guns, and obey.

Adorno and other theorists of the Frankfurt School drew on Freud because they recognized the importance of psychology for understanding authoritarianism. Freud was useful because he seemed to provide a window to otherwise inaccessible workings of the mind. Given that the horrors of Nazism occurred amid the best that twentieth-century European civilization had to offer, it seemed crucial to identify mechanisms hidden in the human psyche, beneath the veneer of civilization, that conduced to barbarity. The value of Freudian psychology for this purpose is of course subject to dispute; its adept practitioners use it to generate allegedly therapeutic insights that positivist psychologists dismiss as untestable poetry. But Freudian psychology per se is beside the point, which is, rather, that critical gender theory needs some coherent way to connect the visible enactment of gender with the internal compulsions to do gender.

As noted earlier, I find Freud less useful for this purpose than analyses of identity, cognition, and emotion coming out of American Pragmatist philosophy, second-wave feminist psychology, and modern social psychology. The proof, in any case, is in what these analyses can deliver by way of insight into how the compulsions to do gender are instilled in us and activated situationally. In this book I am specifically concerned with compulsions to enact manhood and to signify masculine selves. Which is to say I am concerned with how and why it is that males seek to become men, to engage in competition for manhood status, and to strive for manhood status and control in ways that *require* indifference to the suffering of others. How is it that this can occur even when males striving to be men know, at some level, that what they are doing, that what they are helping to make happen, is wrong? Focusing simply on styles of self-presentation is not enough to answer this question; what's needed, in addition, is analysis of why males feel that the doing—what I will call manhood acts—must be done. Critical gender theory must explain these compulsions, linking them to interaction on the one hand, and to political and economic systems on the other.

As the above implies, critical gender theory is concerned with more than gender as it is construed by conventional sociological theory. The latter tends to imagine that gender can be studied separately from psychology and political economy. This is related to the tendency, noted earlier, to reify gender and turn it into a dichotomous variable that can be used to predict measurable outcomes. But even the less-quantified approaches to gender as a form of doing tend to make a similar mistake: gender as doing is typically treated as distinct from the doing that constitutes capitalism.[25]

In what is now conventional sociological discourse, links between gender and capitalism are usually made by invoking "intersectionality." There is no consensus, however, about what this term refers to.[26] It is sometimes meant to refer to the location of people in multiple categories of privilege and oppression. The key insight, though hardly stunning, is that people's experiences are shaped by simultaneous membership in race, class, and gender categories. Let us therefore be on guard against the simplistic presumption that "being a man" (for example) is the same experience for every member of the category. If the goal is to explain patterns of subjective experience and to avoid the fallacy of assuming that people's experiences are determined by a single master status, this is a useful way to look at intersectionality.

Intersectionality can also refer to connections between race, class, and gender as systems of oppression. The idea in this case is that these are "mutually reinforcing" systems. Precisely how this reinforcement occurs is often left unsaid, but the strongest arguments point to how racism and sexism are used—strategically, by capitalists—to justify paying lower wages to women and people of color, to encourage white males to accept minor privileges and illusions of superiority in lieu of better wages, and to undermine working-class solidarity.[27] In this construal of intersectionality, the point is to understand how gender and race are constructed to facilitate economic exploitation. The key recognition here is that race/racism and gender/sexism are not free-floating forms of inequality that randomly popped into existence, but are intimately linked, in understandable ways, to the workings of an exploitive economy.

Both ways of thinking about intersectionality can inform critical gender theory. It's important, as I've suggested, to understand subjective experience and how this experience is implicated in reproducing large-scale social arrangements. Any critical analysis of society must also consider how these institutional arrangements connect. However they are defined, gender, race, and class are so interwoven historically that to understand the shape of one, it is necessary to understand the shape of the others. It is the totality that makes the pieces what they are.

Yet the conventional ways of thinking about intersectionality still treat gender as if it were fundamentally noneconomic. Men and women are still seen as existing prior to economic relationships, and thus the exploitive nature of gender remains hidden. This is akin to the mistake of imagining that workers and capitalists exist in elemental form before they enter into economic relationships with each other. A similar mistake is imagining that men exist prior to exploitive economic relationships. Critical gender theory proposes instead an ontological connection: manhood *emerges from* and is *essential to* maintaining exploitive economic relationships (see Chapter 5). In this view, which I realize will not be congenial to those who are happy with capitalism, the implication is that manhood of the kind that makes holocausts possible will be with us until we create nonexploitive economies.

As I argue in Chapter 2, what began as a set of radical feminist analyses of men and masculinity has become a domesticated academic specialty. The subfield still claims the term "critical," as in Critical Studies of Men and Masculinity, but much of the current work has little to say about exploitation or oppression. What it now amounts to, for the most part, is a feckless project of cataloging "masculinities."[28] The original feminist impetus to study how males fashioned themselves as men so as to subjugate women and benefit from the exploitation of women's minds, bodies, and labor, has faded. This is not to say that no one cares any more about sexism or discrimination; surely they do, when it is easy to see and denounce. But what has been backlashed nearly to extinction is the perspective from which gender, manhood, and masculinity are seen as inherently about domination, not merely self-expression.

To fulfill the aims I have described here, critical gender theory must avoid de-radicalization. By this I mean it must avoid, under pressures to be polite and to celebrate diversity, the tendency to forgo examining the roots of gender in exploitation and oppression. I realize that this is easier said than done.

Institutional space for carrying on critical theorizing about gender is most likely to exist in academia. It is here that assumptions can be questioned and disruptive ideas put forth, or so I hope. Yet academia is a contradictory space; even while it can nurture unconventional thought, it also encourages toning down ideas that might overly upset students; it also channels dissident energy into careerism. And so to the extent that critical gender theory remains solely an academic enterprise, it will be at risk of being made into a career vehicle, or reduced to an "approach" that can be described (as occupying one end of a spectrum) but not endorsed. If it is going to be a force for change, critical gender theory will need support—which is to say, it will need people who carry on the discourse, critically theorize about gender, and thereby seek to transform consciousness and practice—outside the confines of academia.

Whether critical gender theory has any uptake beyond academia will depend in part on its accessibility. Too much theorizing about gender is burdened by unnecessary jargon. There is also a tendency among academic gender theorists to play language games for the pleasure of the author and an audience of hip insiders. Any critical theory that suffers from these problems is limited in its potential to change consciousness and practice in the world at large. Ideas that can't be understood can't be used to make a difference. And so I have tried to write in the common tongue, begging indulgence for the occasional sociologism. I should add that accessibility does not imply acceptability, as if writing plainly makes threatening ideas less so. In fact, in the short run, plainer expression will no doubt make some ideas more threatening and less acceptable. My hope is that in the long run the benefits of clarity will outweigh the risks of rejection.

It is in the interest of accessibility that I have referred to the aims of *critical gender theory* rather than *feminist theory*. What I have called critical gender theory is certainly feminist in its origins, motivating values, and goals. I mean to imply no scholarly, philosophical, or political gaps between critical gender theory and what I have characterized—and, yes, I am lumping much together—as radical second-wave feminism. No doubt some readers will see what I am calling critical gender theory as just socialist (or Marxist or materialist) feminism, with a dose of social psychology thrown in, along with a peculiar focus on manhood.[29] Although this would not be totally unfair, such pigeonholing would be unfortunate, and so I am trying to deter it. There are other theoretical birds here, and they are likely to be lost if the analysis is forced into overly familiar boxes. My hope, then, is that the term *critical gender theory* will enhance receptivity by suggesting that there is more to the analysis (developed in the chapters that follow) than might be implied by the term *feminist theory*, which activates prejudices that can filter out new ideas and information.

I also mean to suggest, by referring to critical gender theory, a parallel to critical race theory. The specific parallel I have in mind is to the latter's recognition of race as inherently about exploitation and oppression. "Race," from the standpoint of critical race theory, is not a matter of happy and harmless cultural differences that are incidentally associated with the geographic distribution of gene pools. Rather, race is seen as a matter of invented belief in the natural superiority and inferiority of different groups, which might or might not correspond to gene pools and phenotypical differences among peoples. Moreover, beliefs about race are seen as invented and used to justify exploitation. Because racial categorization schemes are by definition—and in actuality—hierarchical, they are not something to be celebrated and preserved.

I take a similar stance toward gender. Gender is not, from the standpoint of critical gender theory, something to be preserved or celebrated or played with, but a system of inequality that should be abolished. This more radical view distinguishes critical gender theory from liberal feminism that seeks equal opportunities for women within oppressive hierarchies, from cultural feminism that touts the alleged virtues of femininity, and even from socialist and Marxist feminisms that take gender for granted as natural and eternal. And just as critical race theory compels examination of how people become invested in, and struggle to defend, subcultures and identities premised on racial categories, likewise with gender. Both perspectives put much into question, and both have much potential to disturb.

Another reason I prefer critical gender theory is that I want to connote the importance of analyzing gender as a system of exploitation and oppression. Radical feminist theory recognizes this and should be understood as speaking to everyone who values human dignity and equality. Yet "feminist theory" tends to connote, rightly or wrongly, a primary focus on the oppression of women, rather than on gender itself. From the goal of analyzing and ending the oppression of women there can be no retreat; the exploitation of women by men is the essence of gender as an institution. The liberation sought by critical gender theory is, first and foremost, liberation from this form of exploitation and oppression. My argument, however, is that liberation from gender oppression cannot occur within exploitive economic relations. And so again I want to affirm the importance of taking a broad theoretical view that does not detach gender from the economy and thereby inadvertently protect capitalism from feminist critique. It also seems appropriate to use a term that foregrounds gender rather than a category—women—derived from a gender system. As noted in the discussion of reification, this does not mean letting males striving to be men off the hook. It is, rather, a way to suggest how far-reaching the social transformation will need to be if we hope to prevent Auschwitz from happening again.

*   *   *

One of the first films I saw in a theater was *The Guns of Navarone*, starring David Niven, Gregory Peck, and Anthony Quinn. It was 1961, and I was five years old. I'm not sure why my father took me to see that film. I certainly couldn't follow the story. He probably wanted to see the film himself, and for me the point was just to have an outing with Dad. Years later, when I saw the film as an adult, I realized that some of its images—huge artillery guns built into the side of a mountain, people being shot, massive explosions that send those guns tumbling into the sea—had lodged in my memory. Apparently, it hadn't all been lost on me, even at five.

Since seeing *The Guns of Navarone* over fifty years ago, I have seen many more war films. Probably between fifty and a hundred. Images from those films are also no doubt lodged in my mind, though the films themselves, with perhaps a dozen or so exceptions, are forgotten. There is, however, one film, not a war film in the usual sense, whose images I can readily recall and cannot forget: Alain Resnais's 1955 documentary about the Nazi concentration camps, *Night and Fog*.

Images from Auschwitz figure prominently in Resnais's film. The film mixes footage shot by the Nazis and by camp liberators with postwar footage of the abandoned grounds. We see purses, luggage, clothes, shoes, and hair in floor-to-ceiling piles. We see gas chambers made to look like showers. We see ovens and smokestacks. We see emaciated prisoners staring in disbelief through wire fences. We see mounds of corpses and the faces of once-living men, women, and children. The film is thirty-two minutes long, in black and white, and its images have been with me now for more than thirty-five years.

I saw *Night and Fog* in an undergraduate social psychology course. In conjunction with the film, we read about Solomon Asch's conformity experiments, Stanley Milgram's obedience experiments, and Philip Zimbardo's mock-prison experiment.[30] The lesson I took from this part of the course was that the Nazis were not a special case of social pathology. The same tendencies to conform and obey, and the same processes of bureaucratic control and diffusion of responsibility, were still present in so-called civilized societies and could, under the right conditions, lead to another holocaust. Later I realized that holocausts can occur on different scales. Only four hundred people were killed at My Lai, yet it was the end of a world.

It would be revisionist history to say that seeing *Night and Fog* set me on a path to become a (sociological) social psychologist. My academic career was much more stumbled into than strategically pursued. But since undergraduate days I have remained concerned with how people are shaped by social conditions and with how they can be organized to act in ways that cause great harm to others.[31] I have also tried to understand how to stop this from happening. In 2013, I remain dually haunted by images from Resnais's film and Adorno's essay on education after Auschwitz. Anyone not convinced by the essay should see the film.

I mention these biographical bits to indicate what I think is at stake as I develop the analyses presented in this book. If the stakes were not so high, I might have been more restrained, less radical, more tentative, less insistent. But however my arguments about gender and manhood are received (I anticipate vehement rejection in some quarters), I want to end with a demonstration that challenging the conditions that undermine moral autonomy doesn't *require* going so far as to argue for the abolition of men. By way of example, here is a short essay I wrote to encourage young men to resist the forces that exploit gender to make them collaborators in the perpetration of holocausts.[32]

* * *

SIX LESSONS FOR YOUNG MEN ON THE EDGE OF WAR

Military service was a rite of passage into adulthood for males in my family. Three of my uncles served in the navy. One uncle served in the air force. My father spent three years in the army. As a boy, it seemed natural that I too would enlist when I finished high school. The only question was, Which branch? Then Vietnam came along.

I was fourteen when four students were shot dead by National Guard troops at Kent State University in May of 1970 during a protest against the Vietnam War. At that time I had no clear idea of what was going on in Vietnam or why people were protesting. My concerns that summer ran to baseball, fishing, and playing along the Lake Michigan shoreline. Vietnam was just words and pictures on TV.

But somehow Kent State pierced my boyhood shell. As I recall, my parents were not sympathetic to the students. "The students shouldn't have been there, and the troops felt threatened," one adult in my family said. I wasn't sure what to think. It seemed to me, having attended a strict German Lutheran grade school, that students ought to be attending classes and studying, not rioting. On the other hand, I was pretty sure that no one deserved to be killed for exercising their free speech rights while marching across a campus.

I started high school that fall, and while I didn't hang out with an especially political crowd, I began to pick up, perhaps from older students, a more critical vibe about Vietnam. That was the first time I became aware that some people thought the war was based on lies. Lies about the Bay of Tonkin, about the legitimacy of the South Vietnamese government, about the civilian death toll, and about the motives of US government leaders.

Not that this radically affected my thinking. At that time I had no way to figure out where the truth lay amid the competing views that surrounded me. The adults in my family, as far as I could tell, supported the war out of reflex patriotism. Coming from a working-class family, I also shared the anti-elitist, anti-privilege sentiments behind the demand, wielded against student protesters, to love America or leave it. Merle Haggard's "Okie from Muskogee" resonated more strongly with me than Neil Young's "Four Dead in Ohio."

The views among my high school friends were also mixed. Some despised Nixon and opposed the war. Others were insufficiently bothered by Vietnam to be deterred from seeking admission to the US military academies. One friend went to Annapolis, another to West Point, and another to Colorado Springs. Smart, serious guys. All of them National Merit Scholars.

What astounds me now is that even with the war and protests going on in the early 1970s, and all of us within a couple years of draftable age, we still didn't pay much attention. The war, for all its prominence in the media, was not a main topic of our conversation. If it came up, it was usually because someone had a brother or cousin who'd been drafted, or who'd been killed, or who'd just been discharged. We weren't dissecting the war as a matter of right or wrong foreign policy. Nor were we talking in any serious way about what it would mean to be personally involved. As the teenage male products of US culture, we were not equipped for that kind of conversation.

My uncertainty about military service lasted until the fall of 1973, when an army recruiter visited my high school. The recruitment pitch, as I recall, involved officer training, a commission, a four-year stretch, and then a full ride through college. It sounded like a good deal, especially since I wanted to go to college but wasn't sure how to pay for it. If Vietnam crossed my mind as a reason not to enlist, I don't remember having that thought. Besides, wasn't that mess over with?

Later I talked to my dad about the recruitment offer. I expected him to be pleased that I was even considering it. Not only would I be carrying on the tradition of military service in the family, but I'd do so as an officer and get my college paid for. I also had the impression that my father enjoyed his time in the army. He never said a bad word about it. So I was surprised when I told him about the offer and he said, with unusual directness, "Don't do it."

What I don't remember is him saying exactly why I shouldn't do it. The impression I retain, thirty-six years later, is that he thought the recruiter's promises were untrustworthy, that the risks were too great, and that things were unlikely to turn out well. I also retain a strong impression of caring behind his advice. Maybe that's why I can't remember exactly what he said. He was not the kind of man who would have articulated his caring explicitly, and so he said it in code.

Any lingering thoughts about military service were extinguished before I'd finished my first year of college. Nearly everyone I met there was critical of the Vietnam War and of how US leaders had conducted it. The most credible critics, to my mind, were the many veterans on campus at that time. Every Vietnam veteran I met told a version of the same story: the war was horrifically cruel and wasteful; most of what the military brass and US politicians said in defense of the war was bullshit; the Vietnamese had driven the French out in the 1950s, and now they wanted the United States out, so they could run their own country. One other thing the vets had in common: they had known none of this when they enlisted.

Other vets silently testified to the horrors the rest of us could only imagine. These were the guys who lived mainly in their own heads, moving through campus space with seemingly little connection to the world around them. They were scary, and best avoided when they drank. It seemed obvious to me that only an idiot, or someone who didn't know any better, would want to go through whatever had so badly rattled their minds.

I am fortunate in that I can't say what it's like to be a civilian or a combatant in a war zone. But in the years since I was an undergraduate, I have studied violence, the myths of manhood, crimes of obedience, and geopolitics. So what I can say, I hope, are some things that might make young men less vulnerable to the seductions of war and to the pitches of military recruiters. Had I been in a position to do so, this is what I might have told the young men whose ignorance of history was exploited to make the Vietnam War happen.

Recognize, first of all, that modern war kills more civilians than soldiers. It used to be said that rich old men start wars, while the young and the poor fight and die in them. That's still largely true. But now it's not male soldiers who are most of those being maimed and killed. Forget glorious cavalry charges and heroic infantry battles. On average, 90 percent of the casualties are women, children, and the elderly. This makes all modern wars crimes against humanity. To join the military is to put yourself in a position where you will be forced to be complicit in these crimes. This alone is sufficient reason to refuse to participate.

The second lesson is that being forced to be complicit in butchering innocent people creates a strong incentive to justify doing so. Military training will aid this process. It will teach you to value the lives of your fellow soldiers over those of the "enemy." Nationalism and racism will add to the mix. Eventually, you will be able to see other human beings as slopes, gooks, or hadjis—all

Chapter 2

The Masculinities Industry

In the early 1990s, a sociologist from another university gave a talk in my department about the history of manhood and masculinity in America. Afterward, a local colleague, a generation older, confessed to me that he didn't get it. Masculinity, as he saw it, was a trait that inhered in individual men, to greater or lesser degrees. He could see how this natural variability might interest psychologists. But the idea of studying masculinity sociologically made no sense to him.

There was already at that time a burgeoning sociological literature on men and masculinity, a body of work as intellectually exciting to me as it was baffling to my colleague. I had been reading this literature for several years and had begun contributing to it.[1] It would be fair to say that I was a partisan for the profeminist version of what was uneasily called "men's studies." And so I tried to convince my colleague that it was both possible and worthwhile to get a sociological handle on masculinity. It's been too many years to recall exactly what I said, but it probably ran along the following lines.

The idea that masculinity is a trait that naturally inheres in men is a folk belief. It's an idea that we can study, as sociologists, in the same way we might study any other piece of ideology. We can ask where such notions come from, how they change over time, who embraces them, what consequences follow from their embrace, and so on. But there is a difference between the folk belief in masculinity as an innate quality of men and the sociological definition of masculinity as a form of doing. What this doing consists of are self-presentations and other acts that mark males as men, or as *manly*, according to local cultural conventions. So, to study masculinity sociologically is to study these conventions and how males use them to construct themselves as men.

Again, I don't recall, twenty-some years later, if my colleague found this account satisfactory. He seemed to think it reasonable for sociologists to study cultural conventions (which is something we do all the time), though he also seemed skeptical about the idea that "men" are not objects found in nature, like plants or rocks or bacteria. For my part, I probably felt affirmed in my belief that, the closer an analysis strikes to home or to the self, the less sociological sociologists become.

My brief account of what it meant to study masculinity sociologically drew on work by R. W. Connell and his colleagues published in the 1980s.[2] According to the definition popularized by Connell, *masculinities* (more later about the plural) were "configurations of practice" through which, or as a consequence of which, men as a group maintain power and privileges over women as a group. I thought this was a useful definition for several reasons. One, it denaturalized masculinity and took it out of the psychological realm; two, it included those things men do collectively to uphold male supremacy; and three, it rendered masculinity visible, and thus more amenable to empirical study.

In the definition I offered my colleague, I translated the phrase "configurations of practice" into "self-presentations and other acts that mark males as men." This is an imperfect translation, because it gives more weight to identity and category membership than Connell's definition, which, though somewhat cryptic, is broader. But by including "other acts," I meant to convey the idea that studying masculinity should include looking at those things men do *together* to devalue women, deny them resources, exploit their bodies and labor, and exclude them from positions of power. In fact, a large part of the attraction of this new way of thinking about masculinity was that it offered a way to study men not just from a sociological perspective but from a feminist perspective.

In the late 1980s and early 1990s, when asked to give an account of what "men's studies" was about, I always said, following the party line, that it was about studying men *as men*, rather than as generic humans.[3] This meant studying men, as I said to my colleague, as socially constructed creatures that were constructed differently in different times and places. Most sociologists knew what it meant to study "gender roles" in the form of cultural prescriptions about how women and men ought to behave. Sociologists had done this for years. Yet they had typically assumed that these roles were learned and performed by people who were naturally identifiable as boys or girls, men or women. It was this assumption of naturalness that the new men's studies, flowing from feminism and a more constructionist sociology of gender, directly challenged.

There was another version of men's studies on the rise at the same time. This was the non- and often antifeminist version that proposed to study men's experiences sympathetically, from a "male-positive perspective." In this view, men were seen as no less oppressed by gender roles than women.[4] Proponents of this view said that the women's movement had usefully focused attention on women's gender-related troubles, and now it was time to give equal attention to men. To do so from a feminist perspective, however, was seen as inappropriate, because feminism was hostile to men and thus biased the analysis.

This other version of men's studies was more essentialist than construction-ist. Alleged differences in how men and women thought, felt, and behaved were seen as rooted in biology. Evolution, it was argued (though more often assumed), endowed males and females with different bodies and brains, and culture simply built on top of these natural differences. So although culture was not dismissed, it was relegated to secondary importance as a shaper of women's and men's behavior. What mattered about culture, in this view, was how well it harmonized with nature. When gender roles accorded with men's and women's natural proclivi-ties, the argument went, societies experienced fewer gender troubles.[5] The danger posed by feminism was that it could exacerbate these troubles by demanding cultural changes that contravened natural differences between women and men.

From the standpoint of profeminist men's studies, this other version was seen as naive, reactionary, or both. Proponents of the profeminist view pointed out that it made no sense to talk about men being oppressed *as men*, because there was no more powerful gender group able to do the oppressing. And although it was fine to say that male privileges had costs, to say that "gender roles oppressed men" was to be willfully obtuse, because these roles were, historically, products of male domination. Moreover, the costs men paid for enacting their privileged gender roles were largely self-imposed and borne precisely because the advan-tages—in terms of power, status, and wealth—outweighed those costs. As for the embrace of essentialism, this was seen as an anti-intellectual refusal to question the ideology that portrayed "men" and "women" as natural objects, and thus allowed a fundamental part of the gender order to remain unexamined.

The most recent incarnation of the essentialist, antifeminist version of men's studies goes by the name of *male studies*, a field seemingly dedicated to the oddly joined propositions that men's behavior stems from maleness, and that males are now victims of an antimale culture.[6] Serious social scientific and schol-arly studies of men as gendered beings continue to embrace the "men's studies" label, though different academic associations claim feminist roots and feminist sensibilities to greater or lesser degrees.[7] This work, usually associated with the label "critical studies of men and masculinities," tends to be nonessentialist and realistic in its recognition of gender inequality and men's institutional power. It is this profeminist version of men's studies—its promise, appeal, and evolu-tion—that concerns me here.

To return, then, to the early 1990s:

Part of what was intellectually exciting about this new way of looking at men was that it rejected not just folk beliefs but also conventional wisdom in sociology. Debunking popular beliefs about the inevitability and naturalness of gender roles was a pleasure, and even more so when it was possible to make visible the inequalities and injustices obscured by the notion of gender roles (if it's not clear what's wrong with the notion of gender roles, consider the more obvious wrongness of a parallel notion of race roles).[8] But in the wake of second-wave feminism, this kind of analysis was standard fare for sociologists; it was based on a liberal notion of fairness and a liberal critique of conservative ideology that justified gender inequality by invoking tradition. It was a critique worth making, but hardly radical.

By adopting a strong social-constructionist perspective and putting the naturalness of "men" and "women" into question, profeminist men's studies was more threatening and disruptive than a liberal critique of unequal gender roles. Even though the strong constructionist view—the view that gender, as a matter of subjectivity, identity, and practice—is entirely a matter of culture, not biology, had been around since at least the 1960s, and had been elaborated in the 1970s and 1980s, many sociologists remained essentialists at heart. Yes, gender roles are cultural prescriptions, they agreed. But surely males and females are different kinds of humans with different innate propensities—propensities that, with some cultural nudging, blossom into what we call masculinity and femininity. Right?

The strong constructionist view said no. Even the categories "male" and "female," according to this view, are cultural.[9] There are of course differences in reproductive anatomy, and we can, if we want, categorize humans based on such differences. But the *idea* that males and females are different kinds of people is a piece of culture. Ideas about how people with male and female bodies should be treated and should behave are even more clearly human inventions, ones that vary culturally and historically. The constructionist view also held that any differences in how women and men perceive, experience, and habitually respond to the world—differences popularly thought to reflect innate qualities of masculinity and femininity—are products of social experience, not biology.

Gender, in this view, is an illusion. It is socially real and consequential, in the same way that "race" is socially real and consequential. But anything beyond the brute fact of differences in reproductive anatomy is a consequence of human invention. We look around and see socially coerced differences in appearance and behavior that lead us to believe that we are seeing "women" and "men."[10] From these external differences we infer internal ones. But what we are doing, according to the constructionist view, is seeing what results when humans act on their collective imaginings. And on this basis we suppose that our imaginings reflect a natural, not invented, reality. It was this more radical view that gave the new men's studies, embedded in a feminist sociology of gender, much of its freshness and intellectual punch.

The appeal was also political. A critical men's studies allied with a feminist sociology of gender offered the possibility of seeing more deeply into how patriarchy and gender inequality were reproduced. This gave profeminist male sociologists a mission, which was to find out something useful about how sexism and an unjust gender order could be abolished. It was, moreover, a mission to be fulfilled by studying men—something that male sociologists were well positioned to do, inasmuch as being male conferred the advantages of easier rapport, access, and sympathetic understanding. There was perhaps also the satisfaction derivable from turning a critical eye on men who were political and economic elites, men who benefited not only from patriarchy but from its ally in domination, capitalism.

Profeminist male sociologists also understood the need for personal transformation. To the extent that we were creatures shaped and privileged by a male supremacist gender order, there was a clear need, often sharply noted by feminist women in our lives, for reflection and change. This self-critique was another part of the mission arising from the embrace of a profeminist men's studies. The appeal, at least to male sociologists, was that profeminist men's studies offered a way to apply the insights of sociology to self-transformation, much as radical feminist therapy had once done for women.[11] It was perhaps also more satisfying to think that self-transformation was being undertaken willingly, as part of a larger social justice effort, rather than being compelled by failings in one's personal life.

My account no doubt has its idiosyncratic elements. Other male sociologists might have experienced the emergence of profeminist men's studies differently. Yet there was plenty of writing and conversation that attested to a commonality of outlook, along the lines suggested above, at least among male sociologists (and other male academics in the social sciences and humanities) born in the 1950s and influenced in graduate school by feminist thought. It was not a large community, and many of us knew each other, read each other's work, and talked to each other at conferences. So I don't think my account of the zeitgeist is entirely idiosyncratic.

My reason for looking back is to reflect on the promise of profeminist men's studies and to assess where it's gone these past twenty-five years. In this regard, I expect my critique will be seen by some as harsh or cynical, perhaps especially by those most invested in how "critical studies of men and masculinities" has developed. My complaint, in a sentence, is that the field has lost its feminist edge and has become an academic industry devoted mainly to the endless description of masculinities, often burdened by obscurantist jargon. The problem began, it seems to me, with the pluralization of masculinity and, as a result, a forgetting that manhood is fundamentally about domination.

*   *   *

If masculinity is a form of doing, it makes sense to suppose that it might come in different forms—meaning that there is more than one acceptable way to be a man. It's clear that this is true cross-culturally and historically.[12] But in their discussion of multiple masculinities, Connell and his (the correct pronoun at the time) colleagues took this idea further. They argued that, even within societies, there are, or can be, diverse doings, diverse configurations of practice, that constitute masculinity. The argument included another seemingly simple but key point: even though there might be different acceptable ways of being a man, all such ways are not equally valued; one version of manhood is typically revered above all others.

The version of manhood that is most revered in a culture, the version that commands the greatest respect, is what Connell and colleagues called the hegemonic version. So, in this scheme of things, there is a hierarchy of masculinities, with one form, hegemonic masculinity, being at the top.[13] Again, this was a seemingly simple but important insight at the time, the point being that masculinity is not just about how men relate to women, but about how men relate to each other. Those who can enact the hegemonic version may succeed not only in dominating women, but also in dominating men who enact lesser-valued, or subordinated, versions of masculinity.

"Hegemonic" is not just a synonym for dominant. The term is used advisedly, in its Gramscian sense, to imply widespread acceptance of the superiority of a particular way of being a man.[14] Hegemonic masculinity is thus dominant not by virtue of constant coercion, but by virtue of many processes, operating at different levels of social organization, through which its superiority comes to be taken for granted by most people (much as the superiority of capitalism as a form of economy comes to be taken for granted by most people who grow up in the United States). The idea of hegemony also implies cooperation on the part of women. No version of masculinity can be hegemonic unless most women buy into it, take its superiority for granted, and support men in enacting it.

Masculinity, then, entails more than acts of individual self-presentation. The practices whereby males claim manhood status can include collective acts of valorizing males, men, and masculinity; of devaluing females, women, and femininity; of excluding women from networks, jobs, and positions of power; and of coordinating acts of domination in war, business, and politics. To engage in these sorts of practices, thereby upholding relations of domination and subordination, is what it means to enact a form of masculinity, according to Connell and colleagues. Hegemonic masculinity is the form that is not only most revered when enacted by individual men, but most effective in maintaining power and privilege for men when enacted collectively.

In later work, Connell noted the importance of hegemonic masculinity as a kind of social representation that legitimates patriarchy. It is the "configuration of gender practice," Connell said, "which embodies the currently accepted answer to the problem of the legitimacy of patriarchy."[15] In this view, hegemonic masculinity need not even be concretely enacted by anyone on a regular basis to have consequences; it merely has to be collectively believed in as something men are capable of, thereby legitimating men's societal dominance. Every man, whether able or willing to enact the hegemonic ideal, thus benefits from—derives a "patriarchal dividend" from—the existence of an exalted ideal of manhood, an ideal that says, in effect, *This is the powerful stuff all men are made of, whether it's immediately obvious or not.*

Although this view of masculinity treats it as created by performance, it differs from the standard dramaturgical view (associated with the work of Erving Goffman) by emphasizing that masculinity is not instantaneously and fleetingly brought into being in face-to-face encounters.[16] It is, rather, embedded in culture, social organization, and history. To understand manhood and masculinity it is necessary, according to Connell and colleagues, to connect these performative constructions to larger social conditions, past and present. Men's presentations of self as men are certainly important in this view. But to explain such presentations of self, as well as their consequences, requires taking a wider context into account.

Part of the appeal of this way of conceiving masculinity, as noted earlier, is that it makes masculinity amenable to sociological study. If masculinity is what males do, individually and collectively, to construct themselves as the dominant gender group, then this doing is, in principle, visible and subject to examination. Likewise, hegemonic masculinity as a cultural ideal and tool for legitimating inequality can also be studied. The idea of *multiple* masculinities further enhanced the appeal, and still does, because it implies that there is interesting variation to be discovered. There is, by the light of this conceptualization, not just one set of practices or one way of enacting manhood to be studied, or even one manhood ideal, but many—as many, potentially, as there are groups and categories of men. To each its own masculinity, supposedly.

This way of conceiving masculinity simultaneously opened doors and created problems. One problem is that if masculinity is construed as a configuration of practice, we are obligated, or should be, to say *which* practices constitute a masculinity. Men, after all, do many things. Which of these things can be bracketed off and said to constitute a masculinity? On what basis do we decide? To say that the important practices to include and examine are those that have the effect of reproducing relations of domination and subordination begs the question, because such an effect must be empirically documented, not presumed. We can't know beforehand, before having a careful look, which practices create and reproduce domination.

One way this demarcation problem has been dealt with, or, rather, evaded, is by treating anything people with male bodies do as if it were part of enacting masculinity. This approach treats changing oil in a car, changing diapers, and changing laws all as masculinity-constitutive practices—when done by males. Acts that have contradictory meanings and consequences can thus be lumped together as part of "doing masculinity." By this logic, male soldiers who follow orders to kill people are doing *military masculinity*, whereas males who oppose war are doing *pacifist masculinity*, and those who write about it from their university positions are doing *academic masculinity*. If this sounds silly, well, it is. Yet this is the kind of thing that is now common in the literature.

Masculinities have also been multiplied by invoking categories of race, ethnicity, religion, class, sexuality, and place. Supposedly, then, there is white masculinity, Black masculinity, Asian masculinity, Latino masculinity, and so on; there is working-class masculinity, middle-class masculinity, upper-middle-class masculinity, and so on; there is Jewish masculinity, Christian masculinity, Muslim masculinity, and so on; there is gay masculinity, straight masculinity, and bisexual masculinity; there is urban masculinity, suburban masculinity, and rural masculinity. These categories can also be combined, suggesting that there might be a unique configuration of practice identifiable as white, middle-class, Christian, bisexual, suburban masculinity.

Every possible category of men, it thus seems, has its own brand of masculinity. One might wonder, however, just what it is that these allegedly different configurations of practice have *in common* that makes them each a masculinity. Is the common feature the effect of upholding male supremacy, regardless of what the specific practices might be? Or is it that, within each of these categories of humans, there are some practices engaged in only by people with male bodies, and this is what makes those practices masculinities? The answer is not clear, leaving us with something of a muddle.[17]

The proliferation of masculinities along lines of race, class, ethnicity, and sexuality was an unsurprising development in an era of identity politics and multiculturalism. It was consistent with the spirit of the times to credit each group in society with a culture of its own, in this case a gender culture. There was also a strong affinity between the social justice orientation of profeminist men's studies and the liberal spirit of multiculturalism. But there was something else going on, something rarely acknowledged: a revalorization of manhood and masculinity under the guise of celebrating diversity. To see this, we need to consider again the concept of hegemonic masculinity.

To reiterate, the hegemonic form of masculinity is defined as the most honored form of manhood in a society. What this means, at the individual level, is that there are certain practices in which a male must engage, certain qualities he must display, if he is to be seen as a *real* man, worthy of every bit of status, every right, every privilege normally accorded to men. So what are these qualities? In Western societies, the list typically includes strength, rationality, toughness, competitiveness, generativity, and heterosexual prowess. If this is so, it should be obvious why there emerges a hierarchy of men: not all males are able, willing, or equipped to engage in the practices conventionally interpreted as signifying strength, rationality, toughness, competitiveness, generativity, or heterosexual prowess. Males who can't or won't do these things, males who don't enact the hegemonic version of manhood, are accorded lesser manhood status and may even struggle to be credited as men at all.

From a sociological standpoint, this way of looking at masculinity and manhood makes sense. It's hardly objectionable for analysts of culture to examine status hierarchies and how they are lived out. This is what the conceptualization of hegemonic and subordinated masculinities allows us to do. Yet to call attention to such status hierarchies offends the liberal precept that all people and subcultures deserve equal respect. It seems insensitive to say, or even to accept the implication, that gay men or poor men or gentle men are lesser men. It might also sting a bit to recognize one's own lower place in the masculine hierarchy one undertakes to analyze. The desire to avoid these discomforts led to blind spots.

What happened in the case of profeminist men's studies is that males who did not fit the hegemonic ideal, and thus were seen as lesser men by mainstream cultural standards, asserted their manhood status implicitly by claiming that *differently practiced* masculinities warranted study. "We might not be considered manly or masculine by dominant standards," the subtext ran. "But we, too, are men; we just do masculinity differently, with less or none of that business about always being strong, tough, or heterosexual." Part of the initial impetus for multiplying masculinities, I am suggesting, was that it allowed males who were unable or unwilling (perhaps for laudable reasons) to enact hegemonic masculinity—mostly gay and profeminist academic males—to retain a claim to manhood status. While Robert Bly's mythopoetic men took to drumming circles and sweat lodges to discover their deep masculinity, other men took to academic conferences.

It might seem that it would be a good thing if more men critically analyzed the practices whereby they claim membership in the dominant gender group. And indeed it could have been (and would be, still). If nonelite males had said, in effect, "It's not just powerful men who must be studied and critiqued. We, too, in our attempts to claim manhood status are part of the problem. We must therefore analyze and critique our own 'masculinities' as part of seeing how we contribute to the oppression of women." If *that* had been the principal motive for multiplying masculinities, the field might have developed differently. But as masculinities were multiplied, the idea of analyzing *all* masculinities as oppressive practices was largely lost.

To be clear, I am referring to a particular historical period—the late 1980s and early 1990s—during which certain ideas about how to study men and masculinity were beginning to take hold. My claim is that part of the appeal of these ideas, a largely unconscious appeal, was that they affirmed the manhood status of males who could not or would not enact hegemonic masculinity.[18] Other dynamics came into play in subsequent decades, as more sociologists, male and female, found the rhetoric of "multiple masculinities" useful for getting published. Eventually the plurality notion itself became hegemonic, wielded automatically rather than critically. What ultimately matters, of course, are not inaugural motives but results. For a time, the idea of multiple masculinities sparked insightful studies of variation in oppressive practices by males striving to be men. That time is past.

My account of how profeminist men's studies has developed will no doubt evoke objection. Those who object can cite numerous self-critical essays and books written in the 1980s and 1990s; they can cite writings on *complicit* masculinity (manhood enactments that are "softer" than the hegemonic form, but do not challenge that form and continue to benefit from its existence); they can also cite studies of *compensatory* masculinity (i.e., studies of how men who cannot enact the hegemonic ideal try to compensate for their manliness deficit in ways that harm women). It would be fair to cite this work as evidence that multiplying masculinities did not, by itself, quash the critical impulse underlying profeminist men's studies. I agree, and will suggest later what else helped to de-radicalize the field. Nonetheless, by the middle of the first decade of the twenty-first century, there were clear signs that masculinity was being rehabilitated by disconnecting it from oppression.

*   *   *

As an example of where this de-radicalizing tendency has brought us, I want to consider an essay, "Hegemonic Masculinity: Rethinking the Concept," published in 2005 in *Gender and Society*.[19] The essay is important because of its placement in sociology's top gender journal and because of its authorship by R. W. Connell and James Messerschmidt. As noted, Connell's writings about masculinity date to the early days of profeminist men's studies and have hugely shaped the field. Messerschmidt, too, has been a prolific and influential contributor for decades.

Given its weighty authorship and placement, the essay can be taken as a watershed statement about how sociologists these days ought to think about masculinity.

Connell and Messerschmidt begin by reviewing the original formulation of "hegemonic masculinity" and its subsequent use in studies of men. They then consider critiques of the concept: that the underlying notion of masculinity is confused and unnecessary; that the concept offers no clear guidance as to how to identify the hegemonic form of masculinity in any given case; that the concept inadequately specifies the relationship between men's historically fluid gender enactments and the reproduction of patriarchy on a larger scale; and that the concept tends to obscure the dynamic and contingent relationships between hegemonic and other forms of masculinity. Connell and Messerschmidt grant that the original concept offered a "too simple model of the social relations surrounding hegemonic masculinities" and that it too readily led people to think of hegemonic masculinity as a fixed set of traits.

To upgrade the concept, Connell and Messerschmidt propose that it be revised to better deal with a number of matters: the nature of gender hierarchy, especially the borrowing that occurs among masculinities, and also how women are implicated in the reproduction of hegemonic masculinities; the geography of masculine configurations (i.e., how local, regional, and global masculinities relate to each other); the process of social embodiment (i.e., how socially shaped bodies are implicated in the enactment and reproduction of masculinities); and the dynamics of masculinities (i.e., how men's practices change over the life course and in response to tensions and contradictions). Connell and Messerschmidt conclude by suggesting how to proceed along these lines, but leave the bulk of the work for others to do—which is fair enough, considering the extensive ground they've already managed to cover.

I see nothing about which to quibble concerning Connell and Messerschmidt's account of the concept's original formulation and its subsequent use. A minor complaint, having reviewed the same literature myself, is that Connell and Messerschmidt are perhaps too easily satisfied when they consider how the concept of hegemonic masculinity has been applied.[20] Yes, the concept has been cited thousands of times in studies of men's behavior in all kinds of settings. Indeed, the concept's popularity as a rhetorical totem is not in doubt. It remains an open question, however, just how much insight this profligate citing has generated.

Most studies that purport to describe distinct forms of masculinity—studies that Connell and Messerschmidt cite approvingly as showing the value of the hegemonic masculinity concept—could just as well have been done, and done just as well, by referring to local variations in men's gender-reproducing practices, without invoking any notion of masculinity at all. And for every study that Connell and Messerschmidt cite that uses the concept of hegemonic masculinity properly—that is, to focus attention on what men do to achieve domination—there is another study that simply uses the term because it's au courant for describing men's behavior, even though no analysis is offered of how men's practices create or reproduce domination over women or other men.

Another problem that is not uncommon in the literature is pointing to masculinity, hegemonic or otherwise, as if it were an explanation for men's behavior. Some pattern of men's behavior will be described, and then this behavior will be "explained" by saying that—*aha!*—men are doing a form of masculinity. But of course this is no explanation at all. If masculinity *is* the pattern, *is* the configuration of practice, it cannot also be the explanation for that practice. If rain were cited as the cause for water droplets falling from the sky, the error would be obvious. Connell and Messerschmidt, to their credit, are clear that to invoke masculinity as an explanation for men's behavior is a mistake.

What Connell and Messerschmidt do not fully come to grips with, however, are problems inherent in the concept of masculinity itself. Although they acknowledge the existence of critics who argue that the concept is "blurred" and "ultimately unnecessary to the task of understanding and contesting men's power," they assess only a limited range of what critics have said. They portray critics as objecting to the concept of masculinity mainly on the grounds that it "essentializes the character of men" and fails to allow for the fluid, adaptive, and discursively constructed nature of manhood. These criticisms have indeed been made, but they're the game-tweaking rather than game-changing criticisms.

The criticism that is more threatening to the masculinities industry is that the concept of masculinity has gained us little analytic ground (and perhaps even run us aground). It indeed has been handy to have a conceptual language to use in writing about the behavior of men as men. Surely it's easier to say that men, or some of them anyway, are "doing hegemonic masculinity" than it is to say that they construct themselves as members of the dominant gender group so as to claim rights and privileges that advantage them relative to women and, perhaps, relative to other groups of men. But ease of expression is a vehicle, not a destination. Ultimately, we must have something to say about precisely how it is that males construct and use a gender order to achieve dominance. We might also want to be able to say something about why they do it as they do.

Are the concepts of masculinity and hegemonic masculinity necessary to achieve these goals? Not really. We could just as easily, and perhaps with more clarity, study and talk about the things men do, the individual and collective behaviors in which they engage, to create and uphold dominance hierarchies. In other words, we could study men's oppressive practices, in relation to each other and in relation to women, without relying on the muddlesome notion of masculinity, whether construed as trait or practice. *This* is what some critics of the concept have argued.[21] But Connell and Messerschmidt can't go down this road because it would mean losing the concept they have set out to rescue.

Giving up the concept of masculinity would be threatening in another way. What the concept allows sociologists to do is to take men off the feminist hook by talking about masculinity instead of talking about men's oppressive behavior. To do the latter—to name the dominant group and put its members squarely in the crosshairs—invites backlash and marginalization.[22] Professionally, it's safer to refer to masculinity, hegemonic masculinity, multiple masculinities, complicit masculinity, compensatory masculinity, competing masculinities, and masculinities ad infinitum. This timidity is not specific to Connell and Messerschmidt. It is characteristic of sociology generally. In this case, the language of "masculinity" and "masculinities," originally intended to expose men's oppressive practices, has, ironically, come to shield men from criticism and shield academics from backlash. This, too, is how hegemony works: it turns the language of critique into a language game played for career points.

The confusion seeded by the notion of multiple masculinities is evident in the Connell and Messerschmidt essay in two other ways. One of these has to do with the claim, attributed to critics, that discourse about multiple masculinities "essentializes" masculinity. Connell and Messerschmidt reject this charge:

> The notion that the concept of masculinity essentializes or homogenizes is quite difficult to reconcile with the tremendous multiplicity of social construc- tions that ethnographers and historians have documented with aid of this concept (Connell 2003). Even further removed from essentialism is the fact that researchers have explored masculinities enacted by people with female bodies (Halberstam 1998; Messerschmidt 2004). Masculinity is not a fixed entity embedded in the body or personality traits of individuals. Masculini- ties are configurations of practice that are accomplished in social action and, therefore, can differ according to the gender relations in a particular social setting. (p. 836)

A curious thing about this defense is that it gets the criticism wrong. Connell and Messerschmidt are right to reject the charge of biological essentialism. The conception of masculinity as a culturally and historically variable configuration of practice is, in fact, antiessentialist. But to offer this as defense is to miss the point.

The important criticism, as suggested earlier, is that those who purport to document diverse masculinities are not clear about precisely which of men's practices constitute a masculinity; nor are they clear about what it is that men's practices across settings have in common that makes them each a masculinity. If the only thing these practices have in common is enactment by people with male bodies, then, ipso facto, masculinity must somehow be tied to the male body. What critics have said is that this amounts to an inadvertent essentialism arising from vague definitions and theoretical confusion—and that it's something that needs to be sorted out. No serious critic is leveling the charge of biological essentialism against which Connell and Messerschmidt needlessly defend themselves.

But wait. Connell and Messerschmidt say that masculinity can be "enacted by people with female bodies." If this means that females can present themselves as men, be taken for men, and strive for dominance in the same ways that males do, then indeed there is no necessary link between body type and masculinity—though it would require that females hide their femaleness, because cultural convention dictates that maleness is a criterion for membership in the category "men." If Connell and Messerschmidt are saying that females can *pass* as men, and thus get the rights and privileges of manhood status by doing the same things men who are biologically male do, there is little to disagree with. Females, too, can "do masculinity" in this sense.

It's not clear, however, that this is Connell and Messerschmidt's argument. A few pages later, they say, "bourgeois women may appropriate aspects of hegemonic masculinity in constructing corporate or professional careers." This would seem to imply that it's possible to present oneself as a woman and be taken as a woman—and still do masculinity (the hegemonic version no less). I take their reference to "constructing corporate or professional careers" to imply striving for power and status. They do not say which aspects of hegemonic masculinity are appropriated to aid this striving, but I presume they are alluding to things like outcompeting others, controlling others, and presenting oneself as rational and emotionally tough (or, as it is usually said, "able to make the hard decisions that are necessary to get the job done"). There's no doubt that women can and do act in these ways to advance their careers, just like men. What remains unresolved is the matter of how we ought to think about the relationship between bodies and masculinity.

The logical implication of what Connell and Messerschmidt are saying is that neither a male body nor a presentation of oneself as a man, nor recognition as a member of the category "men," is necessary to engage in a configuration of practice called a masculinity. One can have a female body, be recognized as female, present oneself as a woman, be socially recognized as a woman, and yet do masculinity. It seems, then, that masculinity as a set of practices has no necessary connection to body type, gender identity, or gender category. Any body can do it. But, again, do *what*, exactly? The lack of a good answer to this question is a theoretical problem, one that is still with us because we have tried to turn a folk concept, masculinity, into an analytic concept, without building a theoretical framework to support the attempted redefinition.

first-wave feminism in the early twentieth century, and second-wave feminism in the 1960s and 1970s, third-wave feminism vaunted individual achievement rather than collective struggle to change sexist laws, policies, and institutional practices. Third-wave feminism told young women that these struggles had been won. Feminism was now, supposedly, all about individual women choosing how to enjoy their freedoms and how to take advantage of opportunities for success.[25]

Third-wave feminism was seductive because it induced a false sense of empowerment.[26] Young women could feel empowered even as they conformed to the strictures of a sexist culture, as long as they defined it as their choice to do so. The critiques of fashion, makeup, sexual objectification, name-changing upon marriage, and pornography made by a previous generation of feminists now seemed outdated. If an individual woman chose to participate in these practices, and it felt okay to her to do so, well, *that* was feminism, regardless of how women as a group might be harmed. It was appealing, too, that this kind of free-market feminism did not require overt challenges to men's sexist behavior, the kind of challenges that could get a woman labeled a bitch.

Third-wave feminism also offered a more soothing analysis of gender. Whereas radical second-wave feminism sees gender itself as a system of inequality, third-wave feminism, under the influence of postmodernism and post-structuralism in the humanities, sees gender largely as a matter of display options. So if a young woman fashions herself as a sexual object to satisfy the male gaze (as it used to be said), she can define this not as subordination but as "playing with gender." Gender, in this view, is a kind of put-on by individuals who, if they play it out with ironic distance, need not feel oppressed. In fact, a woman who believes she is choosing to use a conventionally feminine gender display to aid her striving for status and power can construe herself (but only if she chooses) as a feminist.

The popularity of this individualistic feminism made it harder to keep calling attention to men's oppressive practices. Individualism itself, as an outlook on social life, was part of the problem, because it deflected attention not only from the harms sexism does to women as a group, but also from the collective practices in which men engage to maintain power and privilege. If gender is about nothing but individual self-display, as third-wave feminism suggests, it might be offensive at times—if, say, an individual man behaves obnoxiously— but it's harder to see gender as an oppressive system from which men as a group benefit. In this sense, third-wave feminism not only de-radicalized thinking about gender, it de-sociologized it, reducing it to a matter of individual, not institutional, practice.

Thinking about gender as a matter of display options also tended to make a critical view of men's practices seem unfair. If, as third-wave feminism says, women are simply playing with gender when they put on a feminine gender display, aren't men entitled to play, too? Aren't men who opt for a conventionally masculine gender display simply making a choice to which they're entitled? Isn't this just a matter of choosing a "gender style" that feels right and makes a man feel good about himself? After all, if there is nothing wrong with a conventionally feminine gender display, then why get bent out of shape about a conventionally masculine gender display? Let guys be guys! Thinking along such lines did not necessarily lead to the conclusion that individual men should be unaccountable for gross sexist behavior. But it made it harder to hold up "masculinity," however defined, as inherently problematic.

Another de-radicalizing development in the 1990s and 2000s was the resurgence of biological essentialism.[27] A generation earlier, biological essentialism—the view that differences in how women and men think, feel, and behave grow out of biological differences between males and females—had been the default view in the culture. Starting in the 1960s, research and theory coming out of the social sciences and humanities challenged biological essentialism by showing how gender enactments varied historically and culturally, and also how such enactments, including sexual behavior, could change in the lives of individuals, depending on life stage and context. Such variability and fluidity shouldn't be observed, gender scholars argued, if gender is biologically programmed. Other research showed that, when observation is systematic and controlled, and context is taken into account, women and men do *not* think, feel, and behave so differently.[28] It thus seemed clear that not only were gender differences in everyday life matters of social construction, but the belief that there were deeper, more fundamental causes in the genes or the brain was also an artifact of ideology.

But biological essentialism never went away. As Anne Fausto-Sterling, Judith Lorber, and others have said, if people believe in gender differences and in a biological basis for those alleged differences, they will seek, and seek ingeniously, until they find evidence for their beliefs.[29] Because the belief in essentialism is embraced with religious fervor, it is largely impervious to refutation by evidence or argument. And so biological essentialism, useful for making sense of what otherwise seems arbitrary and oppressive to half of humanity, refuses to die. Every generation it rises from the grave in a new form. In the 1990s and 2000s, this new form was called "evolutionary psychology."

The basic idea of evolutionary psychology is that just as organisms evolve physically because bodily variations can confer reproductive advantage, so, too, do behavior patterns evolve.[30] Giraffes have long necks, to take a familiar example, because those of their ancestors who had slightly longer necks, and thus were able to access more nutrients higher in the trees, were more likely to survive and reproduce, passing on their genetic potential for longer necks. The result, after millions of years of selection for longer neck length, is the oddly proportioned but well-adapted animals we see today. Likewise, behaviors that confer a reproductive advantage, presuming they are linked to genetically heritable brain circuitry, tend to be preserved in subsequent generations. Animal behaviors in the wild thus are what they are because those behaviors were adaptive at one time and, absent major environmental changes, remain adaptive. Evolutionary psychology uses this logic to explain human behaviors.

According to evolutionary psychology, if men today are prone to sexual infidelity; if men try to accumulate wealth and use it to obtain the sexual favors of young, fecund women; if men compete with each other and strive for dominance; if men rape women, it is because such behaviors, once upon a time (the Pleistocene era is usually cited), conferred reproductive advantage.[31] Behaviors that increased the chances of a man passing along his genetic material to the next generation tended to be preserved, again presuming that the predisposition to such behaviors arises from heritable aspects of brain circuitry. Evolutionary psychology makes parallel arguments about how women's behaviors—for example, trying to attract and mate with the highest-status males available; seeking a male with the resources and apparent proclivity to be a good provider—similarly reflect successful adaptive strategies.

Critics of evolutionary psychology have objected on a number of grounds: that the behavior patterns it claims to explain are stereotypes that misrepresent how most men and women actually behave; that culture and social organization are far more powerful shapers of human desire and social behavior; that the adaptive pressures faced by early hominins and by hunter-gatherers varied widely and are not accurately known; and that evolutionary psychology, stripped of its scientific pretensions, offers only the banal observation that humans have evolved the capacities to do certain things under certain conditions (e.g., to cooperate or to kill). What evolutionary psychology provides, critics have thus said, is a bunch of "just-so stories" that can be used to justify sexist social practices by implying that these practices reflect the wisdom that evolution has supposedly wired into human beings.[32] Despite these criticisms, evolutionary psychology gained mainstream acceptance in the 2000s. In popular culture and in some corners of academia, it now holds sway.

The resurgence of biological essentialism was also fueled by the increasing use of body-scanning technologies, especially positron-emission tomography and functional magnetic resonance imaging, in studies that looked for differences in male and female brains. Studies that purported to find such differences were often widely reported in the media. Even if these studies were debunked later, the impression was fostered that gender is a consequence of biology. Although this research was typically said to represent the cutting edge in the scientific study of gender, it really just affirmed what most people already believed. If *real* scientists—the ones who wear lab coats and use fancy machines to look into people's brains—say that gender-related behaviors are rooted in the body, it must be true.[33]

It's hard to say precisely how these developments affected social scientists and humanities scholars who studied gender. A few sociologists jumped on the genetic bandwagon because it was a way to get grants, advance their careers, and claim the status-enhancing mantle of science.[34] Most sociologists of gender did not succumb. Most understood that new forms of biological essentialism, especially evolutionary psychology, remained sociologically blind, failing to see gender enactments *as* enactments, failing to see how such enactments are learned and compelled through social processes, and failing, too, to understand how gender culture begins to shape individuals from the moment of birth. Most probably saw evolutionary psychology and brain-scan studies as old gender ideology in new scientific clothes.

Still, it was hard to remain unaffected. Putting forward a strong constructionist view became harder in the face of the popular impression that science had shown such a view to be outdated. Difficulties could arise in the form of student resistance in the classroom, demands by editors and reviewers that one address the latest findings revealing the genetic basis for gender differences, or being cut out of public discourse about gender. If nothing else, enthusiasm for making a strong social constructionist argument could be—and I think was—dampened by the sense that the argument would get little uptake. The harder the cultural current ran against the idea that "men" are social, not natural, constructions, the harder it became to keep advancing that idea.

The original profeminist critique of gender—informed by radical second-wave feminism and by social constructionism—saw it as something to be eradicated. An essentialist view denies that this is possible and sees gender as no less a part of human nature than having two arms and two legs. So, again, as biological essentialism gained ground in popular culture and in academia, it became harder to expound a view of gender as a socially constructed system of domination that humans should strive to transcend. By the end of the 2000s, many sociologists of gender, though not recanting their constructionist views, seemed to accept that gender would be forever with us—that at best it could be done differently but not done away with.[35] This stance of resignation betrayed the original political ambitions of radical feminism and profeminist men's studies. It was, however, congenial to the academic masculinities industry in at least one way: it meant that masculinities, by virtue of being *permanent* features of human social life, were all the more important to study in their infinite variety.

A fourth de-radicalizing current of sentiment emerged following the terrorist attacks of September 11, 2001. After the attacks, paeans were written to the police officers and firefighters who risked and sometimes lost their lives trying to rescue others from collapsing buildings and burning rubble. These songs of praise were, as sociologists are wont to say, gendered. The iconic image of the heroic cop or firefighter was unambiguously male. Moreover, and more importantly, their self-sacrificing heroism was not attributed to a noble work ethic joined with the courage born of urgent need. It was attributed, sometimes explicitly, more often implicitly, to masculinity. Our heroes were heroes not simply because they were compassionate and brave and doing what needed to be done, but because they were men.[36]

After the attacks, an even stronger, indeed overwhelming, current of popular sentiment favored violent revenge and the use of military force. In New York City, first-responders, acting with manly strength and courage, had dealt with the immediate damage and saved those who could be saved. Now it was time for retribution, and for this, too, real men were needed. The job called for men who were skilled in violence and willing to use it without hesitation. Our new heroes, or heroes-in-the-making, were those men who would not only track down and kill the perpetrators but send a clear message to the rest of the world: do not fuck with the United States. The same qualities of manly strength and courage displayed by first-responders would now be deployed to kill as many people as necessary to put the scales back in balance. It was not a propitious moment in which to put forward a critique of hegemonic masculinity.

The moment extended throughout the decade, as the US government sent soldiers first to invade and occupy Afghanistan and then Iraq. Hundreds of media stories, many written by strategically embedded reporters, humanized and heroized these soldiers. Despite occasional blemishes—torture and abuse in Abu Ghraib, civilian massacres in Fallujah and Haditha and Ramadi and Kakarak and Ishaqi—the image of the tough, resolute, get-the-job-done soldier was revived and revalorized. Domestic propaganda urged Americans, no matter their feelings about the wisdom of US foreign policy, to "support the troops" who were "fighting for our freedoms." Part of what was being urged was respect for the qualities of character that made a soldier a good soldier: strength, courage, willingness to sacrifice—in a word, masculinity (as popularly conceived). Even though women were rhetorically acknowledged—"our brave young men *and women* in uniform"—the iconic image of the US soldier was still G. I. Joe, not Jane.[37]

I don't mean to suggest that promilitary propaganda, the intentional and the inadvertent, was so effective that it quashed all feminist or profeminist critique of masculinity. In some quarters, the invasions of Afghanistan and Iraq were seen as more evidence that the critique—especially linking masculinity to violence and a desire for domination—was correct.[38] Nonetheless, over the decade, the energy behind the critique seemed to wane in the face of a cultural revaluing of masculinity as the essential quality of a good soldier. To critique masculinity came to seem vaguely unpatriotic, as if one were failing to appreciate the kind of character so very needed to keep us safe and free in a world full of evildoing bad guys.

My claim, in sum, is that powerful cultural currents in the 1990s and 2000s—multiculturalism, third-wave feminism, the resurgence of biological essentialism, and the valorizing of masculinity as part of a remilitarization of US culture—combined to wither the critical spirit that once led profeminist men's studies to analyze masculinities as configurations of *oppressive* practice. Facing a cultural headwind and hobbled by theoretical confusions, profeminist men's studies devolved into an academic industry devoted to the safe documentation of the myriad ways males style themselves as men. Even worse, by the mid-2000s, profeminist men's studies was fighting a rearguard action against antifeminist backlash claims that boys and men, far from being privileged, were now being bested in school and in the job market by girls and women.[39] From a radical feminist perspective, it seemed that, with the exception of expanded rights for gays and lesbians, the clock of progress had begun to run backward.

*   *   *

It was exciting, at one time, to have a new way to think about masculinity. It was a mistake, however, to try to turn "masculinity" into an analytic concept simply by redefining it as a configuration of practice. As argued here, we could have just as well studied the practices whereby males construct themselves as men without talking about masculinity at all. Perhaps because the word "masculinity" was so present in our minds and so ingrained in our pre-sociological thinking about the nature of men, we believed it represented a real thing in the world, something that must have a tangible form. It would have been wiser to treat masculinity as an ideological illusion—a dominant-group myth to be deconstructed and dissolved.

Despite its utility for avoiding trouble when talking about men and for fueling an academic industry, the concept of masculinity as a configuration of practice has turned out to be an analytic and political dead end. But what would be better? In the next chapter I'll proffer an alternative. By way of a bridge to that alternative, let me say what I think is needed.

If the goal is to understand the *practices* that create and uphold male supremacy, then we need a theoretical perspective that focuses our attention on those practices whereby males construct themselves as the dominant gender group called "men," and whereby they gain psychological and material advantages vis-à-vis women. We need to be able to describe what these practices are, to say what's

Humans are hard to control but susceptible to many means of control. They can be controlled by force, by giving or withholding material rewards, by stirring emotions, and by implanting ideas. When one group is able to use these means to create and maintain an exploitive social arrangement with another group, we can say that dominance has been achieved. Antagonistic interests are inherent in such an arrangement, regardless of how strongly felt those antagonisms might be at any given time.

A sexual division of labor inflected by reproductive necessity *could* be nonexploitive. For this to be the case, the arrangement would have to be free of compulsion and entail no disproportionate benefit to males as a group or females as a group. It would also mean that neither group had more power than the other and that neither group enjoyed higher status or greater privileges. If these conditions obtained, a sexual division of labor could be considered nonexploitive.

A primitive sexual division of labor inflected by reproductive necessity is what might have been found in early hominin groups and hunter-gatherer societies. All societies since the advent of settled agriculture about twelve thousand years ago have been characterized, however, by elaborate gender orders. A gender order can be said to exist when human activity in multiple realms—government, religion, war, medicine, education, sports, art, and so on—is sex-differentiated and normative.[2] Which is to say that males do certain things while females do others, and the arrangement is widely regarded as sensible and proper.

One can plausibly imagine a warrior caste of males—those most adept at violence—forming in response to threats of resource loss or exploitation at the hands of an out-group. This caste and its leaders might come to function as (what we now call) "the state."[3] Even if the external threat abates, a warrior caste, once formed, is hard to eradicate, especially if it has monopolized the means of violence. The possibility of eradicating a warrior caste in one society is also limited by the existence of warrior castes in other societies.[4]

A gender order includes sex-differentiated practices in multiple realms, normative rules that guide such practices, and ideas that explain and justify the practices. It also includes the ingrained dispositions of thought and feeling that are generated by assimilation to these practices and by immersion in their legitimating ideologies. A gender order is constituted, then, by practices, rules, beliefs, and dispositions.[5] Individuals exist within a gender order, which is reproduced by what individuals think, feel, say, and do in everyday life.

To the extent that lifelong participation in a gender order instills dispositions of thought and feeling, the gender order can be said also to exist *inside* individuals. It is both an external and internal social reality.[6]

Human minds are not blank slates. We are, it seems, evolutionarily predisposed to learn some things quickly: facial recognition, language, how to spot cheating.[7] The activation and behavioral expressions of these ancient learning capacities depend on the environment in which humans live. A key feature of this environment, for the last ten thousand years, is an exploitive gender order often called "patriarchy."

The belief that males and females are essentially different kinds of human beings is foundational to a gender order. This is a belief in more than differences in reproductive anatomy. It is a belief that males and females possess, by virtue of their biological maleness or femaleness, different capacities and proclivities for thought, feeling, and behavior. This belief makes it possible to explain and justify the differential treatment of males and females. Without such a background belief, a gender order would make little sense.

Belief in the essential difference of males and females is visibly affirmed by the practices through which males and females fashion themselves into the kind of people called "men" and "women." Such practices must, first of all, *differentiate*. Males must be recognizable as men, and females as women. Ambiguity is anathema to a gender order. Such practices must also appear *natural*. Being a man or a woman must appear to be an effect of biology. If the practices by which males and females fashion themselves as men and women appear to be matters of arbitrary social convention, the essentialist belief that is foundational to the gender order is threatened.

One can plausibly imagine the invention of "men" as the result of warrior-caste males valorizing themselves and their practices, so as to claim extra privileges and benefits. If so, men today are living fossils, holdovers from an earlier stage of human existence. Men survive, as forms of social beings, because humans have not yet evolved beyond hierarchy and exploitation. In a world without domination, men and manhood would be absurd.

Strictly speaking, to claim to be *male* is to identify as a member of a *sex* category; to claim to be a *man* is to identify as member of a *gender* category. It is difficult to speak so strictly, however, when ideology gives us to understand that males *are* men, and that to qualify as a man it is necessary to be male. The claim to being male or female is thus popularly understood to be a claim to membership in a gender category. Indeed, once the belief takes hold that males and females are essentially different kinds of human beings, sex and gender become difficult to untangle.[8]

Untangling sex and gender is necessary for understanding the social construction of gender. Sociologists say this all the time—and then go on to forget this distinction by referring to males as if they were naturally men and to females as if they were naturally women. Avoiding this tendency requires language that rings strange. So, to reiterate, males are not men; males construct themselves as the cultural objects we conventionally know as "men." This is both an individual and a collective project.

The common ground of human experience is larger than the ground created by sex-differentiated or sex-segregated practices. Males and females, men and women, to the extent that they share a common culture and material environment, will possess many of the same cognitive, emotional, and behavioral response tendencies.[9] Such differences as exist are often ideologically exaggerated in the interest of legitimating male supremacy.

In principle, a gender order could be nonexploitive, provided that neither gender group could impose its will on the other in any domain of activity; that neither group was accorded more status, rights, and privileges; that neither group disproportionately benefited from the labor of the other in any domain of activity; and that all socially valued resources were equally distributed across both groups. No modern society fits this description.

In all modern societies, "men" have been constructed and positioned as the higher-status group. As a group, males in the guise of men have enjoyed a near-monopoly on institutional authority, more rights and privileges, and a greater share of societal resources.[10] Males in the guise of men have also been able to exploit women's bodies, minds, and labor, privately and publicly. Gender orders in all modern societies have operated to advantage members of the category "men" at the expense of members of the category "women." All gender orders, as we know them today, are regimes of exploitation.

Religion, it has been said, is what keeps the poor from organizing to kill the rich. Gender ideology, it can be said, is what keeps females from organizing to end their exploitation as women at the hands of males in the guise of men. Gender ideology is what keeps most parties to the arrangement from imagining that things could be any other way. Most people can more easily imagine the end of the world than a world without gender.[11]

The ideological conceit of men is that they are the subjects, the makers, of history, and nature and women are its objects. This conceit induces an inability to appreciate two things: the dependence of humans on nature and the subjectivities of humans in dominated groups. When nature and people are treated as mere objects, atrocities follow.

Precisely how and to what extent men are able to exploit women's bodies and labor depends on the economy in which a gender order is enmeshed. The nature and extent of this exploitation will vary depending on how particular groups of men and women are positioned in the economy and in other social hierarchies. Not all men will be advantaged in the same way or to the same degree. Not all women will be disadvantaged in the same way or to the same degree.[12] All will be affected.

To derive the benefits and privileges associated with membership in the higher-status gender category "men," males must signify that they are, indeed, men. What males must do is to display the signs by which membership in the gender category "men" is indicated. Males must dress, speak, and act in ways that signify both maleness and manliness. Males must learn to perform these acts of signification in accord with local customs and audience expectations. To fail to signify manhood correctly is to lose some or all of the benefits and privileges associated with manhood in a given situation. Laying claim to these benefits and privileges requires, in other words, a good manhood act.[13]

The gender order can be transgressed by pointing to its constructedness, by rejecting belief in biological differences between male and female bodies as the basis for complex social behaviors, and by refusing to construct masculine or feminine selves. It can also be transgressed by exposing gender as an exploitive hierarchy in league with all others. All transgressions will be punished, even if they are only minimally disruptive.

Though it is a semiotic asset, a penis does not make a man. A manhood act makes a man.

Other than genitalia, indicators of sex-category and gender-category membership are imposed on infants and children. This begins with naming, and then includes dressing, hair styling, and provision of playthings.[14] Infants and children

Because members of the category "men" are assumed to be male and therefore naturally possessed of qualities popularly defined as masculine, a successful manhood act will elicit the imputation that the actor possesses at least a rudimentary masculine self, which is of less social value than a fully creditable masculine self. Lack of a male body does not make it impossible to signify a masculine self, but ideology ensures that such a self will never be fully creditable, even if it elicits deference under some conditions.

Sex-segregated activities endow participation in those activities with signifying value. To allow only males to participate in activities that imply a capacity to exert control and resist being controlled is to unequally distribute opportunities to construct masculine selves. If females are allowed to participate—in, say, football, boxing, wrestling, hunting, and combat—then the value of these activities for signifying a masculine self is diminished.[24]

The danger if sex-segregation of activities breaks down is that competent performance by females will show that the competence of males is not attributable to maleness. Females who excel in activities defined as masculine or manly must therefore be defined as freaks of nature. A further danger, if males and females compete directly, is that the illusion of male supremacy will be shattered when females outperform males.

As sex-segregation of activities breaks down, males place greater value on those activities in which uniquely male features—size, strength, and speed—ensure a performance edge. As women have achieved greater equality in US society, football, professional wrestling, and extreme fighting have become more popular with men.[25]

The signifying acts by which a masculine self is constructed can be observed and their guiding rules inferred. Just as the construction of meaningful speech relies on tacit knowledge of grammar, so does the construction of a masculine self rely on tacit knowledge of an *identity code*, a set of guiding rules for assembling bits of signifying behavior into a meaningful whole that elicits desired responses from others. To create a fully creditable masculine self, one must be able to competently deploy the grammar of gender.

To say that males who put on a successful manhood act elicit the attribution of possessing a masculine self is to use analytic language, not the language of everyday life.[26] No male says to himself, "I am going to put on a manhood act so that others will attribute to me a masculine self and therefore grant me all the benefits and privileges that come with being a member of the dominant gender group." Yet *analysts* of gender can use such language to describe what is going on. For the most part, these goings-on are outside the conscious awareness of males who put on manhood acts as matters of habit and unquestioned convention.

An audience might see a manhood act as flawed in some way; an expected part of the act might be missing, or a part might contradict the whole. An act might be seen as wrong for the occasion. If the act is flawed in any of these ways, it may fail to elicit the attribution that the actor possesses a fully creditable masculine self. The actor's social value is thus diminished.

Signifying the *capacity* to exert control and resist being controlled does not necessarily mean coercing others in any given situation. A masculine self is attributed to an actor based on apparent capabilities. These capabilities do not need to be concretely demonstrated on every occasion to be inferred to exist.

Successfully exerting control is a sure way to demonstrate that one can do it, but obvious attempts to exert control are risky because they can fail. A masculine self may thus be more safely constructed by *implying* the capacity to exert control and resist being controlled than by actually trying to control potentially resistant people and objects. What matters is the image of a masculine self that can be induced in the minds of others. Failure can shatter the image.

Exertions of control have greater signifying power if they appear effortless. The lack of apparent effort when control is exercised implies that the actor possesses additional capacities, strength in reserve, that can be drawn upon if circumstances require it.[27] Regulating expression of effort is thus part of the act. "No sweat," the man said on one occasion. "You saw what I could do when I put my mind to it," he said on another.

The acts from which will be inferred a capacity to exert control and resist control depend on culture and context. Displays of esoteric knowledge and lacerating wit will sometimes be taken to signify a masculine self. In other times and places, displays of physical strength and fighting prowess are required. A male must know the local identity code and be able to use it flexibly to meet audience expectations under varying conditions.[28] The ability to do this well can distinguish a male as a man for all seasons.

A manhood act can establish a legitimate claim to membership in the gender category "men," yet be faulty or weak. If so, it will elicit imputations of possessing a less-than-fully-creditable masculine self. A manhood act can thus succeed and fail at the same time. To fail is to fall short of achieving full manhood status.

"Full manhood status" can be thought of in both situational and societal terms. To succeed in eliciting imputations of possessing a fully creditable masculine self by the standards of a given situation is to achieve full manhood status *in that situation*. Yet because realms of activity are differently valued, a masculine self that is fully creditable in one realm may not have the same social value as a masculine self that is fully creditable in another realm. Audience perspective is what matters. One audience's star is another audience's bit player.

The material and psychological rewards attainable through achievement of full manhood status are situation specific. Achieving full manhood status in some situations pays off better than in others. Access to high-payoff situations depends on successfully signifying membership in other privileged social categories.[29] Males who cannot do this can still achieve full manhood status, but only in inferior realms of activity. A gangster who is unequivocally a man is still only a gangster.

On a societal basis, those males who can successfully signify membership in all relevant privileged categories, and who can perform virtuoso manhood acts of their own, define what constitutes full manhood status, assign its value, and determine its rewards.[30] A society in which this is the case can be called patriarchal.

The ideology of biological essentialism says that male and female bodies are signs of deep-rooted differences in capacities and proclivities. A male body is thus taken to be a natural sign of a masculine self. This is an ideological interpretation—*ideological* not only because it is fanciful, but because it serves to legitimate inequality.

A male body is a special kind of signifier. As a sign, it can trump others and affect how other signs—clothes, speech, gestures—are interpreted. A male body can thus be called a *peremptory signifier*.[31] When it comes to eliciting attributions of possessing a masculine self, a male body is an asset; a female body is a liability.

Manhood acts include signification of the actor's biological maleness. For adult males, secondary sex characteristics usually accomplish this signification. Audiences infer from observation of these characteristics that the actor is male. Other signs—clothes, speech, gestures—also come into play. These are usually seen as corroborating the inferences drawn from observation of secondary sex characteristics. But because genitalia are not usually visible, nonbodily signs can be used to mislead. Clothes, speech, gestures, and other signs can be used by adult humans with female bodies to elicit the inference of being male.[32] On this basis, an audience, operating on essentialist beliefs, will attribute to the actor a rudimentary masculine self.

Because secondary sex characteristics are powerful signifiers, much of the semiotic work of putting on a manhood act is experienced as effortless by biological males. Even so, other signs must harmonize with the body apparent. If clothes, speech, and gestures do not also signify maleness and possession of a masculine self, the manhood act will suffer. The actor might still be recognized as male, but will not be seen as possessing a fully creditable masculine self or deserving of full manhood status.

Bodies can signify a capacity to exert control or resist being controlled. A large, muscular male body signifies a greater capacity for exerting control and resisting being controlled than a small, flabby male body. A large, muscular female body might imply a greater capacity for exerting control and resisting being controlled than a small, flabby male body.

A well-muscled and apparently powerful female body can signify a masculine self. In such a case, the signifying effect of muscularity opposes the signifying effect of femaleness but cannot cancel it entirely. Ideology renders femaleness discordant with other signifiers of power. Muscularity and maleness are ideologically concordant, making their signifying value additive.[33]

Faces in which neither mercy nor compassion is evident can be tools for exerting control. Such faces can be accidents of genetic endowment. But they can also be learned. Such faces can be elements of a manhood act. It is not only male athletes in competition who wear game faces.

Mercy can be part of a manhood act when it signifies a capacity to determine the fate of an other.

The bits of signifying behavior that constitute a manhood act are, for most actors, matters of habit and of following unquestioned convention. Manhood acts may thus not be experienced as acts at all, because an "act" is usually understood to be intentionally deceptive. Most of the time, manhood acts are not experienced as phony, deceptive, or inauthentic.[34]

Males first learn to perform a manhood act, and only later realize, perhaps, that what they have learned and been shaped by is an act. To be told, for the first time, "big boys don't cry" is not to receive theatrical coaching. It is to be told how one must strive to *be*.

Human subjectivity is conditionable. Habits of perception, thought, feeling, and behavior are formed as adaptive responses to a social environment and are ingrained in the body. When the social environment includes a pervasive gender order to which individuals must adapt, individual subjectivity will be conditioned accordingly. In this sense, individual subjectivity can be said to be "gendered." We are all creatures of habitus.

The virtual self constructed in interaction might not correspond accurately to an individual's conditioned subjectivity. Character can be read incorrectly. It is always read incompletely. Readings of character, based on interpretations of signifying behavior, can also vary across audiences and between actor and audience. Actors can imagine they possess selves other than those imputed to them. One audience might impute a creditable masculine self, another might not.

Signifying behaviors that elicit attributions of possessing a masculine self and that are matters of deeply ingrained habit can be thought of as elements of a *gender habitus*.[35] Just as the experiences associated with class position can ingrain habits of thought, feeling, and behavior, so can the experiences associated with lifelong sex-category and gender-category membership. Because these behaviors are matters of habit and not usually reflected upon, males often feel authentic as they engage in manhood acts.

Gender habitus is not immutable programming. Habitus can be thwarted by novel circumstances, uncooperative audiences, and conflicting impulses to act. Such problems, if serious enough, can compel reflection, adaptation, and reconditioning. Even so, gender habitus will shape an individual's feelings about the sort of personal changes that "feel right" to undertake. And in contemplating personal changes, *gender* habitus is not the only habitus that matters.

Discrepant elements in a manhood act—signifying behaviors that do not meet audience expectations—can evoke demands for an account. An account is an explanation for the discrepant element, in an attempt to prevent it from damaging the manhood act as a whole.[36] When an audience demands an account, a male may become aware that part of his manhood act has come into question and remedial action is necessary. This can induce awareness that the act, or part of it, is an act. Persistent awareness of the dramaturgical nature of manhood can induce feelings of inauthenticity.

Signifying a masculine self, though largely habitual and often seemingly effortless, is not without costs. The energy expended in remaining alert for opportunities to signify the capacity for control is a cost. The energy expended in guarding against intimations that one is controllable is a cost. Chronic fear of being seen as unable to exert control or resist being controlled is a cost. Shame upon failure is a cost. The one-sided individual development and the distorted relationships that come from an obsession with control are costs. The diminishment of the womanized other is the greatest and most unconscionable cost.

Manhood acts are motivated not only by the promise of benefits and privileges vis-à-vis women, but by fear of shame and humiliation, of being exposed as unworthy of manhood status.[37] Even as males strive to signify autonomy, fear of being diminished in manhood status makes males more controllable. Males can be induced to accept political, economic, or military subordination if they are allowed to take pride in the construction of an illusory masculine self. Resistance to being controlled can also be reduced by defining the capacity to bear suffering as a sign of manhood. A real man can take pain, especially if it arises in a manhood contest.

Males striving to be recognized as men by more powerful men are more controllable than males striving to be human.

A manhood act can include disavowal of the desire to control others. An individual male can try to reject the imputation of being inclined to strive for domination. "I might have a male body and present myself as a man," the subtext runs, "but don't therefore presume that I am an insensitive brute." This is to distance oneself from the self implied by male embodiment. Yet to present oneself as a man is still to claim membership in the dominant gender group. And disavowing a *desire* to control others is not the same as disavowing a *capacity* to exert control or resist being controlled.

Overtly disavowing interest in control can be useful for achieving control. It puts others off guard.

Males can verbally reject male supremacy without rejecting manhood status for themselves. The verbal rejection might be all the more powerful—as a claim to a moral self—because it comes from a member of the dominant gender group.

Males can construct themselves as men and yet oppose sexism, just as whites can oppose racism. Both men and whites nonetheless remain caught in a set of social arrangements that bestow higher-status identities and confer unearned privilege. To fail to challenge these arrangements is to help reproduce them.[38] The question of what constitutes an adequate challenge has no honest answers that are comforting.

Liberals often object to extreme inequalities in wealth or income but do not oppose the capitalist economy that produces these inequalities. Males who construct themselves as men often object to crass expressions of sexism but do not oppose the gender order that systematically advantages them at women's expense.

Immanent social criticism of the gender order asks males striving to be men to please do so in less destructive ways. Transcendent social criticism asks if humanity would be better served if no one tried to construct a masculine self, no one claimed membership in the gender category "men," and no one competed for manhood status. Immanent social criticism presumes the inevitability of men, masculine selves, and manhood contests—and hopes to limit the damage they cause. Transcendent criticism presumes the possibility of abolishing the social formations—economic exploitation, hierarchical control, and the manhood they require—that make damage inevitable.

One need not believe that humans are perfectible to believe that social life can be organized to foster more kindness, compassion, generosity, and cooperativeness. Proposing how humans might improve upon themselves is optimistically presumptuous. It is an invitation to consider what might be, not a request for legislation.

Publicly exorcising the demons enlodged by a patriarchal gender order can help to deny them shelter elsewhere.

Males often experience conflicting impulses to act. Circumstances can answer to impulses to act in ways that would undermine a manhood act. A male might wish to be seen as tough and rational, on the one hand, so as to elicit attributions of possessing a masculine self, and at the same time wish to act with tenderness and compassion, thus risking attributions of weakness. If not for conflicting impulses to act, the cage of gender habitus would be locked more tightly than it is.

Manhood acts cannot be taken lightly. Nor can demands to account for potentially discrediting bits of signifying behavior. To be recognized as male is to be expected, as a matter of cultural convention, to put on a manhood act. It is to be expected to do one's part in reproducing the gender order and upholding belief in its rightness. Failing to do this, and especially failing to account for missteps, is to risk being seen as incompetent, immoral, or insane.[39] A male who fails to put on an expected manhood act is courting interactional trouble.

The subtext of an accountability demand is this: "you are not behaving as you are supposed to behave as a (presumed) male. You are not signifying the kind of self you should possess as a man. Your behavior implies that you are not worthy of full manhood status." The further subtext is this: "get your act together, or suffer the consequences." What is called for is semiotic repair of a damaged claim to privilege.

Manhood acts can be parodied intentionally, as in films such as *The Expendables.* When young males try to emulate the manly characters they see in films, the result is often an unwitting parody of a parody. Sometimes this is funny. Sometimes it is deadly.

A gender order includes routinized practices, normative rules, legitimating beliefs, and ingrained dispositions, but these do not make it determinative of behavior. Routines can be disrupted, rules ignored, and beliefs questioned. Ingrained dispositions can come to awareness, be reflected upon, and altered.[40] Those who are disadvantaged can resist. These are not only possibilities; they are in fact how gender orders change.

On an everyday basis, gender orders are stable and experienced as compelling, because to reject collective routines, shared rules, and widely held beliefs makes it impossible to interact smoothly with others and to elicit their cooperation. A manhood act is helpful for getting along with others when it is what others expect and when they see it as a sign of good character.

Manhood acts are not only about individual males getting along with others; they are about males collectively maintaining the benefits and privileges that come with being members of the gender group called "men." This is why males who want to retain those benefits and privileges disdain manhood acts that fail to construct a sufficiently masculine self. Such acts tend to undermine belief in essential differences between males and females. They also make it hard to sustain belief in the natural superiority of males when it comes to exercising control in ways that warrant extra reward and respect. A bad manhood act by one male can puncture the illusion on which the benefits and privileges of other males depend. Males thus police each other's manhood acts with vigilance.

Manhood acts require cooperative audiences. If an audience does not perceive an actor's expressive action as signifying a capacity to exert control or resist being controlled, a masculine self cannot be constructed. By definition, a masculine self is always a joint creation. A masculine self thus remains vulnerable, despite its alleged hardness and potency. It is the equivalent of a glass house that can be shattered by a carefully thrown word.

Constructing a masculine self depends on shared cultural knowledge concerning the meaning of signs and symbols wielded by actors in a scene of face-to-face interaction.[41] It also depends on shared knowledge of how types of actors relate to each other. These relationships extend beyond immediate scenes of face-to-face interaction. Situationally created selves are always in part the consequences of relationships with others outside the scene.[42]

An individual can signify the capacity to exert control and resist being controlled by invoking relationships to others. This is what occurs in formal organizations. Bosses, whether male or female, are understood to be able to exert control because they will be supported by others in the organization. It is this shared understanding—between boss and worker—that allows a boss to construct a masculine self and leads a worker to comply with a boss's wishes.

Being seen as a member of a dominant group implies to members of a subordinate group that one could, if necessary, draw on the resources of the dominant group to exert control.[43] The greater the perceived solidarity of the dominant group, the more credible the impression of an individual's capacity to exert control. The situational construction of a masculine self is thus always dependent, in part, on presuppositions about male solidarity.

Threats to male solidarity are threats to male supremacy, though male supremacy is hardly threatened by a few dissenting males. Historically, gender heretics have been easily ignored, discredited, or, somewhat less easily, killed—actions that serve to reaffirm male solidarity. To marginalize, discredit, or expunge a heretic also sends a message to others who might find themselves inclined to challenge an exploitive gender order: Do Not Try It.

Being seen as possessing a masculine self implies the possibility of mobilizing the support of others—soldiers, police, bureaucratic functionaries—who are eager to display their capacity for exerting control. It also implies a willingness to take whatever steps are necessary to maintain control. To construct a masculine self is thus always to construct an air of threat.

Constructing a masculine self depends in part on the semiotic skill deployed by an actor in a given situation and in part on shared cultural knowledge about how the bits of an actor's signifying behavior should be interpreted. It also depends on shared knowledge of how an actor stands in relationship to others outside the situation, these relationships being crucial determinants of an actor's ability to exert control. A masculine self is thus a consequence of culture and social organization no less than it is a consequence of virtuoso self-presentation.

No individual cop could get away with pepper-spraying a person in a mass protest if it were not understood that the cop was part of an organized group capable of applying even greater violence, and doing so with impunity. Likewise, no boss could fire a worker if capitalist relations of production were not widely understood, and understood to be enforced by an organized group (police) capable of using physical violence.

A form of social organization—an enduring set of ways for doing things together—can provide greater or fewer opportunities for people to signify capacities for exerting control or resisting control by others. A hierarchical form of social organization requires frequent indication by some actors of a capacity for exerting control over other people. It also provides frequent opportunities to display a capacity to resist being controlled. An egalitarian form of social organization—a form in which people did not try to control others—would provide few, if any, opportunities to construct a masculine self.

Manhood acts are built into the routine workings of all hierarchical organizations and realms of activity where people compete for status and power.[44]

In modern capitalist societies, patriarchal authority is vested in the state, so the state must signify a masculine character. All state leaders and would-be leaders are correspondingly compelled to signify masculine selves. Signs of compassion are permissible, if they do not raise doubts about the ultimate capacity to exert control.[45] The signifying values of a drone fleet and a presidential kill list are not canceled by a teardrop on the podium.

Manhood acts are adaptations to hierarchy. They are essential to the maintenance of hierarchy, and are also undertaken in opposition to hierarchy. The masculine selves thereby engendered are mutually dependent and often mutually destructive.

Constructing a masculine self typically entails signifying rank in any status hierarchy that can plausibly be invoked. Such status claims are about control and resisting control. The normative presupposition is that those of lower status will defer to those of higher status.[46] To claim higher status is to say, "You should defer to me, not I to you. You have no right to expect compliance from me. I have greater social value."

Competition is built into the construction of masculine selves, because one person's success at exerting or resisting control is another person's failure. The zero-sum nature of the game, which can be deadly, tends to escalate the struggle for control. It also tends to dehumanize relationships between males and others, because others come to be seen either as obstacles to signifying a masculine self, or as props useful for doing so. In a society characterized by striving for manhood status through the signification of masculine selves, humans are inevitably reduced from ends in themselves to mere means to ends.

The tragedy of the commons is traceable to the tragedy of manhood, which is the tragedy of collective annihilation arising from competition for status, wealth, and power.[47]

Competitiveness as a manly quality is another name for the refusal to be dominated or to accept subordinate status. Signifying competitiveness is essential to signifying a fully creditable masculine self. A male who is not constantly striving to get ahead, to outdo others, is not seen as worthy of full manhood status.[48] This is a lesson for females/women seeking faux-manhood status in formal organizations. Displaying a desire to get ahead, to achieve rank, is a must.

All systems of exploitation require the construction of masculine selves. All systems of exploitation also require periodic demonstration, lest subordinates forget, that the capacity for exerting control is not merely an imaginary construct. Bodies must sometimes be used to put other bodies back into line.

All systems of exploitation are inherently destructive, even if they yield great wealth for a few and general improvement in the material conditions of life. What such systems inevitably destroy is the human potential of those whose minds, bodies, and labor are controlled so that a few can enjoy all that life has to offer. The perpetuation of such systems requires a cultivated blindness to the human potential they waste. It also requires belief that the least deserving, the exploiting classes, are the most deserving.[49]

Constructing a masculine self requires signifying emotional toughness. This, too, is about control and resisting control. To be emotionally tough is to be undeterrable by feelings of love or compassion. It is to be willing to do whatever is necessary, despite the emotional cost, to compel others to behave as one desires.

Signifying the capacity for emotional toughness can instill fear in others, because it implies a willingness to inflict pain without limit.[50] When this is successful as a control strategy, it undermines others' claims to possessing masculine selves. To frighten others into obedience is to diminish their social value and to implicitly justify their subordination.

In common parlance, when a male is thought to be fully controlled by another, he is said to be unmanned. When resistance to control is advised, it often takes the form, in US culture, of being urged to "man up" or "grow a pair."

Signifying emotional toughness includes showing no fear. To show fear is to indicate that one can be intimidated, hence controlled. To show no fear means that one is not fazed by the prospects of discomfort, pain, or death. Thus one cannot be frightened into obedience. Signifying emotional toughness can be a claim to a self of value equal to the selves claimed by would-be dominators.

Manhood acts that involve signifying emotional toughness by showing no fear often lead to the actor's injury or demise. Such acts are not necessarily failures, from the standpoint of constructing masculine selves. As virtual realities, masculine selves can be imputed to actors who no longer exist. Such actors may enjoy imagined accolades in fleeting moments before their departure.[51]

Most males can imagine circumstances under which they might have to kill another male to prove their manhood. Most males can imagine circumstances under which they would feel compelled to embrace death to prove their manhood. Many males would profess to prefer death to being unmanned. Few males live up to such professing.

The headline of a final compensatory manhood act: MAN KILLS WIFE, KILLS SELF. The headline of a manhood act scripted by elite males and paid for by subordinated others: SOLDIER DIES IN COMBAT. The headline of a manhood act undertaken by elite males: THOUSANDS LAID OFF AS PRODUCTION IS MOVED OVERSEAS. The biblical name for the ultimate collective manhood act: ARMAGEDDON.

Replacing male bodies with a few female ones in a system of exploitation counts as no progress toward creating a sustainable, egalitarian society. Capitalism is not threatened when women construct masculine selves and behave in the manner of capitalists.[52] Gentler exploitation is still exploitation, and it will be preserved with violence if politeness fails.

The capacity to exert control and resist being controlled can be demonstrated by acts of creation and by acts of destruction. In the absence of opportunities to construct a masculine self by creating objects of value, a masculine self can be constructed by destroying objects of value.[53] The greater the value of the object, the more impressive the act. Objects that are defined as soft and weak have little value and are often destroyed profligately, with slight notice or consequence.

Creating, controlling, or destroying an object defined as masculine has greater value for signifying a masculine self than creating, controlling, or destroying an object defined as feminine. These objects are often other human beings.

Anything that can be controlled or resisted can be used as a prop for signifying a masculine self. Even the weather. A young man who goes about in shorts and a T-shirt on a freezing day sends a message: "let it be known that I am impervious to the cold and to the discomfort it might induce in others. If the weather cannot dominate me, neither can you."

Skateboards and cruise missiles can serve equivalent signifying functions for different classes of males.

Anything that can be made into a symbol of resistance or fearlessness can become a prop for signifying a masculine self. Young males can be led to believe that smoking cigarettes signifies death-defying toughness and thus manly indomitability. Young males have been led to this belief by the expenditure of billions of dollars on clever advertising and deceitful marketing.[54] To signify rugged individualism, millions of powerless young males use a mass-marketed prop that weakens and kills them.

Commodities that signify masculine selves are the opiate of the males.

The capacity of individual males to exert control and resist being controlled is negligible in the face of an organized system of exploitation. Males may thus be drawn to collective action through which they can assert a capacity for exerting and resisting control. Participation in the collective manhood act pays a psychological wage to the otherwise powerless individual. Armies, nations, and sports teams recruit by offering these wages.

Manhood acts are performed for others, and it is out of others' interpretations that the imputation of a masculine self arises. But signifying behaviors are also witnessed in the theater of an actor's mind. Individuals perceive and interpret their own signifying behaviors, such as they might be aware of them and, on this basis, impute qualities to themselves. A masculine self can thus be the imagined possession of a self-reflective agent.[55] It may be a hard imagining to sustain, however, if no external audience will validate it.

An actor has knowledge of weaknesses and failures, proscribed desires, and feelings of inauthenticity that an external audience does not. And so it can happen that no fully creditable masculine self is createable in the theater of an actor's mind. The result is chronic shame that can render a man controllable. Relieve this shame by crediting him with a masculine self of glorious magnitude—compare him favorably to Achilles—and he will obey.

Chronic shame because of an inability to construct a fully creditable masculine self can make some men feel oppressed by the social arrangements that privilege men as a group.

A consistent lack of external audience validation—a sense that one's manhood act is not being properly appreciated, or that one is not being credited with a masculine self of the desired level of social value—can spur efforts to compensate. Such efforts can be clumsy or adroit. They can succeed or fail, to greater or lesser degrees. Abject failure may be experienced as requiring the destruction of the failed self.[56]

Only sometimes are compensatory efforts to construct a creditable masculine self consciously undertaken. Males can be drawn, without realizing it, to wielding signs of the capacity to exert control and resist being controlled because doing so elicits rewarding responses from accessible audiences. Signifying acts can be assembled by a gradual process of accretion. This process can unfold without plan, over many years. Males also gravitate toward audiences that are most favorably disposed toward the type of manhood act they are best able to perform. Some men end up riding Harleys; others end up writing books.

Manhood is seductive. Achieving it affords status and privilege and access to resources. It also pays the psychological wage that comes from the ability to identify with the dominant group and its superior qualities, heroes, and accomplishments. Understandably, most males want these benefits, despite the costs. Patriarchal ideology portrays these costs, which are optional, as the inevitable consequences of human existence.

Manhood acts have their exemplars. One can point to Achilles, Odysseus, or the modern equivalents and say, "Now *there* is a *man*." Such a statement conveys multiple subtexts: this is a man worthy of emulation; this is a man against whom other men can be measured; this is a man whose exploits illustrate how far the capabilities of men surpass those of women. No real male needs to match the qualities of these mythical figures for them to be consequential.[57] Consequences follow from using these figures as templates for action, standards of comparison, and as legitimators of male supremacy.

The human invention most useful for constructing a masculine self is the story. Any socially competent male can use this invention. The stories that illustrate how to construct a masculine self and that simultaneously valorize manhood are preserved as what we call *myths*. Manhood and male supremacy are sustained in part by imagining that such myths express deep truths about human nature rather than oppressive desires for status and power.[58]

New stories create possibilities for creating new selves. If we can imagine stories in which there are no men, no women, no whites, no blacks, no capitalists, no workers, we can try to grow into them, try to make them come true.[59]

Chapter 4

Drone Morality

On the evening of Saturday, November 12, 2011, a group of about seventy anarchists took over an unused car dealership building on the main street of Chapel Hill, North Carolina, the town where I live. The takeover was apparently a spontaneous action after a daylong book fair. The building had sat empty for years and was widely considered an eyesore. Inspired in part by the Occupy protests occurring around the country, the anarchist group entered the building and declared their intent to turn it into a community center. News reports quoted members of the group as saying that the building was unlocked and no damage was done to gain entry.[1]

The group spent the next day cleaning the building, setting up a kitchen, and putting posters in the windows ("STOP TAKING ORDERS/START TAKING OVER"). Police took notice of the occupation and went in to investigate. Disputes arose later about whether police warned the occupiers of possible arrest if they didn't leave. Members of the anarchist group knew that they were trespassing, but wanted to make the point that the community's interest in good use of the property should trump the owner's legal right to let it deteriorate. Local officials, although themselves unhappy about the building's condition, did not agree.

The next day, eighteen hours after the anarchists took over the building, the police moved in to evict them. Only seven members of the original group were in the building at the time. The eviction was carried out like a military raid.

Fifteen officers in full body armor stormed the building. They brandished semiautomatic pistols and assault rifles, screaming at people to get on the ground. Uninvolved observers and passersby on the street were treated similarly. Twelve people, including two news reporters, were cuffed and detained. Eight people were arrested. This included seven anarchists arrested for breaking and entering, and one sixty-eight-year-old woman who was passing by and asked an officer what was going on. He ordered her to get on the ground along with everyone else. When she refused, she was arrested for "obstructing and delaying a police officer."

The story made national news, in part because of a dramatic photograph showing police in tactical gear pointing pistols and rifles at people outside the building. A segment of the local community reacted to the raid with outrage. The feeling was that the police had gone overboard, that there was no need for such aggressive, potentially lethal handling of a few protesters who were well-intentioned and doing no harm. There was also anger at how the police had treated reporters and onlookers. There was embarrassment, too, in that the photograph of the raid clashed with Chapel Hill's image of itself as a progressive college town with a high tolerance for protest and diversity. Citizen groups demanded that police, the town manager, and the mayor account for their actions. Hundreds of people signed a petition asking the town council for an independent inquiry into the incident.

In the immediate aftermath of the raid and arrests, the Chapel Hill police chief tried to justify the level of force employed. It was well known, he claimed, that anarchist tactics often included destroying property and booby-trapping occupied buildings. The police also had reason to believe, he said, that the group was distributing dangerous "riot literature." Moreover, the posters in the windows of the building made it hard to tell what the anarchists were doing inside. All in all, the chief concluded, "we believe this [action] was prudent and reasonable, given what we knew." No weapons or traps of any kind were found.

Town officials backed the police. In his public statement, the mayor said, "These [anarchist] actions were clear violations of state law. In these instances, the town will respond in accord with the oath every elected official and law enforcement officer takes—to uphold the laws of our state and nation." The town manager claimed that the actions of the police were justified because they were "consistent with training designed to minimize the potential for unintended consequences and injury." Some members of the town council thought the police had mistreated the reporters on the scene. By a vote of 5 to 4, the council approved a motion to issue an apology to the press.

In response to the public outcry, local officials agreed to investigate themselves. The result was a report issued by the town manager about two months later. In the report, the town manager reiterated his belief that the on-scene police commanders had made the best possible decisions, and that the actions of the police were "appropriate" and "in the community's best interests." The report did note, however, that in the future the police needed to communicate better with the media.

People who were upset by the actions of the police saw the town manager's report as a whitewash. They continued to argue that the police had used a level of force that posed a high risk of injury or death and was vastly out of proportion to any credible threat posed by a few peaceful protesters in an empty building. Many people continued to demand an independent inquiry. Instead, the matter was referred to a never-before-used community policing advisory committee. When the committee recommended an independent inquiry, the town council refused to pay for it.

I recount this story because it illustrates several elements of what I refer to in this chapter as drone morality. By drone morality I mean a tacit moral paradigm that grows out of and reinforces relations of domination and subordination. To say that this is a tacit moral paradigm is to say that its principles usually remain unspoken. These principles operate at the level of deep assumptions and are often masked by other moral rhetorics. My goals here are thus to articulate the basic principles of drone morality, show how they guide action, and show how they produce real-world consequences. As will become clear, I use the term *drone* advisedly; its military and biological resonances are intended.

The first principle of drone morality is this: that which establishes and preserves hierarchical control is good. This is different from saying that *order* is a fundamental good; drone morality valorizes order that results from hierarchical control, or the upward concentration of power and its downward application. It is not just preservation of hierarchical control that constitutes the foremost good from the standpoint of drone morality, but control *by those who have the correct worldview*—in short, control by "legitimate authorities." Drone morality does not question this legitimacy or investigate its undemocratic foundations.

The second principle of drone morality is that what is right and good is to be found by reference to rules, not feelings or moral intuition. Correct action is determined, from the standpoint of drone morality, by application of the correct rule. Empathy is suspect. Feelings are not seen as aids to discerning the nature of a moral problem or how best to solve it; feelings are seen, rather, as impediments to moral problem solving.[2] Drone morality thus valorizes and embraces rules, though rules can be trumped by the imperative to maintain hierarchical control.

The third principle of drone morality is that what extends the human capacity for exerting control is good. Drone morality thus relentlessly and uncritically seeks increased control over all things in the world, including people. From the standpoint of drone morality, the potential costs of increased control are always less than the imagined benefits. Calculations will be adjusted to make the pursuit of greater control seem reasonable. If freedom and privacy stand to be lost, this loss will be seen as outweighed by gains in safety and order.

What I am calling drone morality includes the implications that follow from these basic principles. The first principle—the overriding dedication to hierarchical control—implies that individual moral autonomy and critical thought are undesirable. It also implies that truth, the essential input to critical thought, must be sacrificed if it threatens hierarchical control. The second principle—the valorization of rules over feelings—implies that actions consistent with legitimated rules will be seen as noble and just, even when the consequences are perverse, destructive, and in conflict with the moral intuitions that arise from empathic connection to others.

A further implication is that what is strong is valued over what is weak. From the standpoint of drone morality, that which is capable of exerting control has greater value than that which is controllable. Deference and social honor are thus accorded in correspondence with the capacity to exert control or resist being controlled. Drone morality sees not just that might makes right, but that might makes the world properly ordered, good, and worth living in. It is an affront to drone morality to suggest that what is perceived as weak be allowed to threaten the order established by what is perceived as strong.

Drone morality is embraced by both the strong and the weak. For the strong, drone morality justifies the crushing of dissent and disorder; it provides insulation from the emotional cost of inflicting pain on others; and it legitimates the destruction of that which can be dominated. For the weak, drone morality makes the pain of subordination bearable, mitigates the burden of moral responsibility, and makes self-sacrifice appear noble. Drone morality allows the strong and the weak to maintain a facade of humanity while doing the inhumane things necessary to preserve relations of domination and subordination.

Although I have called drone morality a paradigm and described it in terms of principles and first-order implications, I don't mean to suggest that it constitutes a coherent moral philosophy or consistent guide to moral action. It is, in fact, fraught with contradictions. That which might seem soft and weak—religion, for example—can be valued for its contribution to preserving hierarchical control. That which threatens control—a rival leader, gang, or army—can be respected if it appears strong. Feelings, even those arising from empathy, can be valued if they motivate efforts to maintain control—for example, the feelings that soldiers develop for each other in combat. Rules can be disdained when the weak invoke them to resist elite control.

To reiterate an earlier point: the principles of drone morality are tacit—understood but, like the rules of grammar, rarely articulated. They usually remain unspoken because to make them explicit can threaten hierarchical control. To say "might makes right" is to invite challenge and strife; to say "the law makes right" is to invite obedience and cooperation. To point out that *might* makes the law, interprets the law, and enforces the law is to expose a potentially troubling reality. For the sake of avoiding trouble and preserving the benefits of domination, drone morality must be practiced without being named, or it must be falsely named.

The problem is not with rules or laws per se. The problem, rather, is with a particular way of understanding and using rules and laws. Drone morality makes of the law not a tool of justice but of justification, a way to legitimate action that is ultimately about preserving hierarchical control. The goodness or badness of laws depends, in general terms, on how they are created, interpreted, and enforced, and on the consequences they produce. Drone morality brooks no critical thought about these matters, instead treating the law as either cudgel or, from a subordinate position, an idol to which all must bow.

Though its principles are rarely articulated and often disguised, drone morality can be discerned by looking at what people do. Just as the rules of grammar can be inferred from patterns of speech, so can the principles of drone morality be inferred from patterns of behavior. The relevant behavior is that which involves challenges to authority—which is to say, challenges to hierarchical control—and challenges to unjust social arrangements and practices. Underlying moral principles can be inferred from the ways in which such conflicts are handled.

Let us return, then, to the case of the eviction raid. Drone morality is evident in how the raid was executed, how it was justified, and how officials responded to citizen complaints. I should note that I treat officials' accounts for their actions as data to be analyzed.[3] Post-hoc justifications are not explanations and certainly cannot be taken at face value.

Recall that police officers in body armor rushed the building without warning, pointed loaded weapons at occupiers and onlookers, then forced people to lie facedown on the ground before cuffing and arresting them. It was a display of overwhelming force. The anarchists did not have permission to use the building, and it seems clear that they expected to be evicted eventually. Nonetheless, police and local officials had a great deal of discretion in handling the situation. If the anarchists had refused to leave, they could have been removed and arrested in a civil, or at least far less violent, manner.

No one thought that the anarchists posed a threat to life or property. Their actions might have posed a threat to respect for property *laws*, but the threat, given the anarchists' marginality, was minuscule. So why the blitzkrieg? Because the real threat they posed was to hierarchical control. A bunch of scruffy anarchists simply could not be allowed to flout the property laws that are the basis for economic domination in a capitalist society. The anarchists were, from the standpoint of drone morality, threatening order and disrespecting the authorities responsible for keeping order. They were also, by virtue of their scruffiness and marginality, seen as weak. Hence they had to be swiftly and decisively slapped down. Drone morality allowed for no argument, no negotiation, no accommodation. Control had to be restored.

States resonated widely but did not inspire much mobilization.[5] Nonetheless, the movement's tactics were an affront to drone morality's love of control. Unlike protesters who march through empty downtown streets on a Sunday afternoon and then go home, Occupy folks wanted to stick around and be visible. It was this unruliness—a refusal to disperse when authorities said, *You've expressed yourselves, now go home so we can restore order*—that posed a threat.

In the Chapel Hill incident, property laws that made the anarchists' action illegal were already in place and well understood, and could be readily invoked to justify police action. Elsewhere, in the case of Occupy protests on public or quasi-public ground, new laws were passed, or obscure laws discovered and reinterpreted, to justify evictions. Once occupiers could be defined as *breaking the law*, it became acceptable, from the standpoint of drone morality, to shut them down. And, as in the Chapel Hill case, what drone morality made acceptable to authorities, it also made acceptable to a large share of the public.[6]

Drone morality valorizes the exertion of control and that which enhances control. This principle was reflected in the behavior of police who eagerly employed new technologies—Tasers, chemical sprays, sound blasters—in seeking to compel compliance on the part of Occupy protesters. But there are limits of course, because drone morality is not universal and because its pure application can provoke resistance and loss of control. Though they equipped themselves to do so, the Chapel Hill police could not have shot the anarchist occupiers without causing a breakdown in legitimacy and, probably, disruptive mass protests. Likewise, when Oakland police seriously injured a Marine veteran at an Occupy camp, it provoked a huge backlash. Rules trump feelings from the standpoint of drone morality, but feelings induced by clumsy or excessive exertions of control can lead to action that disregards all rules.

In the case of Occupy protesters in Chapel Hill and around the United States, competing moral paradigms limited what drone morality could accomplish. Police and local officials typically embraced the principles of drone morality and counted on most of the public to do so as well. But human rights and citizenship rights could not be completely ignored in the interest of preserving hierarchical control—not without risking de-legitimation and loss of control. Elsewhere, however, when there is no limiting concern for governmental legitimacy, the consequences of drone morality can be horrific. Drone morality's damage in the case of Occupy protesters in the United States was minor compared with the damage it does to people around the world.

*   *   *

In December 2011, the *Atlantic* published an article with the title "Drone-Ethics Briefing: What a Leading Robot Expert Told the CIA."[7] The author, Patrick Lin, is a professor of philosophy at California Polytechnic State University in San Luis Obispo. As the title suggests, the article consists mainly of a briefing memo that Lin delivered in the fall of 2011 at an event hosted by an outfit called In-Q-Tel, which is described as "the CIA's venture-capital arm." The editorial lead-in to the piece calls it "unnerving." It is indeed a useful window to drone morality.

Although much of the memo is professorial, pointing in detached, academic fashion to ethical issues associated with the use of robotic weapons, it's clear that Lin identifies with his audience. He uses "we" and "us" throughout; he refers to the people against whom robotic weapons will be deployed as "terrorists"; and when he refers to critics of robotic weapons it is to make the point that their objections need to be countered. I mention this not because Lin himself is of interest, but to establish that his memo is congenial to the moral outlook of his audience, an outlook from which the manufacture, sale, and use of robotic weapons are foregone conclusions. The memo, in other words, is not a challenge to these conclusions but an aid to making them palatable. What the memo thus illustrates is not simply drone morality, but the *crafting* of drone morality.

As I will show, the memo offers its audience a way to think about morality itself, and a way to think about the use of robotic weapons as ethical. The lessons about the nature of morality and about what is essential to ethical conduct are largely implicit. By drawing them out, it becomes possible to see how drone morality so readily conduces to evil.

The oft-cited advantages of military robots are that they can be used in combat and in dangerous rescue and reconnaissance missions, thus reducing the risk of one's own soldiers being killed.[8] Robots can also perform a host of noncombat jobs that are dirty or dangerous, and do so without fatigue or complaint. Lin's memo reviews this familiar territory and then goes beyond it. He proposes that another advantage of robots is their ability to "act with dispassion," especially when the tasks are interrogation and torture. Robots, Lin says,

> can solve the dilemma of using physicians in interrogations and torture. These activities conflict with [physicians'] duty to care and the Hippocratic oath to do no harm. Robots can monitor vital signs of interrogated suspects, as well as any human doctor can. They could also administer injections and even inflict pain in a more controlled way, free from malice and prejudices that might take things too far (or much further than already).

Elsewhere Lin notes that "robots don't act with malice or hatred or other emotions that can lead to war crimes and other abuses, such as rape." This dispassion, Lin also suggests, means that robots can be "objective, unblinking observers to ensure ethical conduct in wartime ... and maybe even act more ethically [than humans] in the high-stress environment of war."

Lin does not explicitly describe the nature of the dilemma that arises when physicians are involved in torture. He seems to presume that his audience is familiar with torture and its procedural difficulties. As I understand it, the dilemma is this: torture protocols require that physicians monitor the process, yet physicians are unreliable participants because they feel a professional duty to relieve pain, not aid its infliction. Robots offer a possible solution because they can play the monitoring role without qualms about "doing no harm" getting in the way. The strict letter of the torture protocol is thus met, allowing torture to proceed under cover of law. Dilemma resolved.

Lin says he is not advocating robot-monitored torture, just speculating about it. But the manner in which he speculates teaches several lessons about the nature of morality and about the relationship between moral reasoning and ethical conduct. These are lessons, offered implicitly, that instill and affirm drone morality.

The first lesson is that morality can be detached from empathy. Lin might admit that physicians' reluctance to participate in torture, even as monitors, arises in part from empathy-induced squeamishness. But the more serious problem is that physicians are *duty*-bound and *oath*-bound not to participate in causing harm. There are, in other words, *rules* that get in the way of physicians doing what torturers would like them to do.[9] The simplest lesson to be drawn from this is that morality and ethical conduct are based on rules, not on feelings that might arise upon observing how other human beings are affected by one's actions.

Note that Lin applauds robotic dispassion and cites emotions—malice and hatred—as possibly leading to war crimes, rape, and going "too far." The lesson here is that, to the extent that emotions enter consideration at all, they are seen as interfering with ethical conduct. Robotic dispassion—presumably based on programmed instructions (i.e., rules)—is good; it might even make robots capable of acting, as Lin says, *more* ethically than humans. Human compassion, however, does not enter Lin's consideration as an emotional response essential to morality or ethical conduct. Compassion, in this moral worldview, is not a constraint on abuse but a potential impediment, as in the case of squeamish doctors who are weak players on an interrogation team.

A third lesson implicit in the memo is that moral deliberation can be compartmentalized. Though war crimes and rape are mentioned as matters of concern, war itself is not treated as unethical, a crime against humanity, or a matter about which individuals must think seriously before becoming involved. Likewise, torture itself is not seen as a form of abuse or a matter for moral reflection. What warrants consideration is only the risk of going too far. Lin's memo takes for granted that the moral acceptability of war and torture is determined by higher authorities, not by interrogators or drone operators. I would guess that no one in Lin's audience thought differently.

Emotions appear again in the memo in two other problematic forms. In one case, Lin considers the possible effect of drone warfare on drone operators.

> Some critics have worried that UAV operators—controlling drones from half a world away—could become detached and less caring about killing, given the distance, and this may lead to more unjustified strikes and collateral damage. But other reports seem to indicate an opposite effect: These controllers have an intimate view of their targets by video streaming, following them for hours and days, and they can also see the aftermath of a strike, which may include strewn body parts of nearby children. So there's a real risk of post-traumatic stress disorder (PTSD) with these operators.

The problem identified here is that drone operators may suffer psychological distress from seeing the results of their work. Presumably this distress arises from the emotions induced by seeing children blown apart. Understandably so.[10] But from the perspective of drone morality, as expressed in Lin's memo, the problem is not with blowing up innocent children, but with the possible loss of effectiveness on the part of military personnel. The pain and suffering experienced by victims of a drone attack are not matters for consideration. Nor is the possibility that the feelings of drone operators signal the fundamental immorality of their actions.

A second way that emotions are a problem concerns the reactions of those who face robots in battle or as agents of everyday control. The problem is that robots and robotic weapons could, because of how people feel about them, incite resistance. As Lin puts it,

> sending robot patrols into Baghdad to keep the peace would send the wrong message about our willingness to connect with the residents; we will still need human diplomacy for that. In war, this could backfire against us, as our enemies mark us as dishonorable and cowardly for [being] not willing to engage them man to man. This serves to make them more resolute in fighting us; it fuels their propaganda and recruitment efforts; and this leads to a new crop of determined terrorists.

To put it another way, a potential problem with using robots and drones to kill and control people is that it can cause a public-relations problem, because it makes people feel like insects. This in turn makes people angry and resistant, and more likely to become "terrorists" rather than grateful subjects. Perhaps if the objects of drone attacks were more dispassionate, in the manner of robots, they would behave more ethically and give up their terrorist ways.

The memo contains still more lessons, as offered, again implicitly, in Lin's consideration of "collateral damage." Lest the point be missed, it is worth noting that in the passage below the obligatory adjective *unintended* does not mean *unanticipated*.

> Another worry is that the use of lethal robots represents a disproportionate use of force, relative to the military objective. This speaks to the collateral damage, or unintended death of nearby innocent civilians, caused by, say, a Hellfire missile launched by a Reaper UAV. What's an acceptable rate of innocents killed for every bad guy killed: 1:1, 10:1, 50:1? That number hasn't been nailed down and continues to be a source of criticism. It's conceivable that there might be a target of such high value that even a 1000:1 collateral-damage rate, or greater, would be acceptable to us.

There are a number of lessons implied here: the killing of innocents, although perhaps regrettable, is entirely acceptable; it's important, if only to avoid criticism, to formulate a defensible *rule* about how many innocents can be killed in the process of killing a "bad guy"; military agents of the state have the right to make these determinations based on how important they believe it is to kill a person who resists being controlled; and that maintaining control is so important that it can warrant killing a thousand or more innocent people for the sake of killing one resister.

Lin's memo is a more powerful shaper of consciousness for not bringing to the surface the principles of drone morality that underlie it. To say, "Let's try to generate better PR by nailing down a good formula for how many children we can kill per bad guy," would be to expose these odious principles and their practical implications to the light of conscience.[11] For the sake of avoiding unsettling distress and maintaining control, it is better that drone morality be allowed to operate in the background. To overtly challenge its principles, in the community for which Lin's memo was intended, would be to mark oneself as a troublemaker or outsider and likely lead to excommunication.[12]

Both the preeminent concern with control and the masking of this concern with moral rhetoric are starkly evident in the last paragraph of Lin's memo. In concluding his briefing, Lin says,

> The issues above … give us much to consider, as we must. These are critical not only for self-interest, such as avoiding international controversies, but also as a matter of sound and just policy. For either reason, it's encouraging that the intelligence and defense communities are engaging ethical issues in robotics and other emerging technologies. Integrating ethics may be more cautious and less agile than a "do first, think later" (or worse, "do first, apologize later")

approach, but it helps us win the moral high ground—perhaps the most strategic of all battlefields.

It is the last line that gives away the game. The ultimate purpose of "engaging ethical issues," Lin admits, is not to determine what's right or good; this has, in keeping with the basic principles of drone morality, already been determined. What is good and right is that the United States should dominate. If "engaging ethical issues" aids this goal—by easing the consciences of those who are compelled to kill or by countering the resistance of those who are targeted for subjugation—then it is worth doing. It's just another part of the battle.

Probably without intending it, the last line of Lin's memo contains a key truth: moral philosophizing that is wedded to and serves the principles of drone morality is not moral philosophy at all. It is not a good-faith search for what is right or for the most ethical course of action. It is not an honest attempt to solve the moral problems entailed by conflicts between individuals, communities, and nations. It is indeed, as Lin says, a *battlefield*, the goal being to win—to establish control and dominate—by manipulating consciousness and subduing conscience.

Had not Lin's memo appeared at a convenient time (as I was writing this book), I might have used other memos as windows to drone morality. I am thinking of memos written by John Yoo, assistant US attorney general under George W. Bush, to justify torture; memos written by Bush administration officials to justify the invasion of Iraq; memos written by Obama administration officials to justify the assassination by drone of US citizen Anwar al-Awlaki; and memos written by other Obama administration officials to justify the indefinite detention, without judicial review or trial, of anyone the president deems a supporter of terrorism.[13] These are all works of virtuoso sophistry in which convoluted legal arguments are brought forth as substitutes for honest moral reasoning.

For elites, drone morality is cultivated to preserve legitimacy. The subtext of all the memos, speeches, and briefings that arise from and affirm drone morality is the same: *be assured that we as rational men have examined the moral quality of our actions. After considering the relevant principles and laws, we have determined that our actions are justified. There is, therefore, no need for further deliberation or consternation. Our efforts to rectify the situation at hand must and will proceed. Your cooperation, you should now understand, is as morally warranted as our action.* Elites and their minions might or might not believe in their own act; hideous realities are often known to those who must hide them. What matters, in any case, is that subordinates believe in the act.

From the perspective of a dominant group, cooperation, not just passive assent, is crucial. Drone morality must not only provide legitimation in an abstract sense, it must enable action, or at least neutralize obstacles to action. It must create in the minds of reward-seekers a willingness to "get the job done" as instructed. A chilling illustration of this mentality appeared in a *Spiegel Online* article about the woes of American drone operators, one of whom is quoted as saying, "There was no time for feelings. When the decision had been made, and they saw that this was an enemy, a hostile person, a legal target that was worthy of being destroyed, I had no problem with taking the shot."[14] The operator, in this case a woman, confesses her moral vacancy in the act of following orders and pulling the trigger. Her compliance is enabled by the belief that trustworthy others have determined that remote assassination is consistent with relevant laws and moral principles. Critical thought can thus be suspended and qualms eased. To the extent that this is not entirely the case, to the extent that drone morality does not entirely cancel empathy and moral intuition, distress and trauma are predictable results.

A day after the September 11, 2001, attacks on the World Trade Towers in New York and the Pentagon in Washington, DC, Ward Churchill, a professor of ethnic studies at the University of Colorado, published an essay, "Some People Push Back," in which he referred to the technocrats working in the Towers as "little Eichmanns."[15] He meant by this appellation that the victims were complicit, in the manner of obedient soldiers and citizens in Nazi Germany, in maintaining US global domination through the machinery of international finance. His larger point in the essay was that the 9/11 attacks needed to be understood as reactions to unjust US foreign policies. This was not a popular argument in the United States, but it was one made by many other critical intellectuals.[16]

Churchill's essay, published in an obscure political journal, went largely unnoticed until he was scheduled to speak at Hamilton College in January 2005. Critics of Churchill's radical politics found the essay and brought the "little Eichmanns" line to light. As his critics hoped, outrage ensued and the talk was canceled, ostensibly on the grounds that adequate security could not be provided. Churchill then became the object of investigation by the University of Colorado over charges of academic misconduct. He was eventually fired in July 2007.

Invoking Nazi imagery to describe those working in the Towers was clearly inflammatory, as events proved. But was it unfair? As a blanket indictment, yes. Most victims of the attacks—and certainly the legions of janitors, mechanics, secretaries, receptionists, and clerks who worked in the buildings—would have had no inkling of what Churchill was getting at. They were not uneasily following orders to herd Jews into boxcars. Nor were there any reasonable grounds for expecting them to think that their daily work harmed anyone. Thus to imply their culpability on a scale that associates them with Nazi war criminals is unfair and offensive.

Yet the larger issue of culpability is a dogged one. The proverbial buck must stop somewhere. Someone must be held accountable for enabling and ordering the violence that kills innocents, for managing the organizations that are used to oppress and exploit, and for orchestrating the efforts that cause suffering. Those who are pressed into service or who barely escape victimhood themselves are least culpable in these regards. That charge should fall, as it did at Nuremberg, on those who, knowing better, refine and purvey the drone morality that allows humans to live with themselves while butchering each other.

*   *   *

In the fall of 2006 a local antiwar activist spoke to the students in my social inequality class. He presented a critique of US foreign policy, the use of the US military to intervene in the affairs of other countries, and of the profit-driven "global war on terror." He was a compelling speaker in part because of his twenty years in the military, including stints in Special Forces as an Army Ranger and as an instructor at West Point. No one could dismiss him as a naive pacifist. At the end of his talk, a young woman asked, "If you feel the way you do, why did you join the army?" He explained that it had taken him decades to arrive at his views. "Remember," he said, "in 1970 I was a typical 18-year-old American boy."

I'm not sure that everyone got his point, but perhaps most did. He was a typical American boy in the sense that he saw military service as a rite of passage into manhood and a way to live out his macho fantasies. He was also a typical American boy in that he knew almost nothing about people in other countries, about history or geopolitics, or about the real purposes and consequences of US military intervention around the planet. His ignorance and desire for manhood status led him into the arms of a vast apparatus of violence from which it took twenty years to extricate himself. The same trap captures many young American males today.

The desire for manhood status is no less strong now than when my guest speaker joined the army. The same macho fantasies are fueled by TV shows and movies, martial sports, and now also by computerized video games, especially the "first-person shooter" variety. And to judge from international comparisons of student knowledge of geography, most American boys still know little about the rest of the world.[17] Teens may use the latest high-tech gadgets to connect with each other, but they are not, by and large, connecting with the vast body of historical knowledge and critical analysis potentially available to them. Thus there are still plenty—although what constitutes "plenty" is a matter of perspective—of typical American boys willing to participate in what they imagine to be the manly glories of war.

Turning adolescent fantasies and the desire for manhood status into collectively wrought horrors would not be possible, however, without the inculcation of drone morality. Young men (and, increasingly, young women) must be made willing to relinquish their moral autonomy, embrace the mission of controlling others, and follow rules laid down by elites, even if their moral intuition tells them to do otherwise. This has, of course, always been one of the main goals of military socialization—to overcome the natural human reluctance to hurt and kill others.[18]

The military is not the only place where drone morality is instilled. Children are taught to obey at home and in school. Religious instruction may also instill reverence for rules and authorities, secular and divine. In their teen years, many youngsters also discover the premium put on obedience in the workplace. By the time they reach recruitment age, the habit of suspending critical thought when faced with orders or rules handed down by authorities is well formed. Even so, the military arena is one in which drone morality is especially blatant and virulent.

But I am less interested in obvious efforts to instill drone morality—boot camp is the classic example—than in those that typically pass without notice. The latter, it seems to me, are more dangerous for being harder to see and resist. And so here I want to consider another case of the discursive crafting of drone morality. In this case, the damaging moral lessons are encoded in what might be called a song of praise.

On December 14, 2011, President Barack Obama spoke at Fort Bragg, North Carolina, following the withdrawal of US combat forces from Iraq. The immediate audience consisted mainly of soldiers, but the text of the speech was published in the *New York Times*, so it was also addressed to the nation.[19] The speech touted the Iraq war as a resounding success, an effort of which all could be proud. Such speeches to returning soldiers are often taken by political analysts as little more than rhetoric offered to soothe the pains of loss and sacrifice. On the other hand, such speeches help to create national myths that can have consequences later. For this reason they deserve a closer look, with particular attention to the lies they contain.[20]

It would be fair to say that the US invasion and nearly nine-year occupation of Iraq, far from being a success, was, on the whole, a disaster. The invasion was a crime from the start, initially sold to the American people with lies about Saddam Hussein's "weapons of mass destruction." When it became undeniable that no such weapons existed, the Bush administration offered a series of alternative lies: the invasion was about ousting a brutal tyrant; the invasion was about fighting al Qaeda and other terrorist groups; the invasion was about giving the Iraqi people the gifts of democracy and stable government. Only in the United States was there much confusion about the purposes of the invasion. Elsewhere around the world it was understood as another attempt by the US government to assert control in the Middle East, a region of immense importance to the world economy because of its energy resources.

The results of this three-trillion-dollar effort included 4,500 US soldiers dead and another 32,000 seriously wounded; 150,000 to 400,000 Iraqis killed; and another 2.3 million Iraqis turned into refugees.[21] When the United States pulled out in December 2011, 50 percent of Iraqis were living in slum conditions (up from 17 percent in 2000), 4.5 million children were orphaned, and 600,000 of those orphans were living in the streets. The US-backed government of Prime Minister Nuri al-Maliki reeked with corruption (Transparency International rated Iraq as the fourth most corrupt country in the world in 2011) and was creating an authoritarian police state, complete with the use of violence and torture to quash protest and the press. In January 2012 sectarian violence was resurging and threatening to tear the country apart again.[22] Baghdad, the hub of the occupation and the site of the United States' fortress-like embassy, was named the world's worst city, according to Mercer's 2011 Quality of Living rankings.[23] If these results constitute success, the mind boggles to imagine what failure would look like.

National leaders are of course wont to describe defeat as victory. This is not a failing of personal honesty, but a matter of necessity for maintaining the support of the populace and the military. Lies are thus to be expected. But lies can be packaged differently, and this packaging encodes messages about the moral outlook that is presumed to be shared between leaders and their audiences. In fact, it may be more important in the long run that this moral outlook is affirmed and privileged than that a particular debacle is misrepresented as a success. A failure to do this could make it harder for elites to muster troops and popular support for the next war.

President Obama's speech at Fort Bragg praised the returned soldiers for the traditionally vaunted qualities of soldierhood: hard work, sacrifice, bravery, resolve, strength, endurance, willingness to bear the pain of loss, and loyalty to each other. (Although both women and men are acknowledged in the speech, it's not hard to see that these are qualities conventionally associated with male soldiers and masculine selves.) Obedience was not explicitly cited as a soldierly virtue, though its importance was affirmed in coded language.

Both President Obama and his wife, Michelle, who introduced him, praised the soldiers for "answering the country's call." It was, in fact, Michelle Obama who most clearly underscored the importance of obedience when she said, "Whenever the country calls, you all are the ones who answer, no matter the circumstance, no matter the danger, no matter the sacrifice." To give praise for compliance *whenever, no matter the circumstance*, is to implicitly affirm the importance of doing what one is told and not thinking for oneself. President Obama also offered praise for "your patriotism, your commitment to fulfill your mission"—that is, for your willingness to equate patriotism with following orders, and for your willingness to do your jobs, no matter how corrupt the mission might have been. And lest the notion pass without challenge, it should be said that "the country" did not call any US soldiers to invade and occupy Iraq. The call came from a cabal of war criminals in the administration of President George W. Bush.

There are several parts of the speech that are worth quoting at length, because they illustrate so well how drone morality is crafted in ways even more subtle than the implicit valorizing of obedience. After assuring members of his audience that the country would provide them with continuing benefits as further rewards for their service, President Obama told the following story.

> *Obama:* But there is something else that we owe you. As Americans, we have a responsibility to learn from your service. I'm thinking of an example—Lieutenant Alvin Shell, who was based here at Fort Bragg. A few years ago, on a supply route outside Baghdad, he and his team were engulfed by flames from an RPG attack. Covered with gasoline, he ran into the fire to help his fellow soldiers, and then led them two miles back to Camp Victory where he finally collapsed, covered with burns. When they told him he was a hero, Alvin disagreed. "I'm not a hero," he said. "A hero is a sandwich." (Laughter.) "I'm a paratrooper."
> *Audience:* Hooah!
> *Obama:* We could do well to learn from Alvin. This country needs to learn from you. Folks in Washington need to learn from you.
> *Audience:* Hooah!

To be clear, the bravery and humility of Lieutenant Shell are not in question. In the immediate context of the attack, his actions were indeed heroic. But what exactly is the lesson that "folks in Washington" need to learn from this episode? The lesson does not seem to be that it is wrong to invade other people's countries under false pretenses and put US soldiers in harm's way, nor that war should be undertaken only as a last resort, because it destroys bodies and lives. After the affirming "Hooah!" Obama draws out the lesson:

> Policymakers and historians will continue to analyze the strategic lessons of Iraq—that's important to do. Our commanders will incorporate the hard-won lessons into future military campaigns—that's important to do. But the most important lesson that we can take from you is not about military strategy—it's a lesson about our national character. For all of the challenges that our nation faces, you remind us that there is nothing we Americans can't do when we stick together.

The lesson, it seems, is that we can continue to get away with this kind of thing—invading and occupying other countries, and perhaps doing so more effectively—if we stick together and embrace the can-do spirit of Americanism.

The notion of "national character" is itself problematic; it obscures internal diversity and conflict, and lends itself alternately to chauvinism (as in Obama's speech) or to racism. But if one were to infer a national character from the behavior of the United States vis-à-vis Iraq, what would this character be? A neutral observer might reasonably suppose that Americans are a people who feel entitled to exert control over the affairs of other people; who are willing to kill and injure a great many people as they try to exert control; who feel no remorse for the damage they cause to those whom they are trying to control; who cannot honestly assess the consequences of their actions; and who chronically fail to learn from their mistakes.

In the case of US military interventionism, learning from mistakes is hard because those who make the mistakes do not bear the costs. It is thus important that others be induced to continue to bear those costs. Obama's speech performs precisely this function. After telling the troops that they—the "9/11 Generation," as he identifies them—have earned their place in history, he goes on to say,

> Because of you—because you have sacrificed so much for a people that you had never met, Iraqis have a chance to forge their own destiny. That's part of what makes us special as Americans. Unlike the old empires, we don't make these sacrifices for territory or for resources. We do it because it's right. There can be no fuller expression of America's support for self-determination than our leaving Iraq to its people. That says something about who we are.

The passage above is a breathtaking inversion of reality. It portrays the brutal invasion and occupation of a sovereign nation as a selfless humanitarian project reflecting nothing more than a love for democracy and a desire to help strangers in need. It is this sort of portrayal that leads people around the world to see Americans as dangerously delusional.

In fact, the United States had been meddling in Iraqi politics for decades, meddling that included covertly aiding Saddam Hussein's rise to power in the Baath Party and backing him even as he terrorized his own people. When Hussein invaded Kuwait in 1990 and stopped acting as a well-behaved US puppet, he was marked for removal. Plans for his removal were, as was later revealed in the so-called Downing Street memo, laid down well before claims about weapons of mass destruction were put forth to propagandize Americans into supporting the venture.[24]

Getting rid of Saddam Hussein was thus not about supporting democracy or self-determination—the US ruling class has always been willing to support compliant dictators around the world—but about making clear that disobedience would not be tolerated, especially not in a place rich with the petroleum resources on which the US economy depends. What US soldiers participated in was not a mission to protect America or free the Iraqi people; it was a mob hit that killed thousands of innocent bystanders and ignited local turf wars. It is fair to say, however, that the invasion inadvertently created an opening for the Iraqi people to "forge their own destiny"—mainly by organizing themselves to drive the United States out.

What is made explicit in the passage quoted above is American exceptionalism—the idea that the United States, unlike all other nations and empires throughout time, does what it does not out of desire for resources or control, but because of transcendent values and a commitment to do what's right. This theme of exceptionalism is underscored a few sentences later:

> So here's what I want you to know, and here's what I want all our men and women in uniform to know: Because of you, we are ending these wars [Iraq and Afghanistan] in a way that will make America stronger and the world more secure. Because of you. That success was never guaranteed. And let us never forget the source of American leadership: our commitment to the values that are written into our founding documents, and a unique willingness among nations to pay a great price for the progress of human freedom and dignity. This is who we are. That's what we do as Americans, together.

As postwar speeches to soldiers go, this is standard fare. The Romans, it is worth remembering, never fought a war they didn't publicly claim to be in defense of civilization. In another respect, this passage is remarkable for its unabashed distortion of reality and callous disregard for the costs borne by the Iraqi people, whose freedom and dignity were not advanced but rather trampled upon by foreign invaders.

A truer expression of how political elites think of these costs was once offered by US secretary of state Madeleine Albright in a segment of the television news show *60 Minutes*. When reporter Lesley Stahl asked Albright, in May of 1996, if the deaths of 500,000 Iraqi children due to US sanctions imposed on Iraq since the first Gulf War were worth it, Albright replied, "I think this is a very hard choice, but the price—we think the price is worth it." Albright later claimed that she had been trapped by the question and regretted saying something that made her sound "cold-blooded and cruel."[25] Perhaps if she had had more time to think, she could have referenced, in the manner of President Obama, our "founding documents," the Declaration of Independence being well-understood to justify the killing of any number of other people's children for the sake of delivering freedom and dignity.

Belief in American exceptionalism depends on ignorance of history and political naïveté. A better understanding of the history of the United States—its crushing of the indigenous peoples of North America; its imperialist wars in Southeast Asia, from the Philippines to Vietnam; its armed support for dictators in Central America, South America, and the Caribbean; its similar behaviors in the Middle East, including support for the Shah of Iran until 1979 and current support for Saudi kings—renders claims of American exceptionalism absurd, or at least exposes such claims as myths of the kind that empires always promote.[26] It seems unlikely, however, that such an understanding was much present among Obama's Fort Bragg audience. Even those who knew they were being fed bullshit had strong psychological incentive to believe it.

The myth-making in Obama's speech is not just about the United States and its history. It is also about what it means to engage in mass violence under its banner, as a member of its armed forces. "Never forget," Obama said, "that you are part of an unbroken line of heroes spanning two centuries." "All of you here today," he continued, "lived through the fires of war. You will be remembered for it. You will be honored for it—always. You have done something profound with your lives.... You will know that you answered when your country called; you served a cause greater than yourselves; you helped forge a just and lasting peace with Iraq, and among all nations." The legacy of their efforts, Obama told members of his audience, "will endure ... in the freedom of your children and grandchildren."

Again, those with greater knowledge of history or even of daily world news might find the line about a just and lasting peace among all nations to be risible. But a person who survived combat and saw comrades hurt and killed could hardly be blamed for embracing the idea of having fought heroically for noble goals. Among those who had suffered, or had witnessed great suffering that they had helped perpetrate, who wouldn't want to set aside doubts and believe?[27] The need for national and personal self-justification made the moment of Obama's speech ripe for seeking comfort in drone morality—constituted here by unquestioning belief in the rightness of US attempts to control other peoples, the rightness of rules and orders handed down by elites, and the rightness of limiting the circle of empathy to fellow Americans, lest feelings for the Iraqi people continue to leave consciences troubled.

The effects of speeches like Obama's can extend across generations. Just as the soldiers he addressed at Fort Bragg took comfort in being described as heroes, so will the next generation seek its own accolades, its own claims to timeless

Chapter 5

Capitalism and the Compulsions of Manhood

Years ago when I interviewed people for my dissertation research, a secretary told me that she could never be a manager because, as she said, "I can't separate my business feelings from my personal feelings."[1] I took her to mean that she couldn't fire people, disappoint them, or otherwise cause them emotional pain without being upset herself. Being an effective manager required, as she saw it, the ability to set aside empathy and compassion for the sake of the bottom line. Her observation was not just about herself or the managers with whom she had worked in her career. She was telling me, without either of us realizing it, how capitalist relations of production are maintained.

The term *relations of production* is shorthand for the law-governed and state-enforced arrangements that determine who can do what with a society's major economic resources. When we talk about who legally controls land, labor, raw materials, tools, machines, and other resources used to produce the material necessities of life, we are talking about relations of production. Every society is characterized by some such set of arrangements.[2] You don't have to be a Marxist to understand that where a person is positioned in this scheme of things has a great deal to do with how his or her life unfolds.

In a capitalist society, we don't talk much about relations of production. We take it for granted that the legally conferred condition called "ownership" gives less than 2 percent of the population the right to use land, factories, machines, raw materials, and accumulated capital in whatever ways are deemed profitable, with no overriding concern for meeting human needs.[3] Potentially productive land and property will be allowed to sit idle, if a capitalist so chooses, even if people are starving. If profitability requires it, a person who needs a job can be deprived of that job, just as a whole community can be undermined if capitalists decide that it will be more profitable to move a factory to a country where labor is cheaper and environmental regulations less costly. If necessary, the state will use violence to protect capitalists' property rights, though this is rarely necessary, because property rights are rarely questioned. Capitalist relations of production are thus legally entrenched, backed by force, and culturally hegemonic.

If we talk little about capitalist relations of production, we talk even less about how these relations of production "intersect" with the gender order. It is this intersection that is my concern here. Specifically, I want to consider what it is that capitalist relations of production have to do with males' efforts to signify masculine selves and compete for manhood status. What I want to consider, in other words, is the relationship between men and capitalism. My contentions are that men are necessary to reproduce capitalism and that capitalism is what turns human beings—usually but not always males—into men.

I expect dispute. The obvious objection is that men, masculine selves, and competition for manhood status all predate capitalism. Yes, of course; *Gilgamesh*, the *Iliad*, and the *Odyssey* are epic tales of manhood acts, real or imagined, dating to the origins of Western civilization. But the proper conclusion is not that capitalism therefore has nothing to do with masculine selves and competition for manhood status. The proper conclusion is that capitalism has something in common with earlier economic systems—an overarching quality that is conducive to creating and nurturing the beings we call men. That quality, as I will argue, is the drive to accumulate value by exploiting the labor of others. This is a task that requires men.

*   *   *

"Intersectionality," the matter of how race, class, and gender are connected, has been a topic of much writing and discussion among analysts of inequality in recent decades.[4] And well before intersectionality entered the mainstream of sociological discourse about inequality, Marxists and radical feminists offered analyses of how race/racism and gender/sexism are linked to economic exploitation.[5] So this is not new ground. The problem is that an important part of the ground is often overlooked in current sociological discussions of gender.

As with other concepts that originally referred to objective social conditions, the concept of intersectionality has been *subjectivized* by mainstream sociology. The same thing happened fifty years earlier to Marx's concept of alienated labor. Marx originally defined alienated labor as labor over which workers had no control and which resulted in the appropriation of labor-created value by an exploiting group. Though Marx speculated on the psychological effects of being compelled to perform alienated labor, he did not confuse these effects with the objective social relations that produced them.[6] He did not, in other words, reduce capitalist relations of production to a matter of how workers felt about work.

Then in 1959 Melvin Seeman published an influential article in the *American Sociological Review* on the meaning of alienation.[7] Seeman argued that the concept was ambiguous and needed clearer definition if it was to be of use for empirical purposes. His strategy, however, was not to narrow and sharpen but to psychologize and agglomerate.

"Alienation," as Seeman defined it, referred to a set of unpleasant feelings variably experienced by individuals: powerlessness, meaninglessness, normlessness, isolation, and self-estrangement. American sociologists embraced this reductionist notion of alienation because it allowed alienation to be measured by using questionnaire items. Over the next thirty years, hundreds of studies were done based on this conception of alienation.[8] These studies usefully documented the misery induced by work in a capitalist society, but they left capitalist relations of production—highlighted by Marx's original concept—out of the picture. This was perhaps another reason for the popularity of the subjective approach to alienation. It allowed sociologists to appear to take a critical stance and champion the underdog, without getting into trouble for pointing to capitalism as the source of the problem.

In the last twenty years, discourse on intersections between race, class, and gender has taken a similarly reductionist path. Intersectionality is now most often discussed in terms of variations in individual experience arising as a result of an individual's simultaneous location in race, sex/gender, sexual orientation, and class categories. We are thus reminded, for example, that the experiences associated with being a man differ depending on race, class, and sexual orientation. Likewise, being middle-class is different if you are black, white, or Latino; being gay is different if you are middle class or working class; being black is different if you are upper middle class or poor; and so on until every permutation is covered.

These variations are not unimportant. If we want to understand patterns of subjective experience—how people think, what they value, how they feel—it's surely necessary to take into account the privileged and subordinate categories in which people are located and from which they derive their social identities. A generation earlier, sociologists made generalizations to all of humanity based on studies of married, middle-class, white males in North America. Against the background of this myopia, the injunction to pay attention to how people's experiences can vary because of class, race, gender, and sexual orientation seems revolutionary. The insight that a person's simultaneous location in multiple systems of inequality matters in important ways is certainly not to be abandoned.

Yet there is something missing. Treating intersectionality as all about patterns of subjective experience leaves us with a can't-get-there-from-here kind of problem. Where we would like to get to, I presume, is an understanding of the systems of inequality that *generate* patterns of subjective experience. I also presume a goal of trying to better understand how such experiences matter for keeping systems of inequality going. Documenting variations in experience can't get us to either place. By way of analogy, we could study the shop-floor experiences of a diverse group of workers and never figure out how a capitalist economy functions. Workers' experiences would be part of the story, but the full story could not be told without looking at the institutional goings-on that give rise to those experiences.

A less subjectivist approach to intersectionality treats it as manifested in face-to-face interaction. People are said to "do gender differently" depending on their racial, ethnic, and class backgrounds.[9] This means that they signify their identities as women or men in ways that are affected by other social locations. People are also therefore perceived and treated differently depending on how these multiple locations are simultaneously evident in their self-presentations.

The problem with the interactional approach—an approach compatible with the sociological treatment of gender as a matter of doing or performance—is that it can lead us to think that gender is about nothing but situational self-presentation. Gender, in this view, becomes nothing more than a matter of how males and females freely choose to fashion their presentations of self as women, men, or something else. It thus comes to seem that the only connection between gender and class is that self-presentational styles vary across classes. The idea that gender is necessarily linked to the class system—that is, a system of economic exploitation—is lost. This is a kind of situationalist rather than psychological reductionism, though it has the same obscurantist effect.

In Chapter 2, I argued that the academic penchant for proliferating masculinities was related to the liberal impulse to celebrate diversity. That same impulse underlies the turn toward treating intersectionality as a matter of "appreciating" how individual experiences vary depending on race, class, gender, sexuality, and so on. Again, recognizing this variability is part of resisting the oppressive idea that upper-middle-class heterosexual white male experience is equivalent to human experience, and thus it is worth doing. The problem is that, if this is taken as an end in itself, it can divert attention from analyzing the larger social arrangements in which are rooted the problems of racism, sexism, violence, poverty, and plutocracy.

When sociologists invoke "race, class, and gender" in discussions of inequality, it is usually understood that "race" and "gender" are code for racism and sexism—discriminatory beliefs and *practices* through which white supremacy and male supremacy are maintained. But what about *class*? To what oppressive beliefs and practices does this term refer? The answer, I have often heard, is that it refers to people claiming superiority, or treating others badly, on the basis of education, income, or wealth. Such attitudes and behavior are said to constitute *classism*. The correct term for this is not classism but *elitism*. My point, however, is that reducing class to "classism" is another instance of the subjectivizing that makes it hard to think seriously about how gender is related to economic exploitation.

There are more sophisticated approaches to intersectionality that do not succumb to the subjectivizing tendency. As noted earlier, Marxist and radical feminist scholars have argued that gender and racial categories are invented by dominant groups to legitimate the extreme exploitation of others, or to aid in controlling the exploited by undermining their solidarity. These analyses have also considered how classes are formed—the southern planter class in the United States, for example—as a result of how dominant groups manage to racialize others.[10] Other analysts have considered how race and gender can take different forms and serve different ends depending on the economies out of which they emerge.[11] These approaches are, in the parlance of sociology, structural and historical rather than subjectivist or situational.

What I am aiming for here is an account of how the capitalist class system is reproduced through the engendering of males as men. I take this engendering to include inculcation of desires to signify masculine selves and compete for manhood status. To avoid the subjectivist trap, however, I want to make it clear how external realities—the social conditions under which manhood is enacted—create incentives for compliance that individual males cannot ignore without high costs, both material and emotional. To understand the latter costs requires consideration of both the intersections at which males find themselves as men, and the intrasections that exist within them as men.

*   *   *

For any exploitive economy to function—any economy that involves one group exercising control over resources and labor so as to derive disproportionate benefits from the creation and exchange of goods and services—some actors in the system must be able and willing to control others. If this control imperative is not satisfied, it is impossible to maintain an exploitive economy, capitalist or otherwise. In the absence of coercive control, people will simply produce for themselves and engage in barter or exchange at rates mutually deemed fair, given a shared understanding of the skill and effort that go into the creation of various goods and services. Under such conditions, some producers and merchants—by virtue of skill, effort, and luck—might come out ahead of others. But in the long run no one will come out very far ahead at the expense of others.

What types of actors, then, are *able and willing* to exercise control over others? In Chapter 3, I suggested that the original agents of control in human history were most likely males who, by virtue of greater size, strength, speed, and skill with weapons, were able to effectively coerce the behavior of others.[12] Such a group, I also suggested, could come to form a privileged warrior caste, *privileged* in the sense of either taking or being granted—perhaps out of fear, or out of gratitude for protection—a larger share of a group's resources. Warrior males may thus have become paleocapitalists, the first group to discover the benefits of taking resources from others, extorting others by hoarding resources, and, at the extreme, enslaving others to extract value from their labor. Considering these early relations of production is useful for seeing how manhood today is still tied to economic exploitation.

Let us imagine that once it became clear that there were advantages to being included in an exploiting caste, there was competition for membership. Conversely, there was likely to be struggle to avoid being seen as an exploitable Other. Would a simple display of maleness suffice for being included in the exploiting caste and exempted from exploitation? Within a band, tribe, or clan, perhaps; between groups, probably not. The reason is that for exploitation to be worth the trouble—it takes energy, vigilance, and skill to control humans—the exploited class must be expanded to the largest practical degree. This requires including not just in-group and out-group females, but all males, in-group and out-group, who can be subjugated. So the distinction between exploiters and the exploitable cannot rest on maleness alone. Finer distinctions must be made.

Under the conditions I have described, it makes sense that males would strive to exert control, so as to take advantage of the benefits potentially available through exploiting others. It also makes sense that males would strive to signify the capacity to exert control, so as to avoid being seen as easy targets for exploitation and perhaps also to appear useful to more powerful males, in whose spoils they might share. And if membership in the exploiting group depends on more than just biological maleness, it makes further sense that it would be crucial to master symbolic displays of the capacity to dominate. Being better at this sort of display—what ethologists might call "posturing"—than other males would increase an individual's chances of being included in the privileged group.

I am not arguing that males evolved genetically in a way that predisposes them to strive for dominance. Genes are superfluous here, except inasmuch as male physiology is obviously a genetic endowment, rooted in millions of years of hominid evolution prior to the emergence of anything that could be called an "economy." Nor am I arguing that there was an accidental historical connection between men and economic exploitation, as if the former just stumbled upon the latter. My argument is that the intersection between exploitation and manhood is an ontological one. *Once the survival strategy of exploiting others is chosen, men are needed to make it work.* Every exploitive economic system requires, by definition, exerting control over resources claimed by others and over the labor of others. In which case, humans able and willing to perform these acts of control are necessary, not optional. These are the humans we have come to know as men, humans defined not merely by their maleness but by their capacities to exert control and by acts that signify these capacities.

There are, in other words, no men outside of exploitive relations of production. The impulse to exploit, acted upon by males and enabled by male physiology, is what gave rise to men. Outside of exploitive relations of production, primitive or modern, there would be no need for a category of humans defined and identified by their actual and signified capacities to exert control over others. Absent exploitation or the threat of being exploited, absent the threat of having one's resources stolen, the idea of men as a category of human beings makes no sense. Human reproduction requires *males*; exploitation requires *men*.

It is the threat of being exploited that compels all males, not only those bent on exploitation, to adopt manhood, if only defensively.[13] This is why signifying not only the capacity to exert control but also to resist being controlled is an essential part of a manhood act. In part this is about signifying that one should not be identified as a member of the category of exploitable Others called "women." But there is an additional subtext. In the face of a threat of being exploited, a manhood act says, in effect, *It will cost you more to subdue me than it will cost to take me in as a brother and give me a cut of the action.* What I am calling a "cut of the action" is what other analysts have called the "patriarchal dividend" that accrues to all men.[14]

Just as men are not optional within exploitive relations of production, being a man is not optional for an individual male under these conditions. To refuse to be a man is to invite identification as a target for exploitation. It is to forgo the benefits that come from membership in the exploiting group. Once exploitive relations of production have been established, the ability to signify a masculine self—a self capable of exerting control and resisting control—acquires enormous survival value. Within exploitive relations of production, the benefits and rewards of manhood status compel all males to claim it, even against conscience.

The idea that males who act as men may do so against conscience points to another feature of men. Males who act as men must develop more than the abilities to exert control and to signify capacities for exerting and resisting control; they must also develop a *willingness* to control others, despite others' resistance. In plainer terms, men must be willing to ignore others' pain and suffering for the sake of maintaining control.[15] In the language of the previous chapter, men must be willing to embrace drone morality—a morality that entails a refusal to be deterred by others' anguish or appeals for relief. If these expressions of anguish and appeals for relief were listened to, heard, and *felt*, control and exploitation would be impossible. Part of the social construction of men, therefore, is instilling a willingness to shut down or limit the human empathic response.

I have been writing in a speculative historical mode as a way to expose the logical and necessary intersection between manhood and exploitive relations of production. This is an attempt to gain analytic distance on phenomena we may otherwise be too close to, or too invested in, to see. The goal is to see if and how the same system logic, revealed by looking backward, remains operative in the present. So, then, does manhood under capitalism in the twenty-first century look like the primal manhood I have been describing? In essence, yes.

Under modern capitalism, males still strive for privilege, wealth, status, and power by claiming manhood status and signifying masculine selves. This doesn't mean that all males try to dominate others in every situation. It means that putting on a manhood act is compulsory for males who wish to be socially accepted, to be seen as fully creditable persons, and to avoid abuse and exploitation at the hands of males who are invested in manhood. Precisely how a manhood act is fashioned can vary across time and place. But claiming manhood status is still not optional for males, even if one wants only to enjoy baseline acceptance and respectability. To achieve more than this—to be elevated within the category of men, to exert control over others in an organization, to get ahead of others who are themselves competing to get ahead—still requires crafting a masculine self.

It cannot be otherwise. Though power is exercised less brutally and arbitrarily in modern capitalist societies than in earlier societies built on exploitive economies, modern capitalist societies are nonetheless hierarchical; economic and political power remain concentrated in relatively few hands. Major societal institutions, public and private, are still authoritarian bureaucracies. Modern capitalist societies in Western Europe and North America are less blatantly patriarchal than in the past, but they are still organized in ways that foster and reward the capacity to exert control. And although in some circles it might be seen as crass to baldly celebrate masculinity and male power, this is still done indirectly and relentlessly, through celebrations of military prowess, dominance in sports, and violence in fiction.

What is also true is that to be an effective manager—that is, an effective controller of other people—it is necessary, as the secretary quoted earlier said, to be able to subordinate one's personal feelings to one's "business feelings." One must be willing, in other words, to do whatever is necessary to get the job done, and done in a way that serves the bottom line. Often enough this means causing others to experience emotional distress because their desires must be ignored or overridden. Empathic, compassionate responses—what the secretary perhaps meant by "personal feelings"—would get in the way of doing this. To make a capitalist economy function, to make any hierarchical organization function, requires making people do what they would not otherwise do, and this in turn requires loyalty to the powerful rather than loyalty to humanity.[16] To keep such a system going requires, no less today than in the past, people willing to act like men.

Contemporary sociologists of gender might say that I am describing "hegemonic masculinity," a manner of being a man that involves fixation on control. To invoke hegemonic masculinity here would be to imply that, yes, there is *one version* of manhood that exalts power and control, but there are other versions that do not.[17] But this is not my argument, which is that manhood itself, no matter how it is enacted by an individual male, is inherently an outgrowth of exploitation and fundamentally necessary for its reproduction. Other "masculinities," if one subscribes to such language, are simply other ways of claiming manhood status, under conditions where inclusion in the category "men" brings privileges and reduces the chances of being subjected to certain forms of exploitation. In this sense, all males who identify as men are implicated, if not all culpable in the same ways.

An implication of this view is that in the context of an exploitive economy there is no escaping the problems associated with masculine selves and competition for manhood status. In short, as long as we have capitalism, we will have men. As long as our form of economy pits people against each other, vertically or horizontally, males will try to survive and prosper by signifying masculine selves. To suppose that we can have capitalism—a system that *requires* dominance of others—and not have the kind of human beings necessary to run it, the kind of human beings we call men, the kind who are able and willing to control others, is a fantasy. It is likewise a fantasy to suppose that males, no matter how enlightened about sexism, can ignore the compulsion to signify masculine selves and relinquish the privileges of being men.

To speak of compulsions to enact manhood is not to say that such compulsions cannot be reflected upon and resisted. They surely can. Even so, most male-bodied persons, even the most staunchly feminist, identify as men and enact manhood. This is exactly what one would expect, given the power and inescapability of the external and internal compulsions I am describing here. The possibility of ungendered selfhood depends on changing the cultures and forms of social organization that generate these compulsions in the first place. I'll say more about this, and about prospects for change, in Chapter 7.

The "intersection" between manhood and capitalism—between manhood and any economic system based on exploitation—is a necessary one, by virtue of what exploitation requires and by virtue of what manhood is. This is not an intersection defined by differences in subjective experience or style of self-presentation. Such intersections are important to consider for some purposes, but focusing on them exclusively obscures a connection that is crucial to see if the goal is to understand how economic systems give rise to an oppressive gender order and are sustained by it. The subjectivist approach also makes it hard to see what is ultimately necessary for change. As I have argued, without changing the exploitive economic arrangements that make manhood compulsory, there is no possibility of transcending our fundamentally inegalitarian gender order, which is to say that there is no possibility of transcending gender.

*   *   *

What I have argued so far can be summed up by saying that while manhood is compelled by exploitive relations of production, individual males retain the capacity to reflect upon and resist this compulsion, though in most cases the exercise of this capacity is likely to be deterred by its prohibitive costs. There is, however, a huge gap between capitalism as a system and the manhood acts of everyday life. Skepticism is warranted whenever such a gap is leaped and the claim is made that large-scale social arrangements lead to X, Y, or Z behaviors. If social psychology has taught us anything over the past hundred years, it is that behavior is a response to situations, not to abstract entities such as "society" or "capitalism." Yet social psychology carries its own danger: failing to see how situations are embedded in culture and social organization.[18] And so what is needed is an account of how what happens in situations—the performance of manhood acts—is compelled by and helps to reproduce capitalist relations of production.

Elsewhere I have written about *nets of accountability* and used this concept to explain how situated action—what people do in face-to-face interaction—arises from and reproduces large-scale social arrangements.[19] The component term *accountability* refers to the condition of being potentially subject to demands to explain and justify one's behavior. A demand for an account, evoked by some bit of unexpected or untoward behavior, is not always an explicit, verbal request for an explanation; it can be a raised eyebrow. Accounts can likewise be elaborate or brief. What matters is that the account makes action appear sensible and morally acceptable in the eyes of an evaluating audience.[20]

Accounts are also defenses against being discredited or diminished in social value. To be thus diminished is to be granted less deference, to be taken less seriously, to be accorded less respect, to be seen as the possessor of a flawed self. Accounts are demanded when an actor's appearance or behavior implies lesser social value than at first claimed by an actor or presumed by an audience. Restoring the value of the self requires a good account.

Successful accounts thus accomplish several things: they keep interaction flowing smoothly by making otherwise baffling behavior understandable; they affirm shared understandings of what constitutes acceptable conduct; and they preserve the social value actors claim for themselves and grant to others in face-to-face encounters. To be called to account and be unable to respond suitably threatens both the wayward actor and the situation, which might fall apart in the event of behavior that cannot be made sense of or rendered morally acceptable. Some social psychological perspectives see the giving and interpreting of accounts as essential features of all interaction.[21]

Although we can be held accountable on many grounds (e.g., whether we live up to professed ideals, or perform our jobs in the ways we're supposed to), we are always potentially accountable to gender category.[22] This is to say that we are always expected to present ourselves as either male or female and, according to custom, as either a man if male or a woman if female. We are also expected to present an appropriately gendered self—masculine if male and a man, feminine if female and a woman. Moreover, our manner or style of gender signification must conform to local standards. No matter what these standards are, gender always remains relevant for assessing an actor's social value. If our gender-related behavior violates audience expectations, and if an account is demanded, and if we are unable to give a satisfactory account, we risk being seen as incompetent, immoral, or insane. At the very least, failing to "do gender" properly makes it hard to get along with others.

It is this matter of always being accountable for properly signifying sex-category membership, gender-category membership, and a masculine or feminine self that does much to hold the gender order in place. Individuals simply cannot ignore the consequences of being seen as incompetent, immoral, or insane—consequences ranging from gentle exclusion, to verbal abuse, to physical violence, to incarceration, to death. Thus there are powerful external compulsions to conform to dominant expectations for gender-related behavior. Although there is always the possibility of forgoing the benefits of total conformity to dominant conventions, or of creating protective subcultures within which to flout those conventions (and of course create new ones), most people, most of the time, are kept in line by accountability demands and by the high costs of not responding satisfactorily to those demands.

The concept of accountability helps to explain situational compulsions to claim manhood status and signify a masculine self. As long as there are widely shared expectations for males to do these things, and as long as these expectations are believed to be morally correct, an individual male cannot refuse to be a man without bearing costs that could fairly be called exorbitant. This is especially true when a male faces an audience whose approval is important for economic or emotional reasons. But an analysis of situational pressures isn't enough to explain how capitalism is upheld by manhood acts. Capitalism as a system must somehow be linked to the situations in which manhood acts are performed.

I take it as a given that capitalism, or anything else we might call a social *system*, consists of the patterned ways that people do things together, day after day, in multiple settings, across which people coordinate action. If there were no such regularized "doings together," there would be no system—no economy, no government, no social institutions of any kind. When sociologists talk about these matters they often use the term *structure*. This term reminds us that there is a durable reality to society—a reality that, although humanly made, cannot be wished away. Unfortunately, this language can also lead us to forget that what we call "structures" consist not of material stuff but of human action.[23] If what we are referring to when we speak of systems, institutions, and structures is really patterned human action, then what we need to explain is how these large-scale patterns are preserved. For this, the concept of nets of accountability is useful.

By way of example, consider a student refusing to do a required assignment. A teacher might try to hold the student accountable as a student, saying that anyone worthy of the identity "student" ought to relish the assignment as a learning opportunity (I realize that this is wishful professorial thinking). This form of accountability demand implicitly invokes shared understandings—tacit norms—about how one ought to behave to be worthy of a socially valued identity. For this tack to work, both parties must share ideas about the identity at risk, about its value, about its proper enactment, and about who can affirm it.

But suppose the normative tack failed, perhaps because the student placed low value on the identity "student," or because s/he had different ideas about how to enact it. The teacher might then say, "What's more, if you don't do the assignment, you'll fail the course and won't graduate." This form of accountability demand is different because it implicates other school officials (perhaps also parents and prospective employers). If these other actors do what they're obliged to do, then the student will indeed fail and lose the anticipated rewards of acquiring a degree. Other actors, if they fail to play by the rules, could be held accountable and lose the main benefits and side bets riding on their continued employment.[24] What is operating here, *across situations*, is a net of accountability that keeps everyone in line—everyone, that is, who cares about reaping the benefits that ride on continued participation in the activity system called "school."

By similar logic, situational accountability can be linked to the larger activity system called capitalism. Consider a wage worker who walks off the job, enters the office of the company's chief financial officer, and demands a raise. Imagine the worker making an eloquent, impassioned plea for a higher wage, citing extreme economic hardship. The CFO would no doubt be taken aback by the worker's presence, reject the demand, and order the worker out, perhaps saying, "You're not supposed to be here. If you don't leave right now, I'll call security and have you removed, and then you'll be fired." Perhaps the CFO speaks more gently, but to the same effect. Let us assume that the worker complies. What has just happened?

In threatening to have the worker forcibly removed and fired, the CFO *symbolically* invoked a net of accountability—a set of rule-governed relationships, known to both the worker and the executive, that exist beyond their face-to-face encounter. If the worker had not complied, the CFO could have *activated* the net by communicating with others outside the situation. This would have meant calling security and then later communicating, through proper channels, with whoever was responsible for supervising the dissident worker. In this example, the worker is held accountable, as a worker, upon appearing in the CFO's office (*you are not supposed to be here*), and later, let us suppose, as a low-level employee, when another boss says, "For walking off the job and entering areas of the building you were not authorized to enter, you are now dismissed. Officer Pinkerton will escort you from the premises."

If we say that the chief financial officer's actions make sense in this scenario, it is because we understand that to violate the usual rules of procedure and give the worker a raise would put at risk the material and emotional benefits that ride on the CFO keeping his or her job. If we say that it makes sense for a security guard to show up and remove the worker, or for some supervisor later to fire the worker, it is for the same reason: we understand the net of accountability in which all these actors are enmeshed. We understand that they all stand to lose the material and psychological benefits that ride on keeping their jobs, if they fail to do what is expected of them in the context of the organization.

The lesson of the example is not just that for the sake of keeping one's job it's a good idea to follow the rules. The lesson is that when workers everywhere are held accountable as workers, when executives everywhere are held accountable as executives, when people everywhere are held accountable for doing their jobs, capitalism itself is reproduced. The net of accountability that makes this happen extends beyond any single encounter or organization. The operative net includes many spatially distributed actors: shareholders, regulators, bankers, merchants, legislators, police, judges, social workers, neighbors, partners, spouses, relatives, children. All of these actors can make accountability demands that help to keep others in line, which is to say, keep them wedded to the patterns of action that constitute a capitalist economy.

One might dismiss this example as unrealistic. No worker, it might be claimed, is going to accost an accounting executive as a way to try to get a raise in pay. This is indeed unlikely. But the fact that such things seldom happen makes the point of the example. They seldom happen precisely because there is a net of accountability that keeps workers, accounting executives, and everyone else in line. Anticipation of how this net can be made to operate preempts disruption. Organizational rules can of course be broken or ignored; these are not the laws of physics. But a tight and expansive net of accountability makes violations unlikely, because the costs of violations are prohibitive. This is all that can ever be done in human affairs; even the application of brute force to compel obedience requires enmeshing enforcers in another net of accountability.[25]

Another possible objection is that the example has nothing to do with gender. After all, the gender identity of neither worker nor executive is mentioned. And why would these identities matter, anyway? Even if one can imagine superficial differences in how the people in the example might have behaved, for all practical purposes they would have done the same things, whether men or women. Hence gender is irrelevant. On the contrary, I would say that the example has much to do with the nature of manhood and its link to capitalism.

Recall that the worker's eloquent, impassioned plea for a raise is of no consequence. No matter the strength of the need or the argument on behalf of that need, no raise will be given. The reason it won't is that wages must be set to ensure profitability, in accord with the desires of top managers and shareholders. A manager who raised wages out of sympathy for workers would be removed, humane action being a threat to profits. Recall, too, that for having the temerity to demand a raise, the worker is subject to firing by a lower-level boss and forcible removal by a security guard—actors who serve as drone-like agents of elite control. For all this to happen—for profit to trump compassion, for the profit-protecting rules of elites to be enforced under threat of violence—the enactment of manhood is necessary. The social machinery of capitalism simply cannot operate without a class of people constructed to be willing and able to control others, even when those others are sane, rational, and nonviolent. This is the class of people known to us as men. The bodies involved might be male or female. What matters are the beliefs and values upon which those bodies act and what they do to other bodies.

To suggest that a sympathetic manager could be ousted raises the issue of who can hold whom accountable for what. Capitalist relations of production rest on the codification of these matters in law. A board of directors can hold managers accountable for acting on the legally mandated fiduciary responsibility to maximize return on shareholder investment.[26] Top managers can hold mid-level managers accountable for doing the practical tasks necessary to meet profit goals.

And likewise down the chain of command, this hierarchy of authority also has the backing of law. There are two important points to note about this. One is that the law is an accountability tool formulated by elites to maintain control of the institutions from whose operation they benefit. It can thus be said, per Max Weber, that in a modern capitalist society elite dominance depends on controlling not only the means of violence but also the means of administration.[27]

The second point is that accountability is never simply a matter of one person with more formal authority holding accountable another person with less formal authority. There is always, as I have suggested, an invisibly present *net* of accountability upon which depends one person's power to compel another's obedience in a concrete situation. As in the examples offered above, this net can be invoked symbolically (which often suffices) or, if necessary, activated practically. Moreover, as also suggested, the net includes not just actors in economic organizations but all those who might hold a person accountable for meeting a legal or normative obligation. A child who says, "Daddy, if you lost your job would we have to sell the house and move? Would we be able to go on vacation this summer?" reminds a man of the net in which he is enmeshed. The strand on which a boss tugs in the workplace is connected to another strand on which a child might tug at home.

Between capitalism as a system and the manhood acts of individual males (and collaborating females) are the concrete situations in which accountability operates. These situations are linked by what I have called a net of accountability, a life-encompassing set of rule-governed relationships that powerfully amplify the compulsion to engage in manhood acts in any given situation. The net, it might be said, is what makes the stakes riding on conformity to gender-related expectations so high. Or, to reverse the equation, it is the net of accountability that raises the costs of nonconformity, because nonconformity in one place can incur high costs in many others.

The view I have been offering implies more than an intersection between capitalism and manhood. I am proposing that capitalism and manhood exist in a state of mutual dependence. This is easier to see if we de-subjectivize manhood and see it not only as a matter of individual experience but as a form of social being essential to all exploitive relations of production. To understand how these exploitive relations are maintained, patterns of individual experience must still be examined. We need to consider how compulsions to engage in the manhood acts that reproduce capitalism are generated, experienced, and handled. The concepts of accountability and nets of accountability help to explain the external compulsions. But how do external conditions and events gain the power to compel?

*   *   *

A simple answer to the question of why external compulsions are so powerful rests on the observation that everything we value in social life—every form of material and psychological reward—comes to us through acceptance by others, and acceptance depends on signifying that we share the same values and beliefs as others. Not *all* others, of course, but at least some community whose approval matters and through which resources flow. It was the potential loss of this approval and loss of concomitant resources that I previously alluded to as the "prohibitive costs" of gender nonconformity. Perhaps it is enough to cite this prospect of loss to explain why males are compelled to perform manhood acts. There is just too much at stake materially to do otherwise.

Yet to just cite externally derived rewards leaves unexamined the matter of how it is that males come to so highly value those rewards. It also leaves us unable to go far in explaining variation in the value attached to particular kinds of manhood acts, why those acts are often felt to be sacred and unrelinquishable, or how those acts might change as a result of self-reflection. To make sense of these matters requires attention to what goes on inside males who embrace manhood, signify masculine selves, and compete for manhood status. Because "what goes on inside" is inextricably linked to the outer world, I think of this as an exploration of the *intrasections*—the externally driven inner dynamics—that generate a compulsion to enact manhood.

Some of these dynamics can be brought to light by deconstructing another fictional episode. What follows is a scene originally written to provide grist for classroom discussion. It, too, is set in a capitalist workplace.

Leroy and his crew were in the break room finishing their coffee and sandwiches. It had been a hard morning already, and the men were more subdued than usual. The men had fallen into silence, anticipating a return to work, when Bill, the unit supervisor, stuck his head through the door and looked around, as if to make sure the room was safe before entering.

Bill stepped in and nodded to the men, then nodded again to Leroy. "Pit four needs to be scrubbed before the inspection on Friday," Bill announced, clutching his ever-present clipboard in front of his chest. "And I need some men willing to get in there and get the job done. It's off-schedule, so the company is willing to pay time-and-a-half."

Leroy and his men exchanged glances. "Off-schedule" meant that scrubbing the pit would put them over their exposure limit for the week.

"What about the new suits?" Leroy asked. The old hazmat suits were being retrofitted with better filters and shielding, but so far none had come back from the manufacturer.

"The new suits aren't ready," Bill said. "You'll have to use the old ones."

The men looked at Bill, then at Leroy, but said nothing. They were waiting for Leroy to speak. After a couple beats, Leroy said, "With the old suits, we'll be over limit if we do another scrub before Friday."

"Look," Bill said, lifting his gaze from Leroy and trying to make eye contact with the men at the table, "the South Unit crew is stepping up and doing an off-schedule. Do you want them to make us look like wusses? Should I go back upstairs and say my guys won't do it until they get their pretty new suits?"

Now everyone looked back to Leroy, who was staring hard at Bill. The man on Leroy's left saw a muscle ripple in Leroy's jaw. After a moment, Leroy leaned back in his chair and seemed to relax. "*Double* time," he said.

"What? That's—" Bill started, stopping abruptly. "That's—" he started again, but didn't seem to know where to go from there. His shoulders slumped a notch.

"That's the deal," Leroy said. The men at the lunch table nodded their heads.

"Okay, double," Bill said. "The company will do it because these are special circumstances. But that's between us. I don't want word getting out about that."

I call this the "Radiation Pit" exercise. When I use it in class, I ask students what's going on between Leroy and Bill. Although their interaction can be described in different ways, one thing it would be fair to call it is a manhood contest.

Bill, the supervisor, wants Leroy and his crew to do extra work, putting them over the safe limit for weekly radiation exposure. Leroy responds as the leader of his crew, showing concern for their safety and resisting the boss's attempt to wring more work out of his men for too little extra pay. Bill tries to shame Leroy and his men into compliance by disparaging the better hazmat suits as merely "pretty"—the kind of thing women might care about—and by citing the manhood act of another crew. But Bill clearly needs Leroy's consent, or the men won't work. Leroy has Bill over the proverbial barrel and realizes that he can get more than Bill is offering. Bill makes a show of resistance to Leroy's demand for double pay, but then gives in, asking the men not to say anything about it. In the moment, Leroy has won the manhood contest, seemingly having gotten the better of Bill, and thereby also earning additional respect from the men in his crew. Leroy also won by allowing Bill to save face. The extra work will in fact get done, and Bill has shown that he has the power to dispense rewards that are important to the men.

There is more at stake in this scene than material rewards. Leroy and Bill—and, by extension, workers and higher-level managers—are in a struggle for control *and* for respect based on their abilities to exert control (or resist being controlled). This is the sense in which what is going on is a manhood contest. The material rewards may indeed be important for obvious economic reasons; bills must be paid. But the manhood contest is important for other reasons. What's at stake is not just how much extra money the men will get for how much extra work. What's at stake is their ability to think of themselves as creditable men. A manhood contest, in other words, is not only a struggle for control; it's a struggle for respect from an external audience and an internal audience.

The word "gendered" is overused as an adjective in these matters, but it is fair to say that criteria for self-evaluation are gendered in the sense that males learn to judge themselves worthy or unworthy, as men, based in large part on their abilities to exert control and resist being controlled. To be worthy as a man is to be able to make happen what one wants to make happen, even in the face of resistance. To be worthy as a man is to be able to command the attention and respect of other men. To be *un*worthy as a man is to be unable to exert control or resist being controlled, and to be seen as weak by other men. Even worse is to feel under the control of those who have no rightful authority or moral legitimacy.[28] To claim the identity "man," as males are expected to, is to be tied to these criteria of self-evaluation, criteria that ensure failure.

A system of exploitive economic relations, a system like capitalism, ensures that most males will fail to meet the control criterion by which manhood status is judged. Under capitalist relations of production, most males have no choice, if they want to make a living, but to submit to the power of capitalist employers. Under capitalism, most people, males and females, are denied control over their economic lives. This is most obvious in the workplace, but evident elsewhere as well. Because capitalism concentrates wealth in the hands of a relative few, and because political power concentrates along with wealth, a capitalist society makes it difficult or impossible for most people to exert much control over their lives. A small sphere of autonomy, built around home and leisure activities, is the best most people can expect.

The special problem for males, however, is socialization that instills the criteria for self-evaluation mentioned above. Males learn to strive for the control that affirms their respectability as men and then to judge themselves by their success in exerting or resisting control. They also learn to expect a degree of control as something they are due by virtue of even rudimentary manhood status. Yet capitalism constantly thwarts these ambitions and expectations. *Be a man*, males are told. *Be strong, ambitious, potent, competitive; achieve wealth, status, and power; get ahead of others, and do not let yourself be dominated.* The problem is that, economic and political realities being what they are in a capitalist society, most males will inevitably fail at this kind of manhood.

leadership, they have resisted being exploited more than they already are. Even Bill, whose manhood act is shaky, is allowed to save face. In one sense, every actor in the scene gets the best outcome, materially and psychologically, he could reasonably hope for. Everyone gets to keep his job and meet the accountability demands that are linked to having a job and an income. The *larger* consequence, however, if we add up all the real-world scenes in which workers are granted a modicum of manly credit even as they comply with a boss's orders, is the reproduction of capitalism.

The dynamic I am describing is one that not only reproduces capitalism by emotionally inducing males to seek manhood status by accepting subordination. It can also be seen as the dynamic that underlies fascism and nationalism.[33] Powerless, self-blaming males are drawn to leaders and groups that offer compensatory feelings of power. The kind of fascism I am referring to only sometimes marches in jackboots. More often it takes the form of following orders, unreflectively and uncritically, in a corporation, on a sports team, or in the military—for the sake of the pleasure that comes from dominating others and expunging one's own feelings of weakness.

Though females are neither promised control nor expected to exert it as part of signifying creditable selves, females are still susceptible to the seductions of compensatory power. To be denied control is frustrating. To be controlled by others is demeaning. If males experience subordination differently than females, it is because achieving creditable manhood by exerting and resisting control is expected of males and held out as a real possibility. For females, it is not. Yet of course the same collaborationist strategy—allying with the powerful—that is used by males striving to be men can be used by females identified as women, and used for the same reasons: to overcome feelings of weakness, gain more control over a threatening environment, and to achieve status.[34] Even honorary manhood has its rewards.

Two caveats are important. First, to reiterate a point made in discussing drone morality: the problem is not that rules and laws are devised to regulate human behavior; nor is the problem that there are people who accept the task of enforcement. It seems fair to say that human social life requires both; and in fact we all help to enforce normative rules. The problems I have been pointing to arise from the use of rules and laws to sustain exploitive economic relationships. Rules and laws that are democratically formulated and of equal benefit to all are to be desired. Those imposed from above—imposed, interpreted, and enforced to maintain social and economic relationships that disproportionately benefit the few at the expense of the many—are the problem. My concern here thus has been with how manhood is leveraged to protect the exploitive relations of production that take the form we call capitalism.

A second caveat is that neither control nor coordination is necessarily bad. As a matter of survival, humans must exert a degree of control over nature and things in it. Technology, craft, and invention all require mastery—that is, control—over tools, materials, and bodies. Social order requires that adults exercise control over children and, sometimes, over adults who are damaged and cannot exercise self-control. Indeed, industrial civilization would be inconceivable apart from the progressive expansion of human control over the material world.

So control per se is not the problem, just as rules and laws per se are not the problem. The problem, rather, is surplus control; that is, control sought and exercised for the sake of exploiting the labor, intellect, and bodies of others—control that yields disproportionate benefits for one person or group at the expense of another person or group. This is control that operates against the will and interests, both material and psychological, of those who are controlled. It is control to a degree that would be intolerable in an egalitarian and democratic world.

Coordination of others is likewise not necessarily a problem. Under capitalism, what is often called "coordination" should properly be called domination, because it depends on the economic and psychological disempowerment of those whose actions are directed by others. When the authority relationships through which coordination is achieved are democratically and rationally formulated, subject to reformulation, and do not require people to relinquish their moral autonomy, the situation is different. Such a condition would be the antithesis of capitalism and of authoritarian bureaucracy. It would make manhood obsolete.

* * *

The compulsions to enact manhood are at once internal and external, situational and structural. They are internal inasmuch as males are taught to embrace an essentialist view of gender and to see themselves, at the core of their being, as men. They are internal inasmuch as males learn to evaluate themselves based on their abilities to exert control and resist being controlled. They are internal inasmuch as males learn to stake their feelings of worth on success in claiming manhood status. The compulsions are internal also inasmuch as males learn that feelings of weakness and inadequacy—feelings of failure as a man—can be mitigated by compensatory or vicarious manhood acts, or by subordinate allegiance—again as a man, a brother in arms—with more powerful males, those who seem to have won society's manhood contests and the right to control others.

External compulsions to enact manhood take the form of audience expectations. Different audiences expect different things, of course. But gender signification is not customarily optional. Culture matters, and mainstream culture dictates that males identify as men and be identifiable as men, in accord with local and situational standards. As the point was made earlier, males are always accountable for their gender identification and display. A male who rejects prevailing conventions—who fails to claim manhood status and signify a masculine self—risks being seen as incompetent, immoral, or insane. The economic and psychic costs of such an audience assessment, as also noted earlier, are prohibitive. Thus even males who are critically aware of their internal compulsions to manhood are externally compelled to claim it.

Audience expectations are expressed and felt in situations. Accountability is manifested in situations. Masculine selves are signified and elicit respect in situations. Feelings of powerlessness are magnified or assuaged because of what happens in situations. In each of these regards, situations crucially determine the compulsion, manner, and immediate consequences of manhood acts. There is simply no understanding manhood, or gender more generally, without attention to what people think, feel, and do in face-to-face encounters. A sociology of gender—in fact, any sociology of inequality—without a social psychology of interaction is likely to be a sociology of abstractions, not people.

There is nothing exceptional about these parts of my argument. Other sociologists have said similar things about why we embrace gender identities so firmly and why we feel situationally compelled to signify acceptance of these identities in conformity with prevailing cultural standards. Somewhat more challengingly, and perhaps more originally, I have tried to expose the intersections between situational compulsions to enact manhood, compulsions that are both internal and external, and the structural compulsions that can be described in terms of nets of accountability and the control imperatives of capitalism.

The idea of nets of accountability helps us see why situational accountability demands are so compelling. The force of such demands is magnified because of the extra-situational consequences of failing to meet them. It is not just the disapproval of an immediate audience that keeps us in line. What keeps us in line is the possibility of losing much else that rides on situational approval. The force of a boss's demand for gender conformity may be amplified, for example, by the knowledge that a bank will hold us accountable for making a mortgage payment on time. To understand the force of a situational accountability demand, it is thus necessary to consider the net of relationships in which actors are enmeshed and to understand how action in one situation—the satisfactory job performance that yields a steady paycheck—is contingently linked to extra-situational actions that yield other kinds of rewards, such as home ownership, the pleasures of leisure, respect in the community, and so on.

Though I have discussed them as if they were purely structural, the control imperatives of capitalism ultimately devolve to situations. It is not just that capitalism, as an exploitive form of economy, logically requires social actors willing and able to control others against their will and against their interests. At some point, real bodies must communicate with and act on other bodies in concrete situations. The control necessary to make capitalism work is not just an abstraction; it must be instantiated in situations where actors—usually, though not always, males striving to be men—use symbolic or physical means, or both, to compel the obedience of others. Without such routine, face-to-face impositions of control, capitalism could not exist.

Internal and external compulsions to enact manhood are also mutually reinforcing. Males are conditioned from an early age to derive satisfaction and feelings of self-respect from successful exertions of control and claims to manhood. This socially shaped desire is then met with genuine rewards: approval, respect, inclusion, livelihood, privilege. In a capitalist society, most males who strive to be men can get just enough of what they seek so that, in the absence of alternatives, they will remain attached to the system. Whether what males seek is what they need as human beings is another question (one I will take up in the last chapter).

I have been trying here to oppose the standard reduction of intersectionality to patterns of subjective experience arising from cross-cutting memberships in privileged and oppressed groups. Such experiences and patterns thereof are not uninteresting; examining them can, as suggested earlier, help us appreciate the diversity of experiences generated by life in societies fraught with multiple forms of inequality. But if we want to understand how these societies are reproduced, we will do better to look at other kinds of inter- and intrasections: those between system imperatives and situated gender enactments; between spatially distributed situations and the relations of production they sustain; and between self-presentations and self-worth.

Read through the lens of individualism, much of what I have said in this chapter will seem wrong. I expect the objections to run along these lines: *most men are not obsessed with control. Most men are not constantly striving for control. Most men do not compete unrelentingly for manhood status. Most men are secure in their manhood and feel no need to dominate others to assuage feelings of weakness or shame. As for capitalism, most men never even think about it, let alone stake their manhood on trying to preserve it.* Setting aside for the moment the question of what is true about "most men," these are perfectly sensible objections. Sensible, that is, from an individualist perspective that takes for granted what ought to be explained sociologically.

The individualist fallacy underlying the objections noted above is that the correctness of an analysis of social formations—things like capitalism, gender, manhood—can be assessed by seeing if it corresponds to the conscious intentions and self-understandings of the people whose actions constitute those formations.

If this were true, there would be no need for sociological analysis at all. To understand the social world, all we would need to do is to ask people what they are up to. Helpful informants, unhindered by any need for self-justification, would then articulate their bedrock assumptions and motives, describe their habitual practices in detail, and explain how those practices produce intended and unintended consequences, including the reproduction of whole societies. I hope it's clear why this would be an impossible expectation and a foolish way to try to understand how the social world works.[35]

To make the point more concretely, let me suggest a parallel. If I had written about whiteness, white supremacy, and racial identity in the manner I've written about manhood and capitalism, the objections might look like this: *most whites are not obsessed with being white. Most whites do not strive to signify their whiteness. Most whites do not try to assuage feelings of insecurity by imagining themselves to be superior to people of color. As for white supremacy, most whites never even think about it, let alone stake their sense of worth on trying to preserve it.* The same individualist fallacy underlies these claims. This fallacy, applied to social analysis, would lead us to conclude, for example, that racial privilege, racial hierarchy, and institutional racism do not exist, because most whites claim not to think about such things. That would be a politically convenient and appealing conclusion for whites, but entirely mistaken, as any competent sociologist would recognize in a minute.

Both sets of objections in italics above make the further mistake of assuming what ought to be explained. Once we take the existence of "men" for granted, as if men were elemental constituents of the natural world, we have short-circuited an analysis of the gender order and its intersections with the economy. Once we accept the essentialist ideology that equates males with men, we have been diverted from analyzing the social origins of men.

By starting with ungendered males and then unpacking the process by which they become the social creatures known as men, we can begin to see the deeper, ontological connection between exploitive relations of production and manhood. These are, as argued in this chapter, not distinct social formations that merely intersect. They are aspects of the same social formation, manhood coming into being at the moment when exploitation is institutionalized, just as "whiteness"—or whiteness by any other name—comes into being coincident with the invention of racial hierarchy.[36]

The thoughts and feelings of males striving to be men indeed matter, though not because thoughts, feelings, or intentions determine consequences or determine whether an analysis is correct. They matter, as I've emphasized here, because they are part of what compels males to signify masculine selves and strive for manhood status. But they are only part of the story; the other part has to do with compulsions that are external, both situational and structural, compulsions that manifest in but do not originate in the minds of individual males striving to be men.

If the goal were simply to understand individual males striving to be men, then, yes, we would want to look at the intersections of race, class, ethnicity, and sexuality at which these males-qua-men exist. But if the goal is to understand men as social creatures, or manhood as a social formation, then it is necessary to look at its intersection with other social formations and try to see through the ideologies that naturalize what is socially constructed. What we might thus see is that manhood cannot be decoupled from economic exploitation, an insight that offers good news and bad. The good news is that manhood and its liabilities for humankind are not eternal. The bad news is that change will be harder than we imagine.

Chapter 6

The Limits of Trans Liberalism

My gender dysphoria is political. As can perhaps be surmised from previous chapters, I object not only to the "gender binary" but to gender hierarchy—the existence of privileged and subordinated categories of persons identified on the basis of sex or gender. As I've argued, this is a social arrangement that arose from and perpetuates oppression and exploitation. I hope that humans will eventually transcend this arrangement and relegate gender, along with race and class, to the trash bin of history. Our survival, as I will argue in the last chapter, depends on it. For now, and no doubt for the rest of my time on the planet, living in this world as a member of the privileged sex and gender categories makes me uncomfortable, as does benefiting from other unjust arrangements in which I am implicated.

Another aspect of my political gender dysphoria concerns my gender habitus—the reflexive (not reflective) habits of thought, feeling, and behavior ingrained in me by virtue of the experiences associated with my place in the gender order. I am well conditioned, it seems, to assume or compete for control, to hide emotional vulnerabilities, and to signify a masculine self. None of this takes conscious effort. The effort, rather, lies in trying to transform the costly habitus ingrained by patriarchy into something consistent with my feminist values. It's a work in progress, fraught with the discomfort caused by frequent failure.[1]

Yet for the most part I feel subjectively at ease as a recognizably biological male who identifies and presents as a heterosexual man. As I was growing up, it never occurred to me to identify or present myself as anything but a boy or a man. To the best of my recollection, I was never confused or ambivalent about being male, a boy, a man, or heterosexual. There were times when I disliked competing for manhood status, but this never led me to question any of my gender-related identities. If anything, contesting for manhood status compelled me to get better at signifying a masculine self. Overall, my visible gender expression is not illegible, liminal, variant, transgressive, or queer. Except for times when I'm zipping about in skin-tight spandex (I'm a cyclist), I look like every other middle-aged white male academic with a beard and glasses. It thus seems fair to say that I am, except for my feminist politics, the result of successful socialization into the dominant gender order.

I describe myself in these ways as a prelude to discussing the politics of transgenderism. I am going to begin with a first-person thought experiment, and I suspect that, in the eyes of some readers, the validity of the experiment will depend on who I am, especially my location within and subjective experience of the prevailing gender order. For those who want to assess the experiment on these grounds, I have put my gender cards on the table, so to speak. In the end, however, I hope it will be clear that the validity of my analysis of the politics of transgenderism does not depend on who I am.

The experiment is this: I am going to suppose that I have decided to live as a woman. Because this would contravene the dominant gender order—I would be violating the usual expectation for a biological male to claim the identity "man"—I would need to account for this decision.[2] If I were to present myself as a woman and not be able to offer an account that made sense of this behavior, I would be at risk of being seen (depending on the audience) as socially incompetent, immoral, weird, or insane. And so the experiment is to consider the accounts I might give and how a feminist colleague might respond. I'll say more later about the feminist perspective from which this imaginary colleague speaks.

Suppose, then, that I have decided to live as a woman. Why have I chosen this course of action? my feminist colleague asks. Below are eight possible accounts, each followed by a brief response from my imaginary colleague.

> I have always felt, deep inside, that I was really female. As a boy, I knew that I was really a girl. As a man, I knew that I was really a woman. Living as a woman is just a matter of acknowledging what I have always known to be true about who I really am. Finally, I'll be living in a way that's true to myself and more honest with the outer world.

But being born with a male body and having been raised as a male, socialized as a boy, and treated as a man, how could you possibly know what it's like to be female, or a girl, or a woman? Don't you really mean to say that you often *imagined*, from your perspective as a male, boy, or man, what it might be like to be female, a girl, or a woman? How could you know what it's like to be a female, girl, or woman any more than you, as a white person, could know what it's like to be black? If you believe that knowledge of oneself is based on social location, isn't your claim to know how females, girls, and women experience themselves rather presumptuous?

> I am tired of trying to live up to the expectations of what a man is supposed to be. Trying to be tough and macho all the time has never felt right to me. I don't want to have to try to be like that anymore. I don't want to constantly compete with other men. As a woman, I won't have to face this burden. Instead of treating me like a rival, men will treat me like a lady.

No doubt it gets tiresome to constantly jockey for status. And I can see how it would be hard to stay bottled up emotionally, always pretending to be unfazed by what would cause pain to any normal human being. So it makes sense that you'd want to forgo all that. But this "treated like a lady" stuff is a fantasy. Have you forgotten what's wrong with being put on a pedestal by members of a dominant group? You'll be treated politely, at least superficially, only as long as you never challenge another man's sexism or challenge men for power.

> I don't know how to explain it, but my body just told me that I'm female, that I'm a woman. I've never felt right as a man, never felt totally comfortable. I didn't know what this was about. But now I've finally heard what my body has been telling me all along: I'm a woman. When I finally got the message, I realized this was more than a vague feeling. I *know* I am a woman.

I believe that you felt something in your body, or something you thought was coming from your body. But whatever you felt had to be interpreted. Whatever you were feeling had to be made sense of. So why did you make sense of it this way? It seems odd, given that you had no prior experiential knowledge of what it's like to be a woman, that you could be so sure about what your male body was telling you. Maybe all your body was telling you is that participating in an oppressive system, even as a member of the privileged group, can take a physical toll. Maybe the message is that you should try to change the system, not take a subordinate place in it.

> I've always wanted a kind of intimacy with women that I've never been able to achieve. I've always been jealous of how women seem to bond with each other by sharing emotions. As a man, I've never felt that I could do this. I couldn't make it work, even when I tried. As a woman, I'll be able to achieve this kind of intimacy and finally have the kind of connections with women that I've always wanted to have.

I understand the desire for emotional connection, and I can see how men often miss out on this. Sometimes I think that being a man must be like not being able to breathe, at least emotionally. I suppose that's one of the costs of privilege. And maybe you'll have better luck connecting with others, perhaps especially with women, if you present yourself as a woman. On the other hand, I don't see why this is necessary. Maybe you could achieve the intimacy you want by being a different kind of *person*, rather than thinking that the solution is to switch gender categories.

> I've always been sexually attracted to men, but I know I'm not gay. I'm *sure* I'm not gay. I think what this is really about is a feminine spirit inside me that draws me to men in a sexual way. But as a man, I never felt that I could act on that sexual impulse. It just wouldn't give me what I want. As a woman, I'll be able to be sexual with men in a way that will make me happy.

You know as well as I do that we live in a heterosexist society. As a person with a male body, you're not supposed to be sexual with other people who have male bodies. If you do, others will stigmatize you as gay and perhaps see you as less of a man. Maybe this is how you look at yourself when you think about your sexual attraction to other men. I mean, we all internalize the dominant cultural perspective. So maybe what you're experiencing is internalized homophobia. Maybe thinking of yourself as a woman, or imagining that you have a "feminine spirit," is a way to avoid the shame evoked by thinking of yourself as a gay man. If so, the problem is heterosexism, not your body type or gender identity.

> I feel that I'm entitled to exist as a sexual person, and it seems that whatever sexual energy I have is somehow connected to seeing myself as a woman. As a boy, I found it exciting to dress up in my mom's clothes. I still find it exciting to wear women's clothes. But doing this once in a while isn't enough. I want to feel sexually alive again, and the only way I can do this is to live as a woman.

Well, okay. Sexuality is a strange and powerful thing. Some people will pay a high price to satisfy their sexual desires. If living as a woman is what you need to do to satisfy yours, so be it. You're entitled to "exist as a sexual person," as you say. And you wouldn't be harming anyone. On the other hand, fetishizing gender doesn't do much to challenge sexism or patriarchy. So it's not clear that your transition will have much feminist consequence.

> Being a man and nothing but a man, having to do only the things that are okay for a man to do, limits my expression of gender. I know there is so much

more inside me—a feminine side that is no less complex and compelling than my masculine side. I want to explore this more fully and bring it out. I feel like the only way to do this is to live as a woman. I know I can't do it as a man. What's more, by becoming a woman I will help to subvert the gender binary that limits everyone's gender expression.

If you switch categories and pass as a woman, you won't be subverting the binary. You'll be affirming it as much as most people do. Though I suppose if you identify yourself as a trans woman, you'll at least encourage some people to see gender display as socially constructed. But you've been writing about the social construction of gender for twenty years, so it's not clear how you'll accomplish more subversion by wearing women's clothes. I also wonder why you think that gender expression is necessary for self-expression. It seems to me that you're embracing an essentialist idea that ties self-expression to being male or female. Wouldn't it be more liberating to detach the idea of self-expression from sex and gender entirely?

> I don't want to belong to the dominant group anymore. I don't want to be a member of the oppressing class. I don't want to contribute to reproducing gender inequality by being compelled as a man to be controlling all the time. I want to be in political solidarity with women and resist patriarchy as a woman. That's why I'm transitioning.

I get the point about not wanting to benefit from unearned privilege, and about not wanting to put on a manhood act that adds, even inadvertently, to women's oppression. But there's a question of strategy here. I wonder if you might be more effective in resisting patriarchy as a feminist man, or a feminist man who is critical of manhood. There are awfully few of those. Maybe you could do more subverting of the dominant gender order by trying to be in the world as a different kind of person, or by trying to bring about a world in which gender is not part of our thinking about how to be a good human being. Again, I appreciate your impulse to be in solidarity with women, but maybe the solution is not to find different ways to embrace gender individually. Maybe we need to find ways to collectively abolish it.

> This is just something that feels right for me. It's what I urgently need to do to be happy. I have a *right* to do it, and it's what I'm going to do. I shouldn't have to explain it to anybody. My happiness shouldn't depend on other people's approval of my gender expression. Besides, the only people who can

understand it are people who have the same feelings I do. If you've never had those feelings—of not being the right gender for your body—you can't possibly understand what this is about.

You can of course do what you want. I accept your right to define yourself however you please and to engage in whatever sort of gender display feels right to you, as long as it doesn't harm others. But I'm surprised that you seem to have forgotten that gender is about power and inequality. You seem to be treating it as nothing more than a field for self-expression, a field on which you can do whatever feels right, with no obligation to examine the social origins of your feelings or the social consequences of how you choose to express yourself. This seems to me to be a very unfeminist and unsociological way to be in the world. I hope someday we can have a more probing conversation about these matters. In the meantime, good luck with your transition. Will you call yourself Michelle?

Because s/he does not take my accounts at face value and offer unequivocal support, the feminist colleague in this thought experiment would be called "transphobic" by some. But the questions raised are, I would say—as my real, not hypothetical, self—important ones, if we are going to undertake a serious feminist analysis of the politics of transgenderism. It's not as if this discursive ground is untrodden. But in recent years the celebratory impulse—the impulse to honor diversity, laud rebelliousness, and champion the underdog—has displaced the analytic impulse.[3] As a result, there is not as much critical thinking as there should be about the limits and potentials of transgenderism for changing an oppressive gender order. At the risk of seeming unfriendly or phobic, I want to try to nudge this thinking along.

*   *   *

It might help if I articulate the principles that underlie the version of feminist sociology employed here. Some of these principles are implicit in earlier chapters. For example, that gender is socially constructed is a basic principle of feminist sociology (this is, by the way, not an axiom but a conclusion reached by studying historical and cultural variation in gender beliefs and practices). It is also a basic principle that the gender order is a system of beliefs, norms, and practices that privileges males and men. The gender order is thus neither natural nor neutral; it is a humanly created set of arrangements through which dominance by males and men is maintained. Demonstrably so.[4] It follows from this that when examining any belief or practice that falls under the rubric of "gender," one must consider its possible connections to inequality. Failing to do this is, from a feminist perspective, intellectual malpractice.

Another principle of feminist sociology is that inner realities—thoughts, feelings, and desires—must be no less subject to analysis than external realities. The contents and workings of human minds do not arise from nowhere; they derive from social experience. Thoughts, feelings, and desires must therefore be *sociologized*—that is, traced back to experiences linked to culture and social organization. And, like more visible realities, thoughts, feelings, and desires must also be examined for their possible connections to inequality. In a society in which sexuality is tied to gender, and gender is about inequality, it is not surprising that some people find erotic pleasure in domination or subordination.[5]

Analyzing the social origins of thoughts, feelings, and desires is not as simple as scanning one's biography for formative experiences. Many of the experiences that shape us occur when we are young and might not even be consciously noted at the time.[6] And whatever mental tapes we later replay in trying to get at these experiences are always incomplete and partly invented. Even so, thoughts, feelings, and desires—*especially* feelings and desires—cannot be exempt from analysis, as if they are "just there" and not to be questioned. Feminist sociology includes, it seems to me, a struggle to engage in this kind of critical self-examination, to get analytic distance on one's socialization and to connect the contents and workings of one's mind to the social world that engendered it.

At times I've used the term *gender order* rather than simply *gender* as a way to underscore another principle of feminist sociology: gender is not just a matter of self-presentation, but includes cultural beliefs, normative rules, laws, and collective practices through which what we loosely call "gender" is constructed and maintained.[7] In other words, to understand gender we have to see it as more than individual self-expression. We have to see it as woven into the routine operations of organizations and institutions. Hierarchical control, as argued in Chapter 5, requires masculine selves and men. Thinking along these lines—seeing gender as rooted in social organization, not only in bodies, minds, and symbolic culture—suggests why nonnormative gender display poses little threat to oppression or exploitation. Capitalist corporations and authoritarian governments can tolerate queerness on the margins, as long as core hierarchies remain intact and the reward system induces a sufficient number of people to behave as men.[8]

The principle of intimate connection between institutional arrangements and everyday life is often summed up in the feminist phrase "the personal is political." On the one hand, this is a truism, in that what we are as persons is always and necessarily a consequence, in part, of the relations of power within which we become persons. Indeed, if not for the political and social—if not for all the relationships within which we exist and that make us what we are—there would be no "personal" at all: no mind, no self. It is also true in the sense that the personal choices we make in our everyday lives have political consequences.

But under the influence of postmodern intellectual fashion that derides the possibility of unifying political analyses, "the personal is political" is now often taken to mean that the political is *nothing but* the personal. This is how rebellious self-presentation comes to be seen as equivalent to revolutionary action. This is how feelings of individual "empowerment" come to substitute for building the kind of power that comes only from organization. The missing feminist principle in this case is that social transformation—abolishing an oppressive gender order—requires collective political action aimed at challenging institutional arrangements and the elites who benefit from those arrangements. Rebellious self-expression might be part of the process, but if it exhausts the process, it will be harmlessly assimilated; it will come to naught, even if it feels naughty.

Feminism is usually thought to be concerned mainly with analyzing and rectifying inequalities between women and men. This is true of liberal feminism, which, in its most admirable form, uncompromisingly seeks equal civic and human rights for women. Much of the energy of the first and second waves of the women's movement in the United States was devoted to achieving precisely these aims. And it would be fair to say that such reforms are still urgently needed wherever women are denied equal pay, equal rights to political participation, and equal control over their lives. From the standpoint of liberal feminism, there remains a great deal of important political work to be done, in the United States and around the world.

Radical feminism is unsatisfied, however, with simply giving women equal opportunities to compete with men for privileged positions in exploitive and oppressive institutions. Radical feminism brings gender itself into question and takes intersectionality seriously. This means recognizing that gender must be understood in connection to racism and economic exploitation; that all forms of oppression and exploitation are unacceptable; and that to create an egalitarian society, all forms of oppression and exploitation must be fought. The feminist principle here is that, to borrow from Hegel, "the truth is whole," meaning that to understand and transform one part of an oppressive society, one must seek to understand and transform its other parts.

Taking intersectionality seriously is one way that feminist sociology applies the principle that the truth is whole. Another way this principle manifests is in the claim that gender is "relational." This is usually taken to mean that there are no men without women, no masculinity without femininity; the nature of each depends on its relation to the other. Inasmuch as our folk understandings of gender include the idea that men and women are "opposite sexes" and that masculinity is the opposite of femininity, the point is valid and important. If the

one-page handout about how people respond to difference. I hoped to get participants to reflect not just on the range of possibilities (from repulsion to tolerance
to appreciation to nurturance) but on the blind spots and unconscious biases
that operate when we meet, evaluate, and supervise others who are, somehow,
different. Low turnout aside, I thought the discussion was honest and productive.

One of the participants was a white man who appeared to be in his early
forties. He was an administrator in the accounting department on his campus.
Throughout the session, his comments were constructive and supportive, if a
bit stiffly delivered. "In my department," I recall him saying, "I don't tolerate
discrimination. I judge people based solely on their job performance, and I insist
that others do the same. This is something I learned in the military."

I affirmed his statement by saying that, compared with many civilian
institutions, the military, once it overcame its own practices of segregation, had
a commendable record of ignoring race and rewarding performance. Had it been
a different kind of teaching moment, I would have challenged the claims that
there was no racism in the military and that all it takes to eliminate racism is
a strict application of bureaucratic criteria for assessing merit. But it wasn't the
time or place to push those points. What I did say, was that the military had a
less impressive record when it came to ending discrimination against gays and
lesbians. His response surprised me.

I expected him to say something like *yes, that's true* or *well, no organization is
perfect* or *that will be a tougher form of discrimination to eliminate*. Instead, he said,
"That's a matter of religion." Though I was pretty sure I knew what he meant, I
asked anyway. He said, "People are against homosexuality for religious reasons.
That's not subject to change." This happened near the end of the workshop, and
I didn't want to spoil the positive vibe, so I didn't probe further. But I got the
impression that he saw religious belief as exempt from critique and a legitimate
basis for discrimination.

The more I thought about this later, the more it bothered me. It wasn't just
the appeal to religion to justify discrimination. That was bad enough, but it was
an old story. For millennia, humans have invented gods and holy doctrines to
justify pillage, murder, and exploitation. What bothered me more, especially in
the context of higher education, was the use of religion to deflect a demand to
examine the morality of oppressive behavior. It was as if one could get away with
saying, "My religion teaches me that homosexuality is wrong, and because it's
my *religion*, you can't challenge what I do based on this belief. You can't even ask
me to *rethink* this belief." Well, what if my religion says it's okay to burn Jews? Is
that off limits for discussion? If discrimination against gays and lesbians can be
justified by calling oneself a Southern Baptist, can discrimination against people
of color be justified by calling oneself a Disciple of Odin?

* * *

Fourteen years later I was teaching a graduate course on the sociology of gender. One of the readings was Sheila Jeffreys's book *Beauty and Misogyny*. I assigned the book because I wanted students to confront Jeffreys's critique of oppressive beauty practices in Western societies. Jeffreys does an excellent job, in my estimation, of showing how beauty practices—body shaving, wearing makeup and high heels, plastic surgery—that are today taken for granted as innocuous, originated in, and still help to perpetuate, the exploitation of women's bodies and sexuality. As I expected, Jeffreys's analysis provoked much consternation on the part of students invested in conventional femininity.

Beauty and Misogyny includes a chapter on "transfemininity" in which Jeffreys critiques male-to-female transsexuality.[12] Jeffreys rejects the idea that male-to-female transsexualism originates in biology. She argues instead that male-to-female transsexuals take on the trappings of femininity—the behaviors of subordination in the gender order—because doing so "satisfies masochistic sexual interests." Adopting the "behaviors and appurtenances" of femininity (often to the point of unintentional parody) is thus for some men an exciting sexual hobby, though by the time hormonal or surgical change is sought, much of the early sexual frisson may have worn off. If male-to-female transsexuals tell stories about being women trapped in male bodies, Jeffreys argues, it is because the medical profession makes its assistance conditional on hearing such stories.[13]

About female-to-male transsexuals, Jeffreys has less to say. She again locates the desire for this sort of transition in the oppression of women and lesbians, not in biology. Sexism and heterosexism, Jeffreys argues, make it impossible for some women to happily love women while in a female body. Embracing manhood is thus a response to internalized homophobia. Jeffreys proposes other reasons for female-to-male transsexualism: a history of sexual abuse by men and a corresponding desire to exit the body associated with victimhood; a desire for access to privilege; and the trauma of menopause giving rise to a preference for being a man rather than a despised old woman.[14]

Jeffreys also rejects the claims by transgender and queer theorists that trans is revolutionary or progressive. Rather, she sees male-to-female transsexualism/ transgenderism as conservative, even reactionary, in several ways: it makes the construction of gender identities essential to the project of being human; it embraces the behaviors of domination (masculinity) and subordination (femininity) as unproblematic forms of self-expression; and it locks into place the system of dominant and subordinate gender categories, doing nothing to overturn male supremacy, patriarchy, or the oppression of women. Whereas transsexuals want to retain gender as an aid to sexual excitement, and transgenderists want to retain it as a means of self-expression, real feminists, Jeffreys says, want to abolish it.

When it came time to discuss this chapter, I began by asking students to articulate Jeffreys's arguments. I wanted us to assess the arguments and the evidence Jeffreys musters to support them. It seemed to me that the arguments were straightforward and clearly expressed, and so I was surprised when students—an otherwise sharp bunch of graduate students in sociology—had a hard time doing this. Instead of getting a handle on her arguments, many students wanted to comment, first and foremost, on what they alleged to be Jeffreys's unfriendly stance toward trans people. Other students seemed to have a hard time getting their minds around Jeffreys's argument about the erotic charge that some men derived from femininity. I decided that at our next class meeting I would announce a transition of my own. Here is what I said:

> Before we start today, I want to make an announcement that I know will come as a surprise to many of you. It's something I've struggled to come to grips with all my life, and now seems like the right time to go public. In fact, you folks will be the first to hear this. The thing is, I've been living a lie for a long time. It's true that I look white, was raised white, and have been publicly identified as white, treated as white, and that my ancestry is Northern European. But inside I'm really black. Ever since I can remember, I've known that my true self is black. Sure, I pretended to like country music and folk music, but it was really jazz and blues that stirred me inside. Yes, I know I look like I just stepped out of the L. L. Bean catalog, but that's fake, too. My soul longs for baggy pants, a do-rag, and lots of bling. I want to fully embrace my natural rhythm, get away from having to be scientific and rational all the time, and get in touch with my spiritual, earthy side. I'm tired of dancing like a white guy. So I've decided it's time to start living authentically. I'm going to take drugs and use dyes to darken my skin. I'm going to get a Jheri curl and buy the urban thug wear I've always wanted. I'm going to get some tapes and study Ebonics. I'll even learn to do that cool strut walk that the other black guys do. But most importantly, I'm going to join a black church and every other black organization I can find, because I want to be among my own people. I know they'll accept me, because—having been victims of oppression themselves—they won't want to discriminate against transracial people like myself. And then, when I'm affirmed as the black person I know myself to be, I will thank God almighty because I will be free at last.

I played it straight all the way through, even though by the time I got to the L. L. Bean line everyone knew it was some kind of teaching exercise.

After making the bogus announcement, I asked, What's wrong with this picture? Everyone recognized that the image of blackness depicted in the announcement is a caricature—a white person's racist fantasy about black people. Students also agreed that it was impossible for a person born, raised, identified, and treated as white, and never having been an intimate member of a black community, to really understand what it means, experientially, to be black in America (a point affirmed by the black students in class). It thus seemed clear, after we had talked through the problem of how well people in a dominant group can understand the experience of people in an oppressed group, that any claims by a white person to be "black inside" had to be viewed with skepticism.

I also asked why white-to-black transraciality was a problem from the standpoint of antiracist politics. Wouldn't it be a good thing, I asked, if more white people identified with the struggles of black people? One of the black students reiterated the point that the image of blackness in the announcement is a racist stereotype—hardly a positive way to identify or identify with black people.[15] Another black student said that there was nothing about a white person pretending to be black that would necessarily do anything to combat interpersonal or institutional racism. Someone else said that white people who wanted to fight racism should confront other white people and challenge white privilege, not act out a racist stereotype. I added the point that transraciality, in the sense of just trying to switch racial categories, would do nothing to challenge the notion of racial categories on which racism depends.

After the transraciality discussion, I read another vignette. In this case, fictional Jane transitions to fictional James, and then runs into a problem.

> Jane, a biological female, transitions to James and begins to live full time as a publicly identified man. Jane was always an assertive person, but now, as James, s/he becomes downright domineering and overbearing. When people point this out and say it's a problem, James says, "Look, I'm a *man*. This is how men behave, because they're *masculine*. You're just expressing prejudice against men and masculinity. It's no different from any other form of bigotry."

The question I posed for discussion was, Must the people who find James's behavior obnoxious simply back off? I don't remember who said what, but no one wanted to defend James. No one thought James should get a pass on his controlling behavior simply by claiming that this behavior was an appropriate expression of his newly adopted manly self.

The point of these exercises was to construct parallels to Jeffreys's analysis of transsexuality/transgenderism. I took this tack because it seemed that students had been led to believe that anything less than celebrating "trans" was impermissible—no analysis, questioning, or critique allowed. Using the race parallel avoided this problem and allowed us to see Jeffreys's argument more clearly. The Jane-to-James vignette helped us think about the ethicality of gender-expressive behavior without getting hung up on the idea that people have a right to claim whatever gender identity they want to. In my follow-up remarks at the start of the next class, I said that analyzing these matters sociologically does not preclude compassion for people who suffer under a restrictive, heterosexist gender order. Anyone with any feminist consciousness, I said, should be anguished, too. The question is what to do about it.

*   *   *

Ideologies that legitimate oppressive social arrangements can mislead us about why we're unhappy. The consumerist ideology that props up a capitalist economy leads us to believe that unhappiness stems from a lack of stuff and that the cure is acquiring more stuff. Real satisfaction might come only from a profound reconsideration of one's values and a reorientation to life, yet we misunderstand our troubles and continually struggle to get more of what we don't really need. Which is exactly what keeps the system going and our troubles unresolved.

The achievement ideology that legitimates inequality—the ideology that says everyone has an equal chance to get ahead; that all it takes is talent, hard work, and a willingness to play by the rules—leads us to blame ourselves for not getting farther ahead, even though it's not structurally possible to do so, because there are a limited number of jobs or positions being sought by a vastly greater number of people. So here again we can misunderstand what's wrong. Under the influence of ideologies with which we are propagandized throughout life, we end up blaming ourselves for outcomes that are inevitable—for most people—under capitalism. Which again helps to keep the system going by keeping it out of the critical spotlight.

Ideologically engineered misunderstandings abound.[16] Whites are led to believe that their economic woes are caused by welfare spending on undeserving minorities. Anglo workers are led to believe that their low wages are caused by illegal immigrants. Private-sector workers are led to believe that high taxes are caused by overpaid public employees. We are all led to believe that capitalism has bestowed on us the best possible form of government, one in which every adult enjoys an equal share of political power through the ballot box. All these notions protect the status quo by obscuring the relations of domination and subordination that are the real sources of most people's unhappiness.

Once upon a time, it was understood that feminist theory had a crucial liberatory purpose to serve by "raising consciousness"—that is, by helping people see through distorting ideologies and get a better handle on the social origins of their experiences as women and men.[17] The radical feminist therapy movement of the 1960s and 1970s most pointedly served this purpose for women who misattributed their unhappiness to failures as wives and mothers. Radical feminist therapy countered this self-blame and helped women see that their unhappiness stemmed from being subordinated, as women, in a patriarchal society. Radical feminist *theory* is therapy writ large, the goal being to reveal the ideologically obscured roots of gender-related unhappiness, as a step in the process of transforming individuals and society. Much of the current trans-positive discourse, especially the more libertarian strains, seems to reject the very possibility of achieving this kind of insight through feminist criticism of the gender order.

Defenders of transsexualism and transgenderism like to say, in rejecting feminist critiques, that people are "experts on their own experience."[18] This is true at the level of reportage. If someone wants to know what it's like to be me, I'm the person to ask. I can tell you what it feels like to be in my skin. But this doesn't mean that I can *explain*, or even identify, all the conditions, processes, and ideas that generated the experiences that made me who and what I am. It doesn't mean that I know where all my fears and anxieties originate. Any explanations I can offer will be skewed by ignorance, faulty memory, emotional investments, political blind spots, and inadequate analytic language. My explanations are also likely to be skewed by a need for self-justification. So, too, with everyone, to greater or lesser degrees. These are the limits of being human, no matter how rigorously we examine our lives.[19]

To say that self-understandings are limited and can be distorted by ideology should be uncontroversial. If we were all truly experts on our own experience, if the conditions that shape our minds and bodies were fully transparent to us, we wouldn't need psychology, sociology, history, anthropology, philosophy, and literature—or other people, be they therapists or insightful friends—to help us sort ourselves out. Feminist theorizing is one of these efforts. It can help us see how the ideologies that support the dominant gender order get inside us, cause unhappiness, and mislead us about where those feelings are coming from. And so it is a mistake for anyone concerned with human suffering related to the gender order to dismiss feminist analysis of transsexualism and transgenderism. The results of such an analysis can be challenged in any given case, but to reject the analytic project is to implicitly defend the ideological underpinnings of the patriarchal status quo.

Defenders of transsexualism and transgenderism err when they suppose that showing compassion for those who suffer under the dominant gender order means accepting all the beliefs and practices of those who suffer. The oppressed may indeed see some things, perhaps many things, better than the privileged.[20] There are also things they might not see at all, such as the backstage actions of

use their material property in whatever ways will benefit them, there are gender dysphoric Americans who want to be able to use their bodies in whatever ways will make them happy.

From a radical feminist perspective, transsexualism is disappointing because whatever dysphoria underlies it fails to induce critical reflection on the gender order as oppressive to females and women. Or so it seems, to read its libertarian defenders.[23] It is this libertarian transsexualism that appears conservative from a feminist perspective, even if individuals make what seem like radical alterations to their bodies and everyday lives. From a feminist perspective, transsexualism does no more to combat sexism than "passing as white" does to combat racism.

Transgender advocates and theorists who embrace queer politics are less averse to thinking beyond individual desires and less averse to feminist analysis of gender as a system of inequality.[24] There is common ground on which radical feminists and some transgender theorists stand in seeing the rigid gender binary—males must be masculine men; females must be feminine women—as the heart of an oppressive gender order. There is also more likely to be agreement that gender, gender identities, gender-related desires, and gender enactments are social constructions—hence subject to reconstruction along less restrictive lines, or no lines at all. And many transgender advocates, politically sensitized by their own chafing against the normative gender binary, are involved in antisexist and other social justice work. This is all to the good.

Yet transgender politics, whatever the body radicalism or dissident self-presentations involved, remain liberal politics in regard to the gender order itself. They are the politics of reform, not abolition. As feminist critics have pointed out, to embrace trans*gender*ism is to implicitly embrace the preservation of gender.[25] Even if dominant strictures of self-presentation and sexuality are loosened, transgenderism presupposes that gender is essential to being human. It is precisely this belief that radical feminism calls into question. Why suppose, radical feminism asks, that we must express our humanity in terms provided by a system of domination? Would it not be better—less restrictive and more liberating—to stop believing that who and what we are as human beings depend on reproductive anatomy? Given that its origins and purposes lie in serving male domination, would it not be better to abolish gender than to imagine that we can make it a safe playground for self-expression?

Radical feminism takes its foremost imperative to be ending the domination and exploitation of females and women by males and men. Transgenderism takes its imperative to be facilitating greater happiness among those individuals who feel constricted by prevailing norms of gender-related behavior and want to "do gender" differently. The problem, from a radical feminist perspective, is that the latter is entirely compatible with the continued domination and exploitation of females and women by males and men. As long as doing gender differently leaves room for males (usually) to construct masculine selves and compete for manhood status, fundamental oppressive arrangements will remain intact. Which is why transgenderism, without a radical feminist critique of gender at its core, poses no real threat to male domination. In fact, by diverting political energy into arguments over identity and self-expression, it can have the inadvertent consequence of protecting the institutionalized gender order.

The limits of transgender liberalism are also evident in the failure to reject masculinity. Whereas radical feminists see masculinity as the behavior of male domination, transgenderists treat it as a legitimate expression of one kind of gendered self. Accepting masculinity as a legitimate way in which a female-to-male trans person might express a gendered self is thus, from a radical feminist perspective, to accept the legitimacy of controlling behavior. It is also to accept the idea that females who want the privileges associated with membership in the dominant gender category must be granted the self-expressive latitude to seek those privileges, if they believe it will relieve their gender dysphoria and make them happy. This is analogous to accepting the liberal idea that workers who are miserable in their jobs or unhappy with their wages should try to solve their problems by becoming capitalists themselves.

The failure of transgenderism to mount an adequate critique of masculinity has been abetted by the academic masculinities industry. Part of the de-radicalization of profeminist men's studies, as argued in Chapter 2, has been acceptance of the idea that some ways of claiming manhood status—that is, some "masculinities"—are not oppressive and can even be progressive.[26] Some transgenderists have embraced this idea, claiming that it's fine to express masculinity, as long as it's alternative, inclusive, or at least not hegemonic.[27] Such a claim incorporates the conceptual confusions about males, men, and masculinity discussed in Chapter 2. It's a claim that makes sense only if masculinity is divorced from power; only if masculinity is thought to have no necessary connection to male supremacy or the dominance of women by men; and only if claiming manhood status by signifying some kind of masculine self is thought to have no necessary connection to preserving an oppressive gender order. From a radical feminist perspective, these are incoherent notions. Incoherent and dangerous.

To put matters in terms of the arguments developed in previous chapters, the problem that is elided by liberal pro-trans politics is that to seek manhood status by signifying a masculine self is always and necessarily an act of seeking privilege by signifying the capacity to control others. One cannot be a man in a gender order that privileges members of the category "men" without receiving and benefiting from privileges vis-à-vis females and women. And to seek cred-itability as a man—to elicit the attribution of being a worthy member of the category, deserving of full manhood status—requires signifying a masculine self. In this view, claiming manhood status, no matter what kind of body one is born with, no matter how gentle, inclusive, non-homophobic, or sweet one's self-presentation, is always about taking a privileged place in an oppressive gender order. Liberal pro-trans politics, however, sees the claiming of manhood status as just another self-expressive possibility on the playground of gender. This is the logical equivalent of celebrating "CEO" as a role that one might happily choose or aspire to on the playground of capitalism.

Once *trans people* were defined into existence as a category of people oppressed for being what they cannot help being, it became harder to see men, manhood acts, and competition for manhood status as inherently problematic. Why? Because some members of the group called men are *transmen*. And because they are, by definition, members of an oppressed group, it violates the norms of liberal multiculturalism to suggest that there might be something wrong with what they do to construct themselves as men. If manhood acts are seen as per-formed by members of an oppressed group seeking liberation from oppression, it's hard to sustain the idea—the feminist idea—that there is anything inher-ently wrong with those acts. Liberal multiculturalism, by exempting transmen from critical analysis, has inadvertently extended the exemption to include the practices used by biological males striving to be men.

Part of the liberal argument is that gender is an expression of an authentic self—an expression of who and what we most deeply believe ourselves to be, an expression essential to the pursuit of happiness. Freedom of gender expression is therefore a human right, like the right to free speech or freedom of religion. With the liberal claim about the right to self-expression, I agree. What I have been arguing for, however, is a critical, sociological analysis of gender expressions that we now take to be unproblematic: manhood acts. The liberal view sees these expressions, provided that they cause no obvious, immediate harm, as natural, authentic, valuable, and a legitimate source of pleasure. What isn't seen from this view is how gender identities, gender-related desires, and expressions of gender arise from and sustain relations of exploitation.

In the current historical moment, I endorse the pro-trans emphasis on changing norms of self-presentation to allow a wider range of acceptable gender expressions. Ours would be a more humane society if people were not discrimi-nated against and subject to abuse because their gender displays deviate from dominant norms. To the extent that these norms are elements of culture, culture needs to be changed. On this, radical feminists and transgenderists agree.

The problem, however, is that culture can shift to allow more room for individual self-expression while leaving fundamental oppressive structures intact, and this is what liberal pro-trans politics misses. If all exploitive economic systems require the creation of human beings willing and able to control others, then men will be ever with us. Moreover, they will be ever with us as a category that is privileged precisely because its members cultivate and, when necessary to maintain exploitive economic relations, exercise the capacity to control others. By implication, gender cannot be made nonexploitive without abolishing the structural economic arrangements that give rise to it and that it helps to sustain. Thus to hold on to gender is not to hold on to a quaint but innocuous belief that males and females ought to style themselves in different ways and have fun doing it. It is to hold on to a basic pillar of an oppressive society.

Radical feminism is threatening to both economic liberalism and transgender liberalism because it puts into question, indeed calls for the abolition of, the social arrangements—capitalist relations of production, a gender order that privileges males and men at the expense of females and women—that liberals want only to tweak so as to squeeze a bit more happiness out of the system. The problem here is not one of gradual change versus revolution; radical feminists know full well that social transformation takes time. The problem is that liberalism gets the analysis wrong, failing to see how the arrangements from which one tries to wring a bit more happiness are what ultimately undermine it. It might thus be said that liberal transgenderists have chosen a road that does not lead to the gender-free, egalitarian future where radical feminism wants to go.

No doubt this seems like wild talk. Gender is woven so deeply into most of us that life without it is unimaginable. In the world today, no one can step outside the cultural frameworks that endow our male and female bodies with the meanings that lead us to think of ourselves as women or men. And even if we think in unconventional terms—even if we try to redefine "woman," "man," and how these identities relate to maleness and femaleness; even if we try to imagine alternative gender identities—there remains the seemingly inescapable belief that what we are as human beings must somehow hinge on reproductive anatomy. Trapped in this web of belief about the inevitability of defining ourselves as gendered beings, talk of a gender-free, egalitarian future seems fantastical.

It is often said by radical feminists that transsexual libertarians and transgender liberals go wrong because they advocate the alteration of individual bodies rather than changing the gender order that imposes restrictive, ideological meanings on male and female bodies.[28] I think this is a fair criticism, though queer-thinking transgender advocates and theorists will say that they challenge these meanings by encouraging people, regardless of body type, to reject the gender binary and decide for themselves how to "express gender." The radical feminist critique of this strategy says, *do away with the whole set of meanings. Do away with the idea entirely that people* have *a gender or must* express *a gender to be human.* As should be apparent, this is a critique I endorse.

But I have also tried to take the radical feminist critique of transgender politics a step farther and show that even abandoning the current set of meanings on which the gender order is based is not enough. Semantic change without structural change is like a theocracy that changes the name of God but remains a theocracy. Men by any other name would be the category of humans that emerges to benefit from and sustain exploitive structural arrangements. It is these arrangements from which we must seek to transition, not from our biological bodies or even the labels we put on our bodies.

In thinking about what is possible by way of redefining ourselves, it might be good to remember that the idea of abolishing racial categories would have once seemed fantastical. To those in the grip of the ideological belief that race is biological, it still does. But to those who understand that race is a political fiction invented to legitimate economic exploitation, abolishing race begins to seem, if not imminent, entirely plausible and possible. Based on this understanding— that race is a fiction used to bolster exploitation and inequality—the *necessity* of abolition becomes apparent.[29] The absurdity of seeking a solution to the problem of racialized oppression by "being white differently" or "being black differently" would be obvious. The need for more fundamental changes in meanings and social organization would be clear. So, too, we will come to see, I think, with gender.

If my argument about the ontological connection between exploitive economic relations and the need for men is correct, the possibility of someday transcending gender should seem more realistic. The implication of my argument is that gender cannot be transcended or abolished by applying force of intellect to alter the meanings we now use to define ourselves. We cannot "make gender go away" by thinking hard about it, playing with it, or studying (again and again) how people enact it. We might, however, abolish it by making men and masculine selves unnecessary. This will be the case when we no longer organize social life based on exploitive economies and the authoritarian governments such economies require. When gender is no longer needed to enforce or enhance exploitation, it will, along with race, fade away.

In the meantime, those of us who have been shaped by the dominant gender order cannot help but think in its terms and rely on gender as a resource for self-construction and self-presentation. We cannot ignore the desires it has instilled in us. No more than we can wish gender away as a set of cultural meanings and practices can we wish it away as a shaper of subjective experience. This is the sense in which sociologists are correct to say that although we can decide to do gender differently, we cannot simply decide to undo ourselves as gendered beings.[30] In these regards, we are all—the comfortable and dysphoric, the conformist and dissident—stuck with gender, albeit in different ways and with different consequences.

We can, nonetheless, challenge the narrowness and rigidity of the dominant gender order, along with its heterosexism, privileging of males and men over females and women, and its valorization of control. We can contest meanings and norms in everyday life. We can refuse to participate in the normalized practices that privilege males and men at the expense of females and women. Feminist gender-queering is part of this process. But, again, in the long run we will need to confront and transform the relations of exploitation on which the gender order rests. The abolition of gender will require more than gender radicalism.

Chapter 7

Feminism or Barbarism

For many antiwar activists, the seven-month run-up to the US invasion of Iraq, from September 2002 to March 2003, was a surreal time. Less than a year after invading Afghanistan, supposedly in pursuit of the organizers of the 9/11 terrorist attacks on the Twin Towers and the Pentagon, Bush administration officials were talking about invading Iraq, a country that had nothing to do with 9/11. On the face of it, the idea of attacking Iraq seemed so contrary to fact and reason, so blatantly criminal, that it was hard to believe the American people would stand for it. In October 2002, I published this letter in the Raleigh, North Carolina, *News and Observer*:

> In your October 4 editorial "The push on Iraq" you say, "No one disputes that Saddam Hussein is a threat." I wonder, do you folks read your own newspaper? Do you read any other newspapers?
>
> If you'd been paying attention, you'd know that most of the rest of the world disputes the absurd claim that Saddam Hussein poses a military threat to the United States. Former UN weapons inspectors have said that Iraq is no threat. Retired US generals have said that Iraq is no threat. Most European leaders (other than Bush's echo, Britain's Tony Blair) have said that Iraq is no threat. Nearly all Iraq's neighbors say they do not feel threatened.
>
> Hundreds of thousands of people around the world have marched in the streets to dispute the claim that Iraq is a threat. The real threat to world peace, they have been saying, is the drive by the Bush cabal to achieve world domination.
>
> Most of this has been reported in *The N&O*. How did you miss it?
>
> What is the Bush administration after? Getting rid of alleged "weapons of mass destruction" has nothing to do with it. Nor does protecting Americans

from terrorism. The unabashed goal is US control of Middle Eastern oil and the leverage over the world economy that would come from this control.

But Americans are understandably reluctant to send their sons and daughters to die for Exxon, and so we are being told that a small country beaten down by 10 years of sanctions is a threat to the greatest military power on Earth. That's a lie big enough to make Goebbels blush.

In February 2003, hundreds of thousands of people in the United States, less gullible than newspaper editorialists and pundits, marched in the streets to oppose the seemingly imminent US invasion. But, no matter. The next month, the Bush administration launched a war of aggression of the kind for which Nazi leaders were condemned at Nuremberg.

Protests might have been even wider if mainstream media in the United States had not been so childishly credulous in accepting Bush administration claims about Saddam Hussein's (nonexistent) "weapons of mass destruction" and his (nonexistent) links to the 9/11 attacks. It might have helped, too, if the media had not largely excluded antiwar voices from their coverage. When Americans turned to TV, radio, and newspapers for information about Iraq, what they got was a steady stream of alleged experts, many of whom were former military officers, speculating on how soon and how best to disarm and depose Saddam Hussein. By the fall of 2002, the question, Why invade Iraq? had seemingly been answered; that's not what supposedly responsible grown-ups were talking about. The talk was about *how*.

Even farther in the background was another question: By what right does the United States presume to attack another sovereign nation, one that has not attacked us, and thus inevitably kill, maim, and displace thousands of innocent people? For the most part, it seemed to be taken for granted that, if the threat was at all credible, the United States had the right to use deadly, mass violence to exert control over national leaders on the other side of the world. Later, after the Bush administration's claims about weapons of mass destruction were exposed as lies, after Saddam Hussein was dead, after the US invasion set off a sectarian civil war, after thousands of Iraqis had been killed, maimed, or had their lives disrupted, it was no less taken for granted by most Americans that the United States had a right to be in Iraq to "bring its people freedom and democracy"—at the point of a gun.

After a nearly decade-long debacle and defeat in Iraq, and over a decade creating a similar disaster in Afghanistan, national consciousness in the United States is little changed. As I write this, the talk is about Iran. Mainstream media are more cautious about accepting official claims that Iran's alleged nuclear ambitions pose a threat. By reading carefully, it's possible to learn that Iran does not have nuclear weapons and is not building nuclear weapons, and that its most powerful national leaders (the Grand Ayatollahs) denounce nuclear weapons as immoral. But then it was possible in the fall of 2002, as I pointed out in the letter reproduced above, for millions of ordinary people in the United States and around the world to know that Iraq posed no threat. And yet the invasion was launched anyway—if not with popular enthusiasm, at least without popular rebellion.

The talk now, facts notwithstanding, is how to stop Iran from building a nuclear weapon. The immediate threat is said to be to Israel, Iran's leaders supposedly being eager to wipe the United States' favorite Middle Eastern client state off the map. And, if *this*, what *else* might Iran be capable of? Will we wait, in the infamous words of Bush's secretary of state Condoleezza Rice, for a mushroom cloud over Manhattan to find out? The real threat, of course, were Iran to go nuclear, is that it would be harder for the United States and Israel to bully Iran and to repress anti-imperialist movements in the oil-rich Middle East—movements to which Iran has given support. A desire to forestall this threat to US power has led President Obama to declare that a nuclear Iran is "unacceptable" and that "all options are on the table" to keep Iran from developing nuclear weapons. What form of consciousness underlies such a declaration?

One aspect of this consciousness is the assumption, which is again not disputed in the mainstream media, that the United States has the right to determine whether Iran can possess nuclear weapons. As in the cases of Afghanistan and Iraq, this control prerogative is rarely questioned. If it is questioned, even indirectly, racist propaganda is ready to provide a justification: *Iranians are driven by an irrational hatred for the United States, Israel, and the West; hence they cannot be trusted to possess such powerful weapons. A sensible adult would no more allow Iran to possess a nuclear weapon than give a handgun to a child. And so, yes, if you must ask, the global community of responsible adults, led by the United States, must place limits on Iran's behavior.* Most Americans are willing to accept this modern version of the white-man's-burden ideology. The implicit belief is that we must exert control over the darker-skinned peoples of the world, until such time as we have brought them sufficient enlightenment to ensure that they can run their own affairs in a manner consistent with their best interests and, of course, ours.

Political elites in the United States do not necessarily embrace the ideological justifications they offer to the public. Backstage, political elites in the United States are candid that they are competing with other national elites for control of raw materials, energy resources, labor, and markets. Beliefs about the inherent superiority or inferiority of nations, races, and ethnic groups may be present, but they are superfluous. In fact, racist beliefs can be dangerous if they lead to underestimating one's opponents. The beliefs that matter are more basic: that human life on all scales, from local to global, is a struggle for control; that one strives for control and either achieves it or ends up being dominated and exploited; and that death is preferable to submission. Together, these beliefs are the core of what might be called dominator consciousness.[1]

This form of consciousness is evident in public discourse about Iran and nuclear weapons. Consider that one argument made in *opposition* to sanctioning Iran for its pursuit of nuclear technology is that Iran, even if it succeeded in developing nuclear weapons, would never use them—especially against Israel or the United States—because to do so would be suicidal; it would be to provoke retaliation in kind, hence annihilation. This argument is rarely unpacked beyond making the point that, whatever else they might be, Iran's leaders are not so irrational as to use a weapon that would ensure their own destruction. If this point is conceded, then we need not worry overly much about Iran's nuclear ambitions. As with the United States, France, Britain, Russia, China, India, Pakistan, North Korea, and Israel, let the Iranians have an unusable bomb.

The part of this argument that is rarely unpacked has to do with the presumed rationality of the annihilating counterattack. Such a response is believed to be so reasonable that it can be cited as a certainty. But what assumptions does this entail? Spelled out more fully, the argument goes like this: *if the leaders of [Iran], leaders who are not under the control of their citizenry, launch a nuclear attack on [Israel, the United States], it is right and proper for leaders of [Israel, the United States] to respond in kind and kill millions of people inside and outside [Iran] who had no control over the initial attack.* To accept the reasonableness of an annihilating counterattack, one must accept these assumptions, which boil down to accepting the right of national elites to dispose of the lives of those whom they have come to dominate politically and economically. Dominator consciousness presumes this right; drone morality accepts it (see Chapter 4).

The same logic of dominance that makes a nuclear counterattack seem reasonable is evident in less cataclysmic actions. When bombs, drones, or death squads are used to eliminate "insurgents," concerns about collateral damage cannot be allowed to compromise the effort. Expressions of regret may be mouthed to mitigate outrage, but the deaths of bystanders and innocents are accepted as inevitable and necessary. Necessary, that is, to maintain dominance.

Critics have argued that drones and bombs—because they kill innocent bystanders, and because they're seen as tools of the cowardly—create more insurgents who are eager for revenge. Critics have also noted that killing one leader just makes room for others to rise in the chain of command. The instrumental value of drones and bombs for achieving domination abroad is thus disputed.[2] But there is also an instrumental purpose served at home. Elite males risk appearing effete, pampered, and soft, and so must find ways to appear tough. Wielding drones, bombs, and death squads is perfect macho political theater. It is a safe and effective way to win manhood contests vis-à-vis supposedly anti-American terrorists and to elevate one's manhood status in the eyes of Americans who will not tolerate a president who appears soft and penetrable.[3]

Commitment to dominance as a first principle of existence means that only those actions that ensure dominance will be seen as logical and will, moreover, be seen as justified. Laws or morals that conflict with the logic of dominance must be discarded, altered, or tortuously interpreted so that dominance retains an appearance of honorability. This, too, is political theater. Lawyers and complicit law professors are far more necessary to the manhood acts of elite males than any code of ethics.[4]

To speak of *dominator consciousness* and *a logic of dominance* is to wield theoretical abstractions. Yet these terms point to concrete realities. The US invasions of Afghanistan and Iraq are not abstractions. The use of bombs, drones, and death squads to kill people who resist US control is not an abstraction. Nor are the deaths of hundreds of thousands of civilians who got in the way as ruling-class men in the United States used violence to try to control men in other countries. The logic of dominance, the logic that underlies dominator consciousness, is acted out all around us in ways that produce effects that are plain to see. In fact, part of the problem, from the standpoint of mobilizing resistance to elite dominance, is that these effects are normalized.[5]

The use of military violence to serve the economic interests of the US ruling class is so commonplace that *New York Times* columnist Thomas Friedman barely elicited a raised eyebrow, except for poor taste, when he said, "The hidden hand of the market will never work without a hidden fist. McDonald's cannot flourish without McDonnell Douglas.... And the hidden fist that keeps the world safe for Silicon Valley's technologies to flourish is called the US Army, Air Force, Navy, and Marine Corps."[6] All but the most naive believers in American exceptionalism understand this, even if they prefer to shroud the violent pursuit of economic goals in rhetoric about democracy and freedom. But given the brutality and destruction this entails, why do most Americans accept it? Why is there is so little popular resistance, inside the United States, to the imperial projects of the ruling class?

Some answers come readily to mind. Most Americans are so occupied with work and family and with deriving a few pleasures from leisure and consumption that they have little time or energy left to study, let alone oppose, the foreign policies of US elites; most Americans, even if they oppose such policies, feel powerless to do anything about them; most Americans realize, at some level, that they benefit economically from US imperialism; most Americans are vulnerable to fear campaigns and elite propaganda about the need for violence to keep them safe from foreign enemies; and most Americans embrace the same dominator mentality as do elites, believing that it is better, in the inevitable struggle between nations, to win than lose. There are, then, powerful economic and ideological forces that operate to compel popular acquiescence to the use of ruling-class violence to control people elsewhere on the planet.

Yet all Americans have not always gone along with the use of violence in pursuit of imperial ambitions, especially when the costs have been high and the benefits dubious. The paradigm example from my generation is Vietnam. An inequitable draft, tens of thousands of American deaths, massive waste, horrific misery heaped on a people who had done no injury to the United States, and the lack of convincing justification provoked widespread popular resistance. For elites, the lesson of Vietnam was not that using massive violence to try to control people in other countries is wrong. The lesson was that popular consciousness needed to be better managed and control exerted in less costly, less provocative ways.

Efforts to manage popular consciousness in the cases of Afghanistan and Iraq have included embedding sympathetic reporters in combat units, filtering information through military press conferences, limiting reporters' access to civilian populations, and likewise restricting the flow of upsetting images to audiences back home. It has also included sponsorship of public events celebrating returning soldiers as heroes, the use of rhetoric that equates criticism of US foreign policy with failure to "support the troops," and incorporating pro-military spectacles into sports events (especially football games). These tactics, combined with the lack of a draft, stymied the development of a disruptive antiwar movement over the last decade.

Resistance has also been dampened by the use of bombs, cruise missiles, and drones as tools of control. The economic costs may continue to be high—these are among the most profitable technologies capitalists have ever devised—but costs in terms of lost American lives have been greatly reduced. If no American boots are on the ground, if no American lives are at risk, a major source of domestic resistance to the use of military force is neutralized. When drones are used to kill, the only troubling body counts that might be reported (usually in the foreign press) are those of unfortunate bystanders. To this sort of thing, Americans, on average, have already become inured. Any qualms that remain—about the killing of bystanders or the lawlessness of political assassination—are eased by propaganda that defines every military-age male victim of a missile or drone attack as a "militant" or terrorist.[7]

Control over domestic resistance has been accomplished in other ways as well. In the last decade, Americans have come to understand that they are subject to ubiquitous surveillance cameras in public; warrantless government Internet snooping and cyber spying; indefinite detention if they are designated as supporters of an organization the State Department defines as terrorist; being

groped and humiliated by government agents in airports; being corralled into
pens when attempting to exercise the right to protest; being strip searched if
they are arrested for even the most minor offense; prosecution if they blow the
whistle on government or military misconduct; and being charged with a federal
offense for disrupting any event at which a person under Secret Service protection
is present. Taken together, these measures constitute the establishment of a new,
post-9/11 control regime in the United States.

Most Americans are unaware that since 9/11 there has also evolved a separate
system of (in)justice for Muslim activists in this country. When the government
has gone after Muslim activists, most of whom have no ties to terrorist activity, the
rules of law, evidence, judicial review, and civilized treatment have been bent or
suspended.[8] And even when there has been evidence sufficient to warrant criminal charges, concerns have been raised about the extent to which alleged "terror
plots" were engineered by FBI agents and informers.[9] Americans who are aware
of the government's campaign against Muslim activists and who have publicly
opposed US foreign policies, especially those associated with the so-called war
on terror, understand that the treatment given to Muslims *could* be extended to
other dissident groups—without much public outcry. This awareness, and the
fear that goes with it, serves as another form of preemptive control.

Political and economic elites in the United States must try to control two
categories of people: those in other countries who resist exploitation, and those
in the United States who sympathize with those resisters. People in the former
category are subject to ideological, economic, and military control. Domestic
sympathizers are mainly subject to ideological control, though control can also
be economic: people whose jobs depend on military spending are unlikely to
criticize the policies and practices that sustain this spending; people can lose
jobs for expressing dissident ideas; people can be denied jobs if they acquire an
arrest record for acts of civil disobedience. Domestic dissenters are not immune
to violence as a means of control, but elites know that using violence against their
fellow citizens is costly, and thus tend to use it only as a last resort.

The control apparatus that has emerged in the last decade is a concomitant of perpetual war, which is the kind of war one gets when fighting a tactic
("terror") rather than a specific enemy. Economic exploitation also guarantees
an endless supply of people whose resistance, whatever form it takes, can be
defined as terrorism. The point is that where there is exploitation, there will be
resistance to the control that exploitation requires, and it will be convenient to
define this resistance as illegitimate and needing to be fought. So, barring the
end of exploitation, what we get, and indeed seem to have gotten, is endless war.
The problem, from the standpoint of political and economic elites, is how to
make the American people accept it.

It doesn't work anymore to try to keep people in the dark; the flow of information and critical analysis is impossible to stop. This same flow of information, mainly via the Internet, has made it impossible to propagandize the American people into accepting the enormous numbers of deaths characteristic of past wars. It has also become harder to hide the crimes and atrocities that are inevitable in war. All this enhances the risk of dissent. And the longer a war goes on, the greater the risk—unless elites find ways to greatly reduce troop deaths and to control dissenters without provoking more dissent. In fact, they have.

Troop deaths have been reduced, as noted before, by the use of bombs, missiles, and drones, and also by the use of death squads ("special operations teams," of the type that killed Osama bin Laden) and mercenaries ("military contractors" or, more misleadingly, "civilian contractors"). There is every reason to expect, as counterinsurgency wars rage on, that these technologies and tactics will continue to be used to keep antiwar sentiment from growing.[10] The apparatus used to control domestic dissent is also likely to be extended and refined, to the point where everyone, not only activists, will understand that their every move, even if there is no political intent, can be tracked and potentially used against them. If people thus come to police themselves, there will be no need, or only a rare need, for the application of force. When the will to dissent disappears, there is no need to disappear anyone.

*   *   *

I've met little objection to the claim that the use of remote combat technologies has muted popular opposition to war by reducing US troop deaths. Everyone seems to get this. It is the claim that a *stealth apparatus* of domestic control has taken shape over the past decade, an apparatus intended to facilitate perpetual war, that elicits more skeptical reactions.

Even when I cite the Patriot Act and its enabling of warrantless government snooping and searches; the National Defense Authorization Act and its enabling of indefinite detention of US citizens without judicial review; the Federal Restricted Buildings and Grounds Improvement Act, which makes it a federal crime to engage in disruptive protest in the vicinity of a person under Secret Service protection; the mistreatment of Muslim activists; the criminalization of protest associated with the Occupy movement; the Obama administration's redefinition of due process when it comes to identifying targets for assassination, including US citizens, as "not judicial process"; the FAA Air Transportation Modernization and Safety Improvement Act of 2012, which legalized domestic drone use for police and military operations; and the monitoring of Americans' communications by the National Security Agency—even when I list these developments, many people refuse to believe that we are living in a new era of government control. As few as fifteen years ago, many Americans would have balked at the installation of surveillance cameras on every street corner, the herding of peaceful protesters into Orwellian "free speech zones," and being groped by airport security guards. Today, these practices have been so normalized that to make an issue of them seems alarmist.

Part of what makes stealth control stealthy is its gradual implementation and subsequent normalization. But it is also masked in another way. Some of the skepticism with which claims about the apparatus of stealth control are met comes, I suspect, from confusing the hands of the state with the face of the president. Barack Obama, to take the current example, comes across to many people as smart and caring, principled, committed to doing the right thing, and able to be firm (or appear firm) when the occasion calls for it. His is not the face of fascism. He is clearly a nice guy who wouldn't engineer an evil apparatus of state control. And of course he hasn't, not alone.

Creating and operating an apparatus of state control requires many thousands of willing people: members of Congress and state legislatures; state governors; ambitious, amoral bureaucrats; federal, state, and local police; makers of weapons and surveillance technologies; communications providers; and complicit judges. It also takes years for such an apparatus to be put into place. The administration of any given president might expand or modify it (as did George W. Bush by creating the Department of Homeland Security), but the presidential role, under normal conditions, is to take temporary responsibility for keeping the established apparatus running smoothly. There is, however, one role that only presidents can play.

In American culture, the president is the face of the state, an embodiment of the power that is concentrated in national government. The president must therefore serve not only as chief executive but as an iconic representation of state power. Which means that the president's manhood act is crucial for how Americans feel about the power of the state and the state of the nation. No candidate, male or female, who cannot put on the kind of manhood act that elicits the emotions of which Americans are in need at any given time can be elected. In the early 1980s, Ronald Reagan's John Wayneish swagger was just what many Americans needed after defeat in Vietnam, the rise of OPEC power, and the humiliating "hostage crisis" at the US embassy in Tehran following the Islamic Revolution in 1979.

Presidents must of course tailor their manhood acts and craft multiple faces. Even Reagan, for all his Hollywood macho posturing, had a genial, avuncular side. The latter was key to Reagan's popularity: his manhood act bolstered Americans' faith in the power of the nation, while avoiding the impression that the power of the state would be used against them. Reagan's antigovernment rhetoric was part of the act; it cast him as a warrior fighting an oppressive bureaucracy, while also alleviating fears of what he might do as the man in charge of that bureaucracy. Twenty years later, George W. Bush, a weak echo of Reagan, tried to play the macho part of the role in the same way, but instead of neutralizing the threat of state power by appearing avuncular, Bush did so by being inarticulate and bumbling.

The Bush administration was able to expand the control apparatus of the state without provoking more resistance mainly because of 9/11, but also because Bush's folksy manhood act made these developments seem less ominous. But as the aftershocks of 9/11 began to fade, it was important, if the control apparatus was to be refined and consolidated, to put a new face on state power. After the wreckages of Iraq and Afghanistan, voters wanted a presidential manhood act that promised smarter and more precise use of state power. In comparison to George "Bring It On" Bush and John "Bomb-bomb-bomb Iran" McCain, Obama stood out as being in thoughtful, manly control of his mind and mouth. To young voters, he was also multicultural and cool, and so his rationality, even with its Ivy League polish, did not come across as cold and scary. His warmth and requisite heterosexuality were evident in his family life.

In addressing foreign policy issues, Obama could talk tough, signifying his capacity to deal with "bad guys" who challenge America's power. But Obama's tough talk was measured, unlike the reckless verbal machoism of G. W. Bush or John McCain. Obama's progressive credentials and rhetoric also led liberal voters to imagine that, after eight years of Bush, state power might now be wielded by someone who understood that such power should serve the interests of the working and middle classes, not Bush's upper class of "haves and have-mores." It was, all in all, the right manhood act for the moment. The act was complete when Obama disavowed his minister's radical racial politics and lectured black people on the need for personal responsibility.

It was also the right manhood act behind which to continue the use of violence to exert US control around the planet and solidify an apparatus of state control at home. Many of Obama's liberal backers—people previously outraged by the Bush administration's warmongering and encroachments on civil liberties—were seduced by Obama's charm, even as his administration extended Bush-era policies. The face of state power—constituted most visibly by Barack Obama's manhood act—is now hip, inclusive, and sensitive. It is an image many people wanted to believe in during the 2008 election campaign. Many still do, even as the state control apparatus continues to be refined and extended in steady, piecemeal fashion.

No doubt some observers see Barack Obama's manhood act—his "presidential masculinity," as some would put it—as progressive. Certainly it looks that way in comparison to what it replaced. It is of course a variation on an old theme: the head of state as urbane, whip smart, cool, and contemporary, yet willing to be tough, though not reckless, when it comes to national defense. It worked for John F. Kennedy and Bill Clinton, up to a point. In all such cases, it's important to see the act for what it is—an image crafted for public consumption—and not confuse it with the actions that constitute the exercise of ruling-class power.

This is not to say that the act is inconsequential. In Obama's case the act masks the authoritarian exercise of state power and thereby reduces dissent. When a presidential manhood act appears progressive, inclusive, benevolent—when the face of the state appears to be that of a tender-yet-tough leader—the hands of the state can get away with much. Those being spied upon, imprisoned, or killed are unlikely to be taken in, but the act is not for them. It's for those who would otherwise be made squeamish by lawlessness and violence, who don't like to think about gulags, torture, extraordinary rendition, death squads, or civilian massacres. It's for those who want to feel safe, protected, and righteous.

Presidential manhood acts are also consequential as models. A successful presidential manhood act, one that provides cover for the exercise of power and control, is an example of how to do it, not just in matters of national and international politics but in workplaces and families. All males interested in power learn how to mask that interest by observing other males who have done it well. The trick is to minimize resistance by making one's own striving for control appear benevolent or benign. On whatever scale this occurs, it can be thought of as political theater—the front-stage image-making behind which corpses accumulate.

The notion that a "new masculinity" is emerging in America today is based on mistaking a softer image for a genuine relinquishment of control. But as with the tobacco industry, the new image—*We're reformed! We're responsible corporate citizens now! We really don't want kids to smoke!*—is not the action that counts: continued manufacturing and aggressive marketing of addictive products that cause disease and death. The fresh and friendly PR image masks the industry's deadly business as usual and helps to fend off criticism and regulation.[11] Ruling-class males in the United States have likewise discovered that the achievement of full spectrum global dominance can be aided by a fuller spectrum of emotional display at home.

So what does it matter if a general sheds a tear for those killed in battle, as long as there is no challenge to the arrangements that allow him to send soldiers and civilians to their deaths? What does it matter if a CEO speaks in compassionate tones about devastating a community by moving a factory overseas, if there is no challenge to capitalist relations of production? What does it matter if a president shows love for his wife and children, if there are no policies forthcoming that would improve the lives of people trying to hold working-class families together? Kinder, gentler, more inclusive manhood acts do nothing to change oppressive hierarchies. They do matter, however, for making those hierarchies more emotionally bearable, and thus for preserving them.

In earlier chapters I argued that manhood is a form of social being necessitated by exploitive economic arrangements. Exploitation requires controlling others, and men are the creatures able and willing to exert control. A world capitalist system—or any system that involves one group dominating and exploiting other groups—requires men for its perpetuation. These men, elites and their minions, will be, naturally enough, obsessed with maintaining control, lest the benefits of exploitation be lost. On a global scale, what this gives us is perpetual efforts to exert control, perpetual resistance, and perpetual violence. Brutality and cruelty, perpetrated by males striving to be men, striving to exert and resist control, are inevitable under these conditions.

As long as humans accept exploitation and hierarchy as basic to social organization, males will strive to be men and will, as men, strive for status, power, and the benefits of domination. Violent conflict will inevitably ensue. As long as males cannot imagine existing as other than men, the ultimate consequence may be worse than endless war; it may be annihilation, under the principle that it is better to be dead, and take everyone else with you, than to give up control. Our choice, then, it seems to me, is between feminism—understood as thoroughgoing, radical egalitarianism—and barbarism. Feminist analysis of our current situation is crucial for seeing how far we need to go in transforming social life. The question is whether we can recognize men and manhood—indeed, gender itself—as evolutionary dead ends, and make of ourselves new kinds of social beings with better prospects for peaceful survival.

* * *

Dominator consciousness is not deterred by collateral damage, whether of people or the planet. This is a problem for those whose lives are squandered in conflict, and for those whose lives depend on the health of the planet. Which means, of course, that it's a problem for us all. To the extent that dominator consciousness is the consciousness of males engaged in contests for manhood status, it would be fair to say that such contests are not sustainable. They lead, inevitably, to ecological destruction.

Capitalism and manhood have led us to embrace the belief that endless economic growth is possible on a finite planet. This is the kind of insane belief necessitated by an economic system that requires constant expansion for its short-term success. To accept that unlimited economic growth is *not* possible would require admitting that capitalism is not a rational economic system—an idea that is taboo in mainstream political discourse. It is also the hubris of manhood to imagine that "dominion over the earth" implies no end to the possibility of exploiting the earth to achieve ever greater wealth, status, and power. Capitalism admits to no limits, nor does manhood, and by failing to recognize the obvious, they reveal their mutually reinforcing irrationality.

Manhood contests among capitalist males are likely to be especially destructive, considering the resources that can be wielded in these contests. Wars are the most obvious example. Within a nation, economies and lives can be ruined as men (of both sexes) compete to exert and extend control over capital and corporations. As journalist Matt Taibbi put it in describing the causes of the financial crisis of 2008, "The best way to understand the financial crisis is to understand the meltdown at [American International Group]. AIG is what happens when short, bald managers of otherwise boring financial bureaucracies start seeing Brad Pitt in the mirror."[12] There is more to Taibbi's analysis, but his quip contains an essential truth: reckless endangerment of the common good is to be expected when males compete for manhood status. Neither the environment nor the nation's financial infrastructure is safe.

The commons—the natural world and the public infrastructure—is vulnerable precisely because manhood status is achieved by the pretense of having "done it alone." Part of a successful manhood act is creating the impression that wealth, status, and power have been achieved solely through one's own qualities and efforts. To acknowledge the social conditions that enable achievement, to acknowledge the help and common resources without which no kind of individual success is possible, is to weaken the act. This is why the commons or the public infrastructure is often devalued, perhaps even sacrificed, as manhood contests play out. It is to sustain the illusion of autonomous power upon which manhood status depends. At the same time, it can lead to the very real destruction of the commonwealth upon which we all depend.

It is fair to wonder whether the problem is manhood *or* capitalism. Could we not have an ecologically sustainable manhood without capitalism? We could certainly behave—as a society and a species—in more ecologically responsible ways without abolishing gender, presuming the transcendence of capitalism and plutocracy. But as long as there are dominant and subordinate gender groups, and as long as manhood status is achievable in greater degree by signifying greater capacity for control, manhood contests will persist, as will dominator consciousness. The natural world will thus continue to appear as a resource for signifying and exerting control. It will, as a result, remain at risk of abuse.

Real, existing capitalism, the capitalism we have on our hands now, requires a hardness of mind and heart toward those who must be controlled, lest it not be possible to exploit their labor. Capitalism requires a similar hardness of mind and heart toward the natural world; affection for the natural world cannot be allowed to impede the environmental exploitation necessary for amassing wealth, status, and power. There are of course many individuals—male, female, men, women—whose orientation to the natural world is one of stewardship. But within capitalist relations of production and capitalist plutocracy, the concerns of stewardship will always be trumped by the concerns of profit. If environmental responsibility nonetheless becomes popular, it, too, can be turned into a profitable commodity. Buy green.

The flip side to capitalist refusal to accept limits on wealth and power is the refusal, in US culture, to accept limits on consumption. One should be able to buy, to consume, as much as one can afford, so the belief goes. This is seen as a natural right, which is the right to signify status through possession. The importance attached to this alleged right is related to the gender order. Signifying status through possession—through the acquisition of things over which one can exert control—is often the main way in which contests for manhood status are carried out. This is as true for males who can buy yachts as for those who can afford only bass boats. As the bumper sticker puts it, THE ONE WITH THE MOST TOYS WINS. While the planet loses.

Just as capitalist relations of production require social creatures willing to ignore the agency and dignity of others so as to impose the control necessary for the exploitation of labor, so, too, these relations require social creatures willing to ignore ecological limits. The consciousness that must be cultivated, for capitalist relations of production to be maintained, is that which sees nature as something to be subdued, acquired, and exploited for gain. As ecofeminists have argued, what this reflects is a gendering of nature as female, as something that must be conquered and *owned*, and thereby made useful for males seeking to be men.[13] In the struggle for manhood status, females and nature are seen as valuable for the same reasons: they constitute exploitable resources, and they provide opportunities to signify the capacity to exert control. They are also seen as dangerous for the same reasons: nature and women may threaten manhood status by proving, at times, to be beyond male control.

American belief in the right to consume without limit is also part of what underlies the condition of perpetual war discussed earlier. With only 6 percent of the world's population, the United States consumes 25 percent of the world's energy resources. This amount of energy is needed to support an economy of wasteful, competitive consumption. Between the damage caused by resource extraction, the environmental burden of more and more toxic stuff to be disposed of, and energy depletion, it seems fair to affirm Ernest Callenbach's assessment of international consumer capitalism as a "self-destroying machine."[14]

Perpetual war is necessary to keep the energy flowing and to ensure that it is bought and sold on terms favorable to US and European capitalists. As we have seen, resistance to the exploitation of Third World energy resources to prop up core capitalist economies will be deemed terrorism and met with force. As long as there is manhood status to be attained, and as long as young males are eager to attain it, there will be bodies enough to fly the drones, drop the bombs, and carry out the night raids that protect the ecologically unsustainable American way of life.

When we think of the ecological damage associated with capitalism we usually think of the externalized costs of production—for example, pollution, cancer—and the environmental burden imposed by excess consumption—for example, burgeoning landfills, energy depletion. What we don't usually think about is wasted human potential.[15] But if humans are understood as part of nature, it's clear that capitalism destroys much of what nature bestows upon us. An economic system that locks people into class categories and requires, as a matter of structural necessity, that most people expend their lives working in dirty, dangerous, mindless jobs to generate profit for others is inhumane. It is also wasteful of the intelligence and creativity of the vast majority of people on the planet. Yet this is the economic system that is celebrated by dominator consciousness.

The conventional way that we construe ecological destruction focuses our attention on damage done to nonhuman nature. This is nature that we depend on for survival; we need drinkable water, breathable air, and fertile soil in which to grow crops. And so it is of course crucial to look at how human action affects what is external to us. Our survival depends no less, however, on what is inside us: potentials for critical and creative thought and the capacities to empathize and cooperate with others. Social arrangements that impede the development of these capacities among the majority of humans are not sustainable. Capitalism is precisely this kind of dead-end arrangement. So is a gender order that instills drone morality, stunts empathy, and values domination and control over equality and cooperation.

Because most people in a capitalist economy find little meaning in their work, other than as a source of income, they must seek meaning elsewhere—in family life, leisure and hobbies, and religion. Males, in particular, may find meaning in competitive sports and in war, activities in which it is possible—or believed possible—to signify a masculine self of the highest value and to achieve manhood status unequivocally. When self-creation becomes impossible in the sphere of production (i.e., in the workplace), it is understandable that efforts at self-creation would shift to the realm of consumption. But for subordinate males it may also shift to realms of destruction, realms where an opponent's dignity or an enemy's life can be expunged in a glorious manhood act. As Chris Hedges has argued, war is a force that gives us meaning.[16] I would add that this meaning is in proportion to that which capitalism denies us.

Because we have not yet moved beyond exploitive economies, we tend to believe that what such economies engender—men, manhood contests, struggles for control, hierarchy—are natural and inevitable. Recognizing the social construction of gender challenges assumptions about the naturalness of gender and the inevitability of gender hierarchy. A critical feminist analysis goes further, exposing connections between gender and economic exploitation, arriving at the insight that as long as we have an exploitive economy, we are going to have the social creatures called "men" acting as agents of exploitation and striving for manhood status. Given the increase in human destructive capacity in the twentieth and twenty-first centuries, how much longer this arrangement will persist is anyone's guess. The logical end of the arrangement is, as I've suggested, self-annihilation, through war or ecocide. But if gender and capitalism are indeed social constructions, this end is not inevitable. The alternative is a future in which the human limitations and wastefulness of both capitalism and gender are transcended.

*   *   *

In May 2012, North Carolina amended its constitution to say that henceforth the only legally recognized domestic union in the state would be marriage between one man and one woman. Gay marriage was already illegal in North Carolina, but proponents of what became known as Amendment One sought to enshrine this prohibition in the state constitution. Their fear, it seemed, was that absent a constitutional amendment, a legal challenge might someday allow people with the wrong match of body types to marry each other.

Opponents of the amendment argued that it was wrong to write discrimination into the state constitution, an act reminiscent of the South's ugly history of Jim Crow segregation; that the amendment would make it illegal for public employers to extend health and other benefits to domestic partners; that it would nullify (or complicate the enforcement of) power-of-attorney arrangements between unmarried partners; and that it could be interpreted by the courts as meaning that women in cohabiting unmarried couples are not entitled to protection against domestic violence. The point was also made that, regardless of its practical harms, the amendment was an insult to gay and lesbian people in the state, relegating them to second-class citizenship.

Supporters of the amendment insisted that fears of its practical harms were exaggerated. They argued that domestic partner benefits can be provided contractually; that power-of-attorney arrangements would not be affected; and that protection against battery and assault does not hinge on marital status. They also insisted that the amendment was not meant to insult anyone. Its purpose was simply to further affirm the widely shared belief that marriage can be properly entered into only by heterosexual couples. A few supporters argued in secular terms, claiming (contrary to evidence offered by family researchers) that heterosexual marriage is always best for children, hence the state has a legitimate interest in protecting it.

Most of the amendment's supporters unabashedly cited the Bible and "God's will" as providing all the justification they needed. Some church leaders and lay people cited religious teachings that led them to oppose the amendment, but for the most part religion was enlisted on behalf of heteronormativity. To dispel any doubts about what God wanted, Billy Graham, North Carolina's archevangelist, took out full-page ads in fourteen newspapers a few days before the vote. Above Graham's resolute, far-gazing countenance, the text read, "At 93, I never thought we would have to debate the definition of marriage. The Bible is clear. God's definition of marriage is between a man and a woman. I want to urge my fellow North Carolinians to vote FOR the marriage amendment on Tuesday, May 8." It passed by a vote of 61 percent to 39 percent.

It is commonplace to say that Western, monotheistic religion has served as an ideological bulwark for male supremacy. All manner of sexist and heterosexist practices have been justified by invoking God and God's will (which is often said to be inscrutable, except when it comes to the propriety of men controlling women). This is what one would expect, given that men have been the primary inventors of gods and religions. Of course men are going to posit an Alpha Male in Charge and insist that as it is in heaven, so shall it be on earth. To reject such an arrangement can thus be construed as blasphemous rejection of the sacred pattern—male dominance—on which the universe is organized. Indeed, to reject God is to reject manhood.

For what is God but manhood writ large and extended beyond family, tribe, and nation to the universe as a whole? I don't mean by this that God—or whichever god in the pantheon is said to be most powerful—is simply cast as male and as possessing the ultimate masculine self. I mean that to conceive of God *at all* is to conceive of power as concentrated in a dominant being, a being that must be revered *because* of that immense power. This is what God is in Western, monotheistic religions. To worship "God" is thus to worship power. In everyday secular life, the principle of worshipping power is reflected in the deference accorded to men and masculine selves. Manhood contests are just strivings by males to be gods in their own domains.

To reject the rightness of males striving to be men, of striving to win manhood contests, is to reject the idea that there is virtue in achieving power over others. From there it is a short step to doubting that ultimate power, the defining feature of God, confers ultimate virtue. Bringing manhood into question—which brings hierarchy and control into question—is thus to challenge the implicit principle by which God is said to deserve human reverence and worship. It is to suggest that humans stop believing that power, embodied in real persons or imaginary beings, ought to command our highest respect. And so the equation can be reversed: to reject manhood is to reject God, or at least the power principle by which "God" is constructed.

There have been movements, inside and outside Western, monotheistic religions, to de-gender God and get away from the image of an all-powerful, judgmental male on high. God has thus been redefined, or at least renamed, as a Creator or Creative Force. Although these terms evoke less scary images, they still imply that there exists something, whatever it might be called, that is *God* by virtue of its immense power and that, because of this power, deserves human reverence and worship. What the power principle also implies is that the Creator or Creative Force deserves human reverence and worship because *in relation to this something-that-is-God,* humans are weak and ignorant. Again, labels aside, the god entity or force is *God* because of its alleged power, and it is power that ought to compel human awe and subservience. Which is much the same outcome sought by antagonists in manhood contests.

There is also of course the even fuzzier notion that God is love, a notion congenial to New Age spiritualism and secular multiculturalism, and which means almost nothing. God is what, intense human affection? Or perhaps the idea is that love is wonderful and yields so many wonderful things that we should treat it *as if* it were sacred. That in itself is not a bad idea. But there is no need to invoke God to express it. In fact, the value of love is better appreciated, more sensibly appreciated, if we understand love as a human capacity and construction, not a divine force, divine though it might feel to be smitten.

Contrary to some strains of atheism, I don't think it irrational to believe in gods. Things happen that are hard to explain; many of the underlying causes are difficult or impossible to see. Over time, forces that were once invisible to us—microbes, gravity, cellular decay, electrons, neurotransmitters, dark matter—have become known. Yet there is plenty about how the world works that remains mysterious. And so it makes sense that humans would posit invisible forces that beget the unsettling things we see and experience. It also makes sense that humans would personify these forces, invent gods that can be invoked as explanations and appealed to as interveners, as a way to cope with anxiety and the dread of permanent death at the hands of a universe that seems indifferent to our existence. In these respects, gods are among humanity's most useful creations.

The problem is that these creations have been and continue to be wielded as tools of control. God and gods are invoked not merely to tell comforting stories about how the universe began, or how life came into being, or what happens after death. They are invoked as powers that establish rightful order, in the social world as well as the natural world. What God tells us, wielders of "God" would have us understand, is how we ought to organize ourselves and behave. Not surprisingly, the social order and behavior that God is alleged to approve often coincide with the order most pleasing to whoever does the alleging. Of course, others might see matters differently, claiming that God really does not endorse slavery, war, or forced motherhood, or they might cite the wishes of a different god. Gods, like swords, can be crafted and wielded to resist control as well as to impose it.

If power and virtue are inherent in any notion of God, then any invocation and characterization of God—with a capital G, as in monotheistic religions—is a claim to power. It is a claim to know how the greatest force in the universe wants things to be done. This is in part about exerting control by inducing in others a desire to obey a Heavenly Father, or live in harmony with the will of a Creator, on whose behalf the invoker of God purports to speak. But it is also about claiming a *rightful authority* to control others. The rhetoric of "God" is thus not only an aid to pulling off a manhood act by exerting control over others, it is also a means for turning a project of domination into a sign of God-blessed manly virtue.

Dominator consciousness finds instrumental value and comfort in the idea of God. The instrumental value comes, as suggested above, from the utility of the idea for controlling others; the comfort comes from the feeling of rightness that the idea of God lends to acts of domination and to the exploitive hierarchies thereby created. Ideas of God and the religions built on these ideas can do more, however, than legitimate domination from the standpoint of the dominant. These ideas and belief systems can make subservience seem ordained and inevitable, even noble. They can also—and here I mean the demand to believe in God and follow religious doctrines as matters of faith—undermine the critical intellect necessary to resist domination. Religious faith thus can be seen as a great inducer of drone morality: a willingness to accept hierarchy and obey without question, and feel good about doing so.

Despite the impression I might have created here, I do not normally invest much energy in trying to disabuse people of their metaphysical beliefs. The universe is an overwhelming place from an earth-bound human perspective. Science notwithstanding, we are awash in mysteries. Horrible things happen for no apparent reason. Life is complicated. Moral choices are often difficult and imperfect. Our bodies decay and betray us. Mortality is an ever-present source of dread. Loved ones suffer and die. Hope is hard to maintain. In the face of these aspects of human existence, it's understandable that many people turn to religion for answers and comfort. It's something that I find hard to begrudge.

On the other hand, I begrudge the invocation of God and the use of religion to control others, establish exploitive hierarchies, and hold these arrangements in place. I also object to the irrationalism—the denial of scientific facts, suspension of critical thought, abandonment of logic, acceptance of authority on faith—that many religions demand of their adherents. These are not just curmudgeonly objections that might be raised in friendly debate over a glass of wine with companionable theologians. They are objections based on recognizing the harm that notions of God and religious belief systems have done historically and continue to do. The harms arise not because of beliefs in people's heads, but because of the actions that follow from these beliefs: the creation of oppressive laws, the exploitation of women's bodies and labor, and the killing of those who refuse to submit to being controlled.

Defenders of religion argue that, for all its ill use, religion has been and continues to be a force for good in the world, mainly by providing rules for moral conduct and motivating people to follow those rules. Defenders are also wont to say that, over the course of human history, religion has had more good results than bad. I will grant the former point, with one qualification: religious teachings to the effect that we should treat our fellow creatures with compassion and respect have indeed motivated humans to do good things—*but religion is by no means necessary for this*. Secular moral philosophies are entirely adequate to the task. To claim otherwise is to claim that humans, as individuals or groups, have never behaved in virtuous ways except because of belief in the supernatural. This is nonsense.

I must reject the second claim—that religion, on the whole, has produced more good results than bad—on the grounds that there is no control group, no alternative earth or human history, to which anyone can point to fairly assess the effects of religion. One might as well claim that, on the whole, humans have accomplished more as carbon-based life-forms than as silicon-based life-forms. This would be a silly claim, one not subject to sensible evaluation. As for religion, one could just as well claim that human existence has been poisoned by religion and that without religion we would be much farther along as a species. Again, it's an impossible claim to assess.

The better question to ask is whether humans have a brighter future with or without God and religion. This is a disturbing question for those whose sense of order and morality is tied to notions of God and religious commandments. Without God, religious commandments, and the threat of eternal punishment for bad behavior, humans will degenerate into beasts, or so it is that the priests of the ruling classes have led many people to believe. Perhaps this is not such an irrational fear, given that capitalism—the economic sea in which we have all been baptized—encourages ruthless striving, discourages empathy, and rewards domination. Nor is it irrational for the weak to want a moral staff with which to fend off the depredations of the strong. Under these conditions, it makes sense to conjure a powerful Parent in the Sky as a device for keeping life from becoming any more nasty, poor, brutish, and short than it is.

In the long run, however, there is little hope for freeing ourselves from earthly depredations if we continue to sacralize power and domination. As long as humans worship a God entity because of its purported power, humans will worship the powerful on earth, accepting their subjugation to the winners of manhood contests even as they accept subjugation to God. The results will include the continued legitimation of exploitation, the control and violence that exploitation requires, the waste of enormous human potential, and the destruction of the planet as men continue to seek wealth, status, and godlike power. And as long as religious belief comforts people as they wait for justice in an afterlife instead of creating it on earth, so, too, shall exploitation continue and so, too, shall we face the possibility of extinction at the hands of those who would prefer Armageddon to equality.

*   *   *

Psychologist Steven Pinker would have us believe that humans are becoming more empathic and less violent. I suppose it can seem so, if one measures violence, as Pinker does in his 2011 book *The Better Angels of Our Nature: Why Violence Has Declined*, using global population as the denominator so that even modern episodes of mass killing can be said to constitute destruction of a smaller proportion of humankind than occurred in past wars.[17] It helps, too, to overlook deaths caused by structural violence, which includes destruction of infrastructure—water treatment plants, drug factories, hospitals, food supplies—through military or economic means. The 500,000 Iraqi children who died because of ten years of US economic sanctions against that country do not register on Pinker's radar. Perhaps the better angels of our nature are still learning to speak Arabic.

Robert Kagan is Pinker's Panglossian counterpart in the discipline of history. In Kagan's 2012 book *The World America Made*, we are told that the period since World War II has been a "golden age for humanity," a period characterized by more democracy, less poverty, and an absence of major wars.[18] According to

Kagan, these developments are results of US global domination, a Pax Americana. In his review of Kagan's book, historian Andrew Bacevich writes this passage:

> And grateful though we may be for so far having avoided World War III, Kagan's golden age has seen some very considerable bloodletting. Noteworthy episodes of violence include the following, with their respective death tolls in parentheses: the partition of India (1,000,000), the Korean War (3,000,000), the French Indochina War (400,000), the Algerian Revolution (537,000), the Vietnam War (1,700,000), the Cambodian Genocide (1,650,000), the Iran-Iraq War (700,000), the Soviet war in Afghanistan (1,500,000), the Rwandan Genocide (800,000), the Second Congo War (3,800,000), and the Second Sudanese Civil War (1,900,000), not to mention the US war in Iraq (weighing in with a relatively modest 150,000 civilian corpses). None of these catastrophes earn more than passing mention in Kagan's account.[19]

That's 17,137,000 deaths in large-scale violent conflict since the end of World War II. If we add the deaths of Iraqi children by economic sanction, the 35 million military and civilian deaths in World War I, and the 60 million in World War II, the total for the last approximately one hundred years comes to 112,637,000. If humans were to slaughter each other in similar numbers in just the next fifty years, this would constitute progress by Pinker's manner of reckoning, because the toll would represent a smaller proportion of the world's population.[20] A future Kagan might declare it a new golden age.

How satisfying one finds the state of the world and its current trajectory depends on what one takes into account and takes for granted. It depends, too, on the standards by which things are measured and progress is assessed. If we assume a world in which hierarchy and economic exploitation are the norms, in which millions of people are inevitably caught up and killed in struggles for wealth and power among politically and economically elite men, in which most people embrace racial, tribal, or national identities that limit the bounds of empathy, in which most people remain in the grip of superstitions that legitimate exploitive hierarchies, in which most people have little control over the conditions of their lives, then perhaps we will be satisfied if the next century is proportionally less murderous than the last.

Even by ordinary American standards, not radical feminist ones, it would seem that we face serious trouble. Wars fought over energy resources will become perpetual as those resources dwindle. The earth will be ravaged all the more recklessly to extract the energy resources that remain. Political power will continue to concentrate along with the concentration of wealth in the hands of individuals and corporations. More and more aspects of the commons will be privatized and sacrificed for the sake of private profit. Freedom to challenge capitalist plutocracy will shrink as the surveillance state expands. The latter will include the use of domestic drones and cyber spying to monitor people's speech and behavior. Pollution caused by unregulated production and heedless consumption will toxify the air and water and accelerate global warming. Rising sea levels caused by global warming will require population shifts that will spark more conflicts over resources. Even as new technologies give us the capacity to be more materially productive, more people will experience chronic economic insecurity.

The same problems are evident whether one takes a feminist perspective or looks at things from a commonsense perspective that values ecological sustainability, freedom of thought and association, community and cooperation, and democracy. One doesn't need to be a radical to be worried. A feminist perspective sets higher standards, however, and suggests where to look for the roots of these problems.

As per the discussion in Chapter 6, I don't mean by a "feminist perspective" a liberal view that attends mainly to whether women have opportunities to attain positions of power within oppressive hierarchies. I mean a view that is radically egalitarian and aims to abolish these hierarchies. This is indeed a high standard, one that won't be met for a long time.[21] Yet what a feminist perspective tells us is that if there is a to *be* a long run for humanity, it will depend on transcending the exploitive economic, political, and social hierarchies that bring perpetual violence, the destruction of the earth, and the gross waste of human potential. A radical feminist perspective also refuses to take gender for granted, instead seeing it as a human construction that is, at root, about domination and economic exploitation. In which case, as I have argued in this book, there is no preserving gender without preserving domination, and there is no preserving economic exploitation, in any form, without preserving manhood and manhood contests and the violence they entail.

If this analysis has any uptake, it will be in small quarters, limited to those who do not believe that we have reached the end of history and that what history has so far made of us is all we can be. For the most part, I expect dismissal on grounds of unrealism—on grounds that gender and the propensity to create hierarchy are, if not untouchably innate, woven too deeply into what we are as creatures to be eradicable. It is hard to dispel such beliefs, especially because so much casual observation seems to support them. Yet we can also observe that there are conditions under which humans are cooperative, empathic, selfless, and egalitarian, and under which gender seems to disappear. It is clear that we possess these potentials as well, even if the forms of social life we've created do not universally nurture these potentials.[22] The question is whether it is realistic to think we can create new forms of social life to do this. Which is to say, to survive as a species.

The view from which my analysis appears unrealistic defines human progress as evident when millions die horribly in wars that fall short of apocalypse; that imagines peace to be attainable through violence rather than justice; that expects to infinitely extract resources from a finite planet; that seeks aid and legitimacy from imaginary beings; and that can't imagine an alternative to an economy based on exploitation and waste. Excuse me if I don't find this to be the more sensible or reassuring view. To me this seems like what C. Wright Mills called crackpot realism.[23] I would prefer to think—not as a matter of faith but as a matter of what can be observed about human potential—that we can do better. What it will take is recognizing not just that there are better angels of our nature to be brought forth, but that those angels will appear only when we stop expecting them to be gendered or dominant or striving for more resources than anyone else. Nor will the age they define, if we are able to bring them forth, be golden or divine. It will be human, only more so.

Notes

CHAPTER 1

1. Adorno's essay is available at http://pedsub.files.wordpress.com/2010/11/adornoeducation1.pdf. It can also be found in T. W. Adorno, *Critical Models: Interventions and Catchwords* (New York: Columbia University Press, 2005).

2. On the concept of sociological mindfulness, see Michael Schwalbe, *The Sociologically Examined Life*, 4th ed. (New York: McGraw-Hill, 2008).

3. Klaus Theleweit's *Male Fantasies* (Minneapolis: University of Minnesota Press, 1987) has become the standard Freudian take on the Nazi cult of masculinity. For another view, see Stephen Haynes, "Ordinary Masculinity: Gender Analysis and Holocaust Scholarship," *Journal of Men's Studies* 10 (2002): 143–163.

4. See Michael Schwalbe, *Rigging the Game: How Inequality Is Reproduced in Everyday Life* (New York: Oxford University Press, 2008).

5. For those new to critical theory, David Held's *Introduction to Critical Theory: Horkheimer to Habermas* (Berkeley: University of California Press, 1980) and Stephen Brenner's *Critical Theory: A Very Short Introduction* (New York: Oxford University Press, 2011) may be useful starting points.

6. Brian Fay examines the positivist, control-oriented epistemology underlying contemporary social science in *Social Theory and Political Practice* (London: George Allen and Unwin, 1975).

7. See Fay, *Social Theory and Political Practice*, and also his *Critical Social Science: Liberation and Its Limits* (Ithaca, NY: Cornell University Press, 1987).

8. A good explication and debunking of the achievement ideology can be found in Jay MacLeod's *Ain't No Makin' It*, 3rd ed. (Boulder, CO: Westview, 2009).

9. See the American Anthropological Association's statement on race at www.aaanet.org/stmts/racepp.htm.

10. For introductions to critical race theory, see Richard Delgado and Jean Stefancic, *Critical Race Theory: An Introduction* (New York: New York University Press, 2001) and Kimberle Crenshaw, Neil Gotanda, Gary Peller, and Kendall Thomas, *Critical Race Theory: The Key Writings That Formed the Movement* (New York: New Press, 1996).

11. My intellectual roots are in symbolic interactionist social psychology, as traced to the American Pragmatist philosophers William James, Charles S. Peirce, John Dewey, and George H. Mead. My particular leanings are Blumerian (see Herbert Blumer, *Symbolic Interactionism: Perspective and Method* [Englewood Cliffs, NJ: Prentice Hall, 1969]). I also draw from other perspectives in modern social psychology (see Jane McLeod, Ed Lawler, and Michael Schwalbe, *Handbook of the Social Psychology of Inequality* [New York: Springer, 2014]). The feminist sources that have influenced my thinking are many, though I owe special debts to Marilyn Frye's *The Politics of Reality* (Freedom, CA: The Crossing Press, 1983); bell hooks's *Feminist Theory: From Margin to Center* (Boston: South End Press, 1984); and Sandra Bartky's *Femininity and Domination* (New York: Routledge, 1990).

12. I take my understanding of decolonizing the mind from Frantz Fanon's *Black Skin, White Masks* (New York: Grove Weidenfeld, 1967) and Paulo Friere's *Pedagogy of the Oppressed* (New York: Continuum, 1992).

13. Frye, "Oppression," in *The Politics of Reality*, pp. 1–16.

14. Sherryl Kleinman and Martha Copp, "Denying Social Harm: Resistance to Lessons about Inequality," *Teaching Sociology* 37 (2009): 283–293.

15. Sherryl Kleinman, Matthew B. Ezzell, and A. Corey Frost, "Reclaiming Critical Analysis: The Social Harms of 'Bitch,'" *Sociological Analysis* 3 (2009): 47–68.

16. Fay, *Social Theory and Political Practice*, pp. 92–110; *Critical Social Science*, pp. 80–83.

17. On reification, see Schwalbe, *The Sociologically Examined Life*, 4th ed., pp. 22–23.

18. Henry A. Giroux, "What Education Might Mean after Abu Ghraib: Revisiting Adorno's Politics of Education," *Comparative Studies of South Asia, Africa, and the Middle East* 24 (2004): 5–24.

19. In *Critical Social Psychology* (London: Routledge and Kegan Paul, 1983), Philip Wexler argues that abstract intellectual analysis is not enough to deter people from fascism. Because the appeal is largely emotional, critical analysis—and its delivery—must take emotion into account. Richard Rorty made similar arguments about the importance of emotion, especially empathy induced by literature, for overcoming tendencies to the inhumane treatment of others (see Rorty, *Contingency, Irony, and Solidarity* [Cambridge: Cambridge University Press, 1989]).

20. The distinction between *biological sex* and *socially constructed gender* is usually made on Day One in undergraduate sociology of gender courses, and in the first chapter of most undergraduate sociology of gender textbooks. Sociologists vary in the degree to which they see biological sex as influencing gender-related behaviors, though most see biological influences as overwhelmed by culture. In this sense, even moderate social constructionist views pose a threat to belief in gender essentialism. The view I'm taking here is radically constructionist.

21. There is by now a vast literature that constitutes profeminist men's studies. See, for example, Michael Kimmel, Jeffrey Hearn, and R. W. Connell, *Handbook of Studies on Men and Masculinities* (Thousand Oaks, CA: Sage, 2005). More can be found in Michael Flood's online *The Men's Bibliography* (http://mensbiblio.xyonline.net/).

22. The modern classic articulation of the "doing gender" perspective is Candace West and Don Zimmerman, "Doing Gender," *Gender and Society* 1 (1987): 125–151. See also Sarah Fenstermaker and Candace West, *Doing Gender, Doing Difference* (New York: Routledge, 2002).

23. Perhaps no one has done more to promote the postmodernist idea of gender as performative plaything than Judith Butler. See her *Gender Trouble* (New York: Routledge, 1990).

24. See Sheila Rowbotham, *Woman's Consciousness, Man's World* (Baltimore: Penguin, 1973); Michele Barrett, *Women's Oppression Today* (London: Verso, 1980); Sylvia Walby, *Theorizing Patriarchy* (Cambridge, MA: Blackwell, 1990); Catherine MacKinnon, *Toward a Feminist Theory of the State* (Cambridge, MA: Harvard University Press, 1989). For more recent assessments, see Deborah L. Rhode, *Speaking of Sex: The Denial of Gender Inequality* (Cambridge, MA: Harvard University Press, 1999); Susan J. Douglas, *Enlightened Sexism: The Seductive Message That Feminism's Work Is Done* (New York: Henry Holt, 2010); and Barbara J. Berg, *Sexism in America: Alive, Well, and Ruining Our Future* (Chicago: Lawrence Hill, 2009).

25. For an exception, see Joan Acker, *Class Questions, Feminist Answers* (Lanham, MD: Rowman and Littlefield, 2006).

26. Hae Yeon Choo and Myra Marx Ferree, "Practicing Intersectionality in Sociological Research: A Critical Analysis of Inclusions, Interactions, and Institutions in the Study of Inequalities," *Sociological Theory* 28 (2010): 129–149; Sylvia Walby, Jo Armstrong, and Sofia Strid, "Intersectionality: Multiple Inequalities in Social Theory," *Sociology* 46 (2012): 224–240.

27. A classic analysis is Oliver Cromwell Cox's *Class, Caste, and Race* (New York: Monthly Review Press, 1948). See also William Staples and Clifford Staples, *Power, Profits, and Patriarchy* (Lanham, MD: Rowman and Littlefield, 2001); Richard Della Fave, *Race and Revolution* (Palm Coast, FL: PhotoGraphics Publishing, 2008); and Heidi Hartmann, "Capitalism, Patriarchy, and Job Segregation," *Signs* 1 (1976): 137–170.

28. For another expression of this critique, see Douglas Schrock and Michael Schwalbe, "Men, Masculinity, and Manhood Acts," *Annual Review of Sociology* 35 (2009): 277–295.

29. Zillah Eisenstein's edited volume *Capitalist Patriarchy and the Case for Socialist Feminism* (New York: Monthly Review Press, 1978) could be added to the list of influences mentioned earlier. Some other profeminist men's studies scholars embrace a compatible outlook, though few have publicly worn the socialist-feminist label. But see Andrew Tolson, *The Limits of Masculinity* (New York: Harper and Row, 1977) and Victor J. Seidler, ed., *The Achilles Heel Reader: Men, Sexual Politics, and Socialism* (New York: Routledge, 1991).

30. See Solomon Asch, "Studies of Independence and Conformity. A Minority of One against a Unanimous Majority," *Psychological Monographs* 70 (1956): 1–70; Stanley Milgram, *Obedience to Authority* (New York: Harper and Row, 1974); and C. Haney, W. C. Banks, and P. G. Zimbardo, "A Study of Prisoners and Guards in a Simulated Prison," *Naval Research Review* 30 (1973): 4–17. See also Zimbardo's more recent *The*

Lucifer Effect: Understanding How Good People Turn Evil (New York: Random House, 2007).

31. My enduring fascination with how social conditions shape individuals was first inspired by reading Hans H. Gerth and C. Wright Mill's *Character and Social Structure: The Psychology of Social Institutions* (New York: Harcourt Brace, 1953) as an undergraduate.

32. The essay was first published on the *Common Dreams* website. It can be found at www.commondreams.org/views06/0816-21.htm.

CHAPTER 2

1. Michael Schwalbe, "Male Supremacy and the Narrowing of the Moral Self," *Berkeley Journal of Sociology* 37 (1992): 29–54; "Making the Sociological Personal and Personal Political—For Men, Too," *Masculinities* 1 (1992): 17–18; "Why Mythopoetic Men Don't Flock to NOMAS," *Masculinities* 1 (1993): 68–72; and, somewhat later, *Unlocking the Iron Cage: The Men's Movement, Gender Politics, and American Culture* (New York: Oxford University Press, 1996).

2. Tim Carrigan, R. W. Connell, and John Lee, "Toward a New Sociology of Masculinity," *Theory and Society* 14 (1985): 551–604.

3. Harry Brod, "The Case for Men's Studies," in H. Brod, ed., *The Making of Masculinities: The New Men's Studies* (Boston: Allen and Unwin, 1987), pp. 39–62.

4. For overviews of various strains of thought in men's studies during this period, see Michael Messner, *Politics of Masculinities* (Thousand Oaks, CA: Sage, 1997) and Kenneth Clatterbaugh, *Contemporary Perspectives on Masculinity*, 2nd ed. (Boulder, CO: Westview, 1997).

5. This argument was associated with what came to be known as the "men's rights" perspective. See George Gilder, *Sexual Suicide* (New York: Bantam, 1973); Herb Goldberg, *The Inevitability of Patriarchy* (New York: William Morrow, 1974); and Warren Farrell, *The Myth of Male Power* (New York: Simon and Schuster, 1993).

6. Male studies has its own foundation (www.malestudies.org) and is now publishing a journal (http://newmalestudies.com/OJS/index.php/nms).

7. In the early 1990s, a rift occurred between the explicitly profeminist men's studies scholars associated with the National Organization for Men Against Sexism (NOMAS) and another group of scholars less committed to feminism. As a result, there exist today the NOMAS-affiliated Men's Studies Association (www.nomas.org/mensstudies) and the American Men's Studies Association (http://mensstudies.org/). The latter publishes *The Journal of Men's Studies* (www.mensstudies.info/journals/the-journal-of-mens-studies/). If there is a journal that could be said to be associated with the former, it would be Michael Kimmel's *Men and Masculinities*.

8. Imagine a Martian anthropologist studying the pre–Civil War US South. The Martian asks why the dark-skinned humans are laboring hard in the fields while the light-skinned humans are sipping mint juleps in the shade. A member of the latter group explains that this arrangement is a matter of people playing their proper race roles, and

action to change sexist laws, policies, or practices is required, either—just individual choice, regardless of the roots of those choices in patriarchy. For a discussion of the false empowerment problem, see Sherryl Kleinman, Martha Copp, and Kent Sandstrom, "Making Sexism Visible: Birdcages, Martians, and Pregnant Men," *Teaching Sociology* 24 (2006): 126–142. For an example of the kind of critical self-analysis required by a liberatory feminist project, see Sandra Bartky's *Femininity and Domination* (New York: Routledge, 1990).

27.   Belief in biological essentialism was boosted by a spate of popular books purporting that new findings in "brain science" reveal that differences in neurophysiology underlay differences in how girls/women and boys/men think, feel, and behave. See, for example, Deborah Blum, *Sex on the Brain* (New York: Penguin, 1998); Michael Gurian, *The Minds of Boys* (San Francisco: Jossey-Bass, 2005); Leonard Sax, *Why Gender Matters: What Parents and Teachers Need to Know about the Emerging Science of Sex Differences* (New York: Three Rivers, 2006); Louann Brizendine, *The Female Brain* (New York: Three Rivers, 2007) and *The Male Brain* (New York: Broadway, 2010).

28.   Epstein, *Deceptive Distinctions*; Eleanor Maccoby and Carol Jacklin, *The Psychology of Sex Differences* (Stanford, CA: Stanford University Press, 1974); Janet Shibley Hyde, "The Gender Similarities Hypothesis," *American Psychologist* 60 (2005): 581–592.

29.   Lorber, "Believing Is Seeing"; Anne Fausto-Sterling, *Myths of Gender: Biological Theories about Women and Men* (New York: Basic, 1985).

30.   For an introduction, see David M. Buss, *Evolutionary Psychology: The New Science of the Mind*, 4th ed. (Upper Saddle River, NJ: Pearson, 2011). See also David M. Buss, ed., *Handbook of Evolutionary Psychology* (New York: Wiley, 2005).

31.   Randy Thornhill and Nancy Wilmsen Thornhill, "The Evolutionary Psychology of Men's Coercive Sexuality," *Behavioral and Brain Sciences* 15 (1992): 363–375; Randy Thornhill and Craig T. Palmer, *A Natural History of Rape: Biological Bases of Sexual Coercion* (Cambridge, MA: MIT Press, 2000).

32.   See Stephen Jay Gould, "Darwinian Fundamentalism," *New York Review of Books* (June 12, 1997) and "Evolutionary Psychology: An Exchange," *New York Review of Books* (October 9, 1997). For other critiques, see Jerry Fodor, "The Selfish Gene Pool," *Times Literary Supplement* (July 27, 2005); and David J. Buller, *Adapting Minds: Evolutionary Psychology and the Persistent Quest for Human Nature* (Cambridge, MA: MIT Press, 2005).

33.   Books that have debunked claims that new findings in brain science can explain gender differences tend to get relatively little media attention. See, for example, Cordelia Fine's *Delusions of Gender: How Our Minds, Society, and Neurosexism Create Difference* (New York: Norton, 2011) and Rebecca M. Jordan-Young, *Brain Storm: The Flaws in the Science of Sex Differences* (Cambridge, MA: Harvard University Press, 2011).

34.   Christopher Shea, "The Nature-Nurture Debate, Redux," *The Chronicle Review* (January 9, 2009).

35.   See "'Doing Gender' as Canon or Agenda: A Symposium on West and Zimmerman," *Gender and Society* 23 (2009): 72–122.

36.   Michael Kimmel, "Declarations of War," *The Chronicle Review* (October 26, 2001). Kimmel, long identified as a profeminist sociologist and men's studies scholar,

lauded the "traditional masculinity" that supposedly led men to make heroic sacrifices during and after the terrorist attacks of September 11, 2001. "Traditional definitions of masculinity," Kimmel said, "certainly have their imperious sides, brimming with homophobia and sexism. But they also contain the capacity for quiet heroism, selfless sacrifice, steadfast resolve, deep wells of compassion and caring, and, yes, a love that made these men magnificent." By highlighting masculinity as the force behind men's magnificent behavior, Kimmel essentializes masculinity—by implying that it is a special quality inherent in men—and valorizes it. Women, however, behaved in no less heroic, self-sacrificing, resolute, compassionate, caring, and loving ways during and after the attacks. To what gender-wide character trait should their magnificent behavior be attributed?

37. In early 2013, US secretary of defense Leon Panetta announced a phased-in lifting of the ban on women in combat roles. For the Pentagon, this was largely a matter of efficient deployment of personnel in the era of an all-volunteer military. Both male and female bodies are needed to carry on war, and women had already been serving in near-frontline support roles, near enough to account for more than 130 deaths and 800 nonfatal casualties in Afghanistan and Iraq from 2001 to 2012. From a liberal standpoint, lifting the ban was hailed as a victory, as was the earlier move to end discrimination against gays and lesbians in the military. A more critical view might see the problem differently. The solution to the problem of militarism is not to put weapons in the hands of women, but to abolish the institutions that compel women and men to use weapons in the service of ruling-class interests.

38. Cynthia Enloe, "Wielding Masculinity Inside Abu Ghraib: Making Feminist Sense of an American Military Scandal," *Asian Journal of Women's Studies* 10 (2004): 89–102; Laura Sjoberg and Sandra Via, eds., *Gender, War, and Militarism* (Santa Barbara, CA: ABC-CLIO, 2010).

39. For a sampling of this genre, see Christina Hoff Sommers, *The War against Boys: How Misguided Feminism Is Harming Our Young Men* (New York: Simon and Schuster, 2001); Kay S. Hymowitz, *Manning Up: How the Rise of Women Has Turned Men into Boys* (New York: Basic, 2011); and Hanna Rosin, *The End of Men and the Rise of Women* (New York: Riverhead, 2012).

CHAPTER 3

1. My theses on the origins and evolution of male dominance are informed by Gerda Lerner, *The Creation of Patriarchy* (New York: Oxford University Press, 1996) and Peggy Reeves Sanday, *Female Power and Male Dominance: On the Origins of Sexual Inequality* (Cambridge: Cambridge University Press, 1981).

2. On the concept of a gender order, see R. W. Connell, *Gender* (Malden, MA: Polity, 2002).

3. This is essentially Max Weber's notion of the origins of the state. See his 1918 essay "Politics as a Vocation," in H. H. Gerth and C. Wright Mills, eds., *From Max Weber: Essays in Sociology* (New York: Oxford University Press, 1958), pp. 77–128.

4. David D. Gilmore, *Manhood in the Making* (New Haven, CT: Yale University Press, 1990).

5. These ingrained dispositions are cognitive and muscular, emotional and erotic. They are formed through social experiences that are consequences of the culture and social organization to which we are assimilated. Explicit instruction may play only a small part in this shaping process. We are, in any case, gendered creatures not merely as matters of definition, but also as matters of conditioned subjectivity.

6. Following Peter Berger and Thomas Luckmann, *The Social Construction of Reality* (New York: Anchor, 1966).

7. Alice H. Eagly and Wendy Wood, "The Origins of Sex Differences in Human Behavior," *American Psychologist* 54 (1999): 408–423; Jaime C. Confer, Judith A. Easton, Diana S. Fleischman, Cari D. Goetz, David M. G. Lewis, Carin Perilloux, and David M. Buss, "Evolutionary Psychology: Controversies, Questions, Prospects, and Limitations," *American Psychologist* 65 (2010): 110–126; David M. Buss and David P. Schmitt, "Evolutionary Psychology and Feminism," *Sex Roles* (2011) DOI 10.1007/s1199-011-9987-3.

8. The so-called gender binary is an enormously powerful cultural prescription that says there are two and only two genders, men and women, and that males must be men and females must be women. When it is forgotten (when one's sociological guard is down) that this construal of gender is a human invention, it is easy to collapse gender into sex and thus to equate males with men and females with women. When this mistake is made, a great deal of confusion ensues.

9. Cynthia Epstein, *Deceptive Distinctions: Sex, Gender, and the Social Order* (New Haven, CT: Yale University Press, 1988); Eleanor Maccoby and Carol Jacklin, *The Psychology of Sex Differences* (Stanford, CA: Stanford University Press, 1974); Janet Shibley Hyde, "The Gender Similarities Hypothesis," *American Psychologist* 60 (2005): 581–592.

10. Allan Johnson, *The Gender Knot*, 2nd ed. (Philadelphia: Temple University Press, 2006).

11. The line "religion is what keeps the poor from murdering the rich" is usually attributed to Napoleon Bonaparte. Fredric Jameson is often credited with the line "it is easier to imagine the end of the world than to imagine the end of capitalism." But Jameson precedes this phrase with "someone once said." See his essay "Future City," *New Left Review* 21 (2003): 65–79.

12. The point is that one must always take note of how systems of inequality intersect. For a classic statement, see Kimberle Crenshaw, "Mapping the Margins: Intersectionality, Identity Politics, and Violence against Women of Color," *Stanford Law Review* 43 (1991): 1241–1299. See also Chapter 1, note 26.

13. For more on the roots of this view in dramaturgical social psychology, see Michael Schwalbe and Heather Shay, "Dramaturgy and Dominance," in J. McLeod, E. Lawler, and M. Schwalbe, eds., *Handbook of the Social Psychology of Inequality* (New York: Springer, 2014), in press.

14. Gregory Stone, "Appearance and the Self: A Slightly Revised Version," in G. P. Stone and H. A. Farberman, eds., *Social Psychology through Symbolic Interaction*, 2nd ed. (New York: John Wiley and Sons, 1981), pp. 187–202.

15. Allan Johnson, *Privilege, Power, and Difference* (New York: McGraw-Hill, 2006).

16. The point again is about the need to consider intersectionality. The "patriarchal dividend," to use R. W. Connell's term, can be greater or lesser depending on where a male is located in race, class, sexual, and other social hierarchies. As a result of these locations, males are also differentially equipped with the cultural capital needed to put on a compelling manhood act.

17. Judith Lorber, "Believing Is Seeing: Biology as Ideology," in J. Lorber, *Paradoxes of Gender* (New Haven, CT: Yale University Press, 1994), pp. 37–54.

18. Daniel Chambliss, "The Mundanity of Excellence: An Ethnographic Report on Stratification and Olympic Swimmers," *Sociological Theory* 7 (1989): 70–86.

19. In face-to-face interaction, some information about ourselves is expressly given, some is "given off" by manner and appearance. The latter is typically under less control than the former; in fact, we are often unaware of all the information that we're giving off about who and what we are. See Erving Goffman, *The Presentation of Self in Everyday Life* (Garden City, NY: Doubleday Anchor, 1959), pp. 1–16.

20. Goffman, *Presentation*, p. 252.

21. Michael Schwalbe, "Goffman against Postmodernism: Emotion and the Reality of the Self," *Symbolic Interaction* 16 (1993): 333–350.

22. *Creditable*, not credible, is the correct term here. What matters—in terms of how an episode of face-to-face interaction plays out—is the social value accorded to the virtual self created by an actor's expressive behavior. To be creditable is to be worthy of the social value normally accorded to a particular kind of self in a given situation.

23. The literature on "female masculinity" examines how females, in various times and places, have adopted and adapted styles of self-presentation typically used by males who wish to claim the gender identity "man" and signify possession of masculine selves. My argument is that females can of course wield signifiers that elicit attributions of possessing a masculine self—that is, a self with the capacity to exert control and resist control—but that, owing to patriarchal convention, a female body is a semiotic liability in this kind of self-construction project. The literature on female masculinity, as I read it, gives less emphasis to signifying the capacity to exert and resist control, and more emphasis to satisfying and signifying sexual desire. See Judith Halberstam, *Female Masculinity* (Durham, NC: Duke University Press, 1998), and "The Good, the Bad, and the Ugly: Men, Women, and Masculinity," in J. K. Gardiner, *Masculinity Studies and Feminist Theory: New Directions* (New York: Columbia University Press, 2002), pp. 344–367.

24. Michael Messner, *Power at Play: Sports and the Problem of Masculinity* (Boston: Beacon Press, 1992).

25. Mariah Burton Nelson, *The Stronger Women Get, the More Men Love Football: Sexism and the American Culture of Sports* (New York: Avon, 1995).

26. Analytic discourse sometimes entails the invention of new terms, sometimes the specialized definition of terms familiar from everyday speech. The goals should be to use terms that aid the cognitive grasp of some phenomena of interest and also to be clear about what those terms mean. I've tried to do this with *manhood acts* and *masculine self*, giving these terms meanings that are useful for analysis but that do not necessarily

carry the same meanings in ordinary English. On the problem of finding an appropriate language for sociological analysis, see Howard S. Becker, "Goffman, Language, and
the Comparative Strategy," in H. S. Becker, *Telling about Society* (Chicago: University
of Chicago Press, 2007), pp. 223–237.

27. Jack Sattel, "The Inexpressive Male: Tragedy or Sexual Politics," *Social Problems*
23 (1976): 469–477.

28. Lest this thesis be misunderstood, I am saying that there are multiple ways to
signify a masculine self, not that there are "multiple masculinities."

29. See, for example, Robert Jackall, *Moral Mazes: The World of Corporate Managers*
(New York: Oxford University Press, 1988).

30. Michael Kimmel, "Masculinity as Homophobia: Fear, Shame, and Silence in
the Construction of Gender Identity," in H. Brod and M. Kaufman, eds., *Theorizing
Masculinities* (London: Sage, 1994), pp. 119–141.

31. Michael Schwalbe and Douglas Mason-Schrock, "Identity Work as Group Process," in B. Markovsky, M. Lovaglia, and R. Simon, eds., *Advances in Group Processes*
13 (1996): 115–149.

32. In the Google era, it is easy enough to find lists. For a list of "Top Ten Women
Who Were Really Men," see http://listverse.com/2008/09/04/top-10-men-who-were
-really-women/. For something more substantial than a list, see Diane Wood Middle-
brook, *Suits Me: The Double Life of Billy Tipton* (New York: Mariner, 1999).

33. Jarred Martin and Aymarlin Govender, "'Making Muscle Junkies': Investigating
Traditional Masculine Ideology, Body Image Discrepancy, and the Pursuit of Muscularity in Adolescent Males," *International Journal of Men's Health* 10 (2011): 220–239.

34. An act that began as a self-conscious act can feel authentic, if the actor comes
to believe in it. See Michael Schwalbe, "We Wear the Mask: Subordinated Masculinity
and the Persona Trap," in P. Vannini and P. Williams, eds., *Authenticity in Culture, Self,
and Society* (Burlington, VT: Ashgate, 2009), pp. 139–152.

35. Pierre Bourdieu, *Masculine Domination* (Stanford, CA: Stanford University Press,
1998), pp. 5–53. See also Leslie McCall, "Does Gender Fit? Bourdieu, Feminism, and
Conceptions of Social Order," *Theory and Society* 21 (1992): 837–867.

36. Accounts are given to repair damaged identities or to deflect potential damage.
See Marvin B. Scott and Stanford M. Lyman, "Accounts," *American Sociological Review*
33 (1968): 46–62. Accounts are likewise given to uphold and repair the virtual selves
being constructed in interaction. Anyone who undertakes to construct a manhood act
and elicit imputations of possessing a masculine self needs to master a repertoire of repair
accounts and also be able to improvise.

37. Kimmel, "Masculinity as Homophobia." See also Michael Kaufman, "The
Construction of Masculinity and the Triad of Men's Violence," in M. Kimmel and
M. Messner, eds., *Men's Lives*, 2nd ed. (New York: Macmillan, 1992), pp. 28–50.

38. Johnson, *Privilege*, p. 106, on "passive oppression."

39. This is West and Zimmerman's argument about why people enact gender in
conventional ways. It isn't that we *can't* act differently or imagine acting differently. The
problem is that if we fail to "do gender" properly (according to local norms) it will be
hard to get along with others, because we will be seen as weird, socially incompetent,

nonsensical, immoral, or possibly insane. See Candace West and Don Zimmerman, "Doing Gender," *Gender and Society* 1 (1987): 125–151.

40. For an example, see Michael Messner, "White Guy Habitus in the Classroom: Challenging the Reproduction of Privilege," *Men and Masculinities* 2 (2000): 457–469.

41. Much of this knowledge is tacit and consists of shared cognitive presuppositions. See Erving Goffman, "The Interaction Order," *American Sociological Review* 48 (1983): 1–17.

42. Michael Schwalbe, "Situation and Structure in the Making of Selves," in C. Edgley, ed., *The Drama of Social Life: A Dramaturgical Handbook* (Burlington, VT: Ashgate, 2013), pp. 75–92.

43. I have discussed this elsewhere using the concept "nets of accountability." See Michael Schwalbe, *Rigging the Game: How Inequality Is Reproduced in Everyday Life* (New York: Oxford University Press, 2008), pp. 170–182; and Schwalbe and Shay, "Dramaturgy and Dominance."

44. Joan Acker, *Class Questions, Feminist Answers* (Lanham, MD: Rowman and Littlefield, 2006).

45. Pierette Hondagneu-Sotelo and Michael Messner, "Gender Displays and Men's Power: The 'New Man' and the Mexican Immigrant Man," in H. Brod and M. Kaufman, eds., *Research on Men and Masculinities: Theorizing Masculinities* (Thousand Oaks, CA: Sage, 1994), pp. 200–219. See also Michael Messner, "The Masculinity of the Governator: Muscle and Compassion in American Politics," *Gender and Society* 21 (2007): 461–480.

46. Deference in interaction is not always a matter of acquiescing to the demands of a higher-status or more powerful person. More often, presuming interaction between status equals whose interests are not antagonistic, deference is a matter of showing ritual respect for the self of an other. See Erving Goffman, "The Nature of Deference and Demeanor," in E. Goffman, *Interaction Ritual* (New York: Pantheon, 1967), pp. 47–95.

47. Owed to Sinikka Elliott.

48. Arthur Brittan, *Masculinity and Power* (New York: Basil Blackwell, 1989), pp. 77–107.

49. Sam Gindin, "Anti-Capitalism and the Terrain of Social Justice," *Monthly Review* 53 (2002): 1–14.

50. Carol Cohn, "Sex and Death in the Rational World of Defense Intellectuals," *Signs* 12 (1987): 687–718. See also Tim Curry, "A Little Pain Never Hurt Anybody: Athletic Career Socialization and the Normalization of Sport Injury," *Symbolic Interaction* 16 (1993): 273–290; and Don Sabo, "Pigskin, Patriarchy, and Pain," in Kimmel and Messner, *Men's Lives*, pp. 158–161.

51. Rachel Kalish and Michael Kimmel, "Suicide by Mass Murder: Masculinity, Aggrieved Entitlement, and Rampage School Shootings," *Health Sociology Review* 19 (2010): 451–464.

52. Nor is justice served when members of previously excluded racial minority groups attain power in exploitive social hierarchies and behave in a manner indistinguishable from dominant group members. See Wendell Berry, *The Hidden Wound* (San Francisco: North Point, 1989).

.org/ama/pub/physician-resources/medical-ethics/code-medical-ethics/opinion2067
.page.

10. The psychological distress associated with killing another human being usually decreases with distance. Although killing by drone is remote, pre-kill drone surveillance can give drone operators a close look at a victim's daily life, thus heightening the prospects for distress and post-traumatic stress disorder. See Dave Grossman, *On Killing* (New York: Back Bay, 2009), esp. pp. 43–49, 284–293.

11. These odious principles were briefly on prominent display when Joe Klein, a writer for *Time Magazine*, in an interview on MSNBC's *Morning Joe* program (October 23, 2012), spoke in defense of Obama's drone program, despite the collateral deaths of children. "The bottom line," Klein said, "is whose four-year-old gets killed? What we're doing is limiting the possibility that four-year-olds here will get killed by indiscriminate acts of terror." As journalist Glenn Greenwald pointed out, this is the same sociopathic rationalization used by terrorists who kill civilians, including children, who have nothing to do with US foreign policy.

12. Carol Cohn describes how "defense intellectuals" speak casually of sanitized mega-deaths and refuse to include in their conversations people who raise concerns about the human suffering caused by bombs and war. See Cohn, "Sex and Death in the Rational World of Defense Intellectuals," *Signs* 12 (1987): 687–718.

13. Despite a lawsuit brought by the ACLU and the Center for Constitutional Rights, as of January 2013, the Obama administration's memo supposedly offering a legal rationale for the targeted killing of US citizens remained secret. See "Judge Backs Obama Administration on Targeting Killings of Terrorism Suspects," *Washington Post* (January 2, 2013).

14. Nicola Abé, "Dreams in Infrared: The Woes of an American Drone Operator," *Spiegel Online International* (December 14, 2012). Available at www.spiegel.de/international/world/pain-continues-after-war-for-american-drone-pilot-a-872726.html.

15. Ward Churchill, "Some People Push Back: On the Justice of Roosting Chickens," *Pockets of Resistance* (2001), p. 20. The essay is reprinted in Churchill, *On the Justice of Roosting Chickens: Reflections on the Consequences of US Imperial Arrogance and Criminality* (Oakland, CA: AK Press, 2003).

16. See, for example, Chalmers Johnson, *Blowback: The Costs and Consequences of American Empire* (New York: Metropolitan, 2000). An updated version of Johnson's book, published in 2004, was a best seller. The "blowback" argument applied to the 9/11 attacks was unpopular in some ideological quarters, but it was widely embraced by hard-nosed policy intellectuals on the left and the right. Churchill's mistake was to issue an indiscriminate and incendiary statement about who deserved to suffer from the blowback.

17. A 2006 *National Geographic*–Roper survey found that 63 percent of Americans aged eighteen to twenty-four could not locate Iraq on a map of the Middle East, though the US had invaded that country three years earlier. The study also found that 70 percent could not locate Iran or Israel. See John Roach, "Young Americans Geographically Illiterate, Survey Suggests," *National Geographic News* (May 2, 2006). A more recent study found similar results. See "Geography 2010: National Assessment of Educational

Progress at Grades 4, 8, and 12," Institute of Educational Sciences, National Center for Education Statistics, US Department of Education, NCES 2011-467.

18. Grossman, *On Killing*, pp. 251–263.

19. "Obama's Speech to Troops at Fort Bragg," *New York Times* (December 14, 2011).

20. There is a vast literature that deconstructs the lies told by political elites to justify war. By way of recent works, I recommend David Swanson's *War Is a Lie* (Charlottesville, VA: WarIsALie.Org, 2010) and Chris Hedges's *War Is a Force That Gives Us Meaning* (New York: Anchor, 2003). See also Chris Hedges, "War Is Betrayal," *Boston Review* (2012) July/August, pp. 32–37. A more visual and visceral antidote to these lies is Ernst Friedrich's classic *War against War!* (Seattle: Real Comet Press, 1967).

21. The consequences of the US invasion and occupation of Iraq are documented in a variety of sources. See "The US Is Blind to the Price of War That Is Still Being Borne by the Iraqi People," *Guardian/UK* (December 19, 2011), www.guardian.co.uk /commentisfree/2011/dec/18/us-blind-price-paid-iraqis; "Post-American Iraq by the Numbers," *Informed Comment* (December 14, 2011), www.juancole.com /2011/12/post-american-iraq-by-the-numbers.html; "The Iraq War Disaster," *In the Middle* (December 15, 2011), http://raedinthemiddle.blogspot.com /2011/12/ iraq-war-disaster.html; "Iraq, Afghanistan, and the End of US Supremacy," *Tom-Dispatch* (January 3, 2012), www.tomdispatch.com/post/175484/tomgram%3A _engelhardt%2C_lessons_from_lost_wars_in_2012/.

22. "Iraq: Intensifying Crackdown on Free Speech, Protests," *Human Rights Watch* (January 22, 2012), www.hrw.org/news/2012/01/22/iraq-intensifying-crackdown-free -speech-protests; "Baghdad Car Bombs Kill 14, Injure Dozens," *CBC News* (January 24, 2012), www.cbc.ca/news/world/story/2012/01/24/iraq-bombings.html. The violence continued throughout 2012 ("At Least 20 Die in Series of Bomb Attacks throughout Iraq," *New York Times* [November 14, 2012], www.nytimes.com/2012/11/15/world /middleeast/Iraq-attacks.html?partner=rss&emc=rss&smid=tw-nytimes) and continues as of this writing ("Violence in Iraq Swells at Year's End, Leaving at Least 3 Dozen Dead," *New York Times* [December 31, 2012], www.nytimes.com/2013/01/01/world /middleeast/attacks-in-iraq-leave-at-least-3-dozen-dead.html). For an up-to-date accounting of violent civilian deaths attributable to the US invasion, see Iraq Body Count (www.iraqbodycount.org/).

23. In 2012, Mercer continued to rank Baghdad as the world's least livable city. See www.mercer.com/qualityofliving.

24. For more on the Downing Street memo, see http://downingstreetmemo.com/. The Wikipedia entry provides a useful summary of the memo and the controversy it sparked. See http://en.wikipedia.org/wiki/Downing_Street_memo. Some political commentators (e.g., Christopher Hitchens) dismissed the significance of the memo on the grounds that it was an open secret, hence no big deal, that Western powers, mainly the United States and Britain, were eager to install a friendlier regime in Iraq. Those who found the memo damning said it showed how intelligence claims about the imminent danger posed by Saddam Hussein were contrived to suit a policy of aggressive war and regime change.

25. Madeleine Albright, *The Mighty and the Almighty: Reflections on America, God, and World Affairs* (New York: Harper Perennial, 2007), p. 55.

26. Howard Zinn's *A People's History of the United States* (New York: Harper Perennial, 2005) is a good antidote to the myth of American exceptionalism. So, too, is William Blum's *Killing Hope: US Military and CIA Interventions since World War II* (Monroe, ME: Common Courage, 2004, updated edition).

27. Many veterans struggle to reduce the dissonance between the idea that they are decent, intelligent people, and the idea that they have been duped into helping to violently oppress others. One way to reduce this dissonance is to embrace the myth of having performed honorable, patriotic service to protect their loved ones and fellow citizens against an evil, threatening enemy. Obama's speech, like all such speeches by political elites, exploits this general psychological tendency to seek relief from painful cognitive dissonance.

28. There is a long history of ex-soldiers, having experienced the horrors of war and seen the truths hidden by the lies of politicians, becoming powerful and eloquent antiwar activists. See, for example, Iraq Veterans Against the War (www.ivaw.org/). The problem, of course, is that the power of elites to propagandize, combined with the prospect of achieving manhood status through participation in collective acts of domination, ensures that many young males will continue to seek soldierhood and, without a critical perspective from which to examine their lives, justify it.

29. For example, Oded Na'aman, "The Checkpoint: Terror, Power, and Cruelty," *Boston Review* (July/August 2012): 39–45.

30. The brutally honest words of Marine general Smedley Butler are worth quoting: "I spent 33 years and four months in active military service, and during that period I spent most of my time as a high-class muscle man for Big Business, for Wall Street and the bankers. In short, I was a racketeer, a gangster for capitalism. I helped make Mexico and especially Tampico safe for American oil interests in 1914. I helped make Haiti and Cuba a decent place for the National City Bank boys to collect revenues in. I helped in the raping of half a dozen Central American republics for the benefit of Wall Street. I helped purify Nicaragua for the International Banking House of Brown Brothers in 1902–1912. I brought light to the Dominican Republic for the American sugar interests in 1916. I helped make Honduras right for the American fruit companies in 1903. In China in 1927 I helped see to it that Standard Oil went on its way unmolested. Looking back on it, I might have given Al Capone a few hints. The best he could do was to operate his racket in three districts. I operated on three continents." See Hans Schmidt, *Maverick Marine: General Smedley D. Butler and the Contradictions of American Military History* (Lexington: University Press of Kentucky, 1998), p. 231.

CHAPTER 5

1. Michael Schwalbe, *The Psychosocial Consequences of Natural and Alienated Labor* (Albany: SUNY Press, 1986), pp. 207–208.

2. Peter Knapp and Alan Spector, *Crisis and Change Today: Basic Questions of Marxist Sociology*, 2nd ed. (Lanham, MD: Rowman and Littlefield, 2011).

3. The size of the capitalist class depends on precisely how one defines a capitalist. When I refer to "less than 2 percent" of the US population, I am referring to large-scale capitalists who own and control the major means of production. This excludes small businesses that employ fewer than ten workers. See Erik O. Wright, Cynthia Costello, David Hachen, and Joey Sprague, "The American Class Structure," *American Sociological Review* 47 (1982): 709–726. See also Wright, *Class Counts: Comparative Studies in Class Analysis* (New York: Cambridge University Press, 1996).

4. See Patricia Hill Collins, *Black Feminist Thought* (New York: Routledge, 1990); Leslie McCall, "The Complexity of Intersectionality," *Signs* 30 (2005): 1772–1800; Hae Yeon Choo and Myra Marx Ferree, "Practicing Intersectionality in Sociological Research: A Critical Analysis of Inclusions, Interactions, and Institutions in the Study of Inequalities," *Sociological Theory* 28 (2010): 129–149. There is of course a Wikipedia page on intersectionality.

5. For example, Oliver Cromwell Cox, *Class, Caste, and State: A Study in Social Dynamics* (New York: Monthly Review Press, 1948); Sheila Rowbotham, *Woman's Consciousness, Man's World* (New York: Penguin, 1973); Michele Barrett, *Women's Oppression Today* (New York: Verso, 1980). Earlier considerations of "intersectionality," though discussed in different terms, can be found in the writings of Friedrich Engels, Rosa Luxemburg, Emma Goldman, and W. E. B. Du Bois.

6. Karl Marx, *Karl Marx: Early Writings*, T. B. Bottomore, ed. and trans. (London: C. A. Watts [1844] 1963). See also Schwalbe, *Psychosocial Consequences*, pp. 7–27.

7. Melvin Seeman, "On the Meaning of Alienation," *American Sociological Review* 26 (1959): 753–758.

8. For discussions of alienation studies over the last fifty years, see Melvin Seeman, "Alienation Studies," *Annual Review of Sociology* 1 (1975): 91–123; Kai Erikson, "Work and Alienation," *American Sociological Review* 51 (1986): 1–8; and Chris Yuill, "Forgetting and Remembering Alienation Theory," *History of the Human Sciences* 24 (2011): 103–119.

9. Candace West and Sarah Fenstermaker, "Doing Difference," *Gender and Society* 9 (1995): 8–37. See also "Symposium on West and Fenstermaker's 'Doing Difference,'" *Gender and Society* 9 (1995): 491–513. The idea that gender is done differently depending on race, class, sexuality, and ethnicity underlies the "multiple masculinities" approach to studying men critiqued in Chapter 2.

10. Philip J. Wood, *Southern Capitalism: The Political Economy of North Carolina, 1880–1980* (Durham, NC: Duke University Press, 1976); Theodore W. Allen, *The Invention of the White Race: Racial Oppression and Social Control* (London: Verso, 1994).

11. Michael Omi and Howard Winant, *Racial Formation in the United States*, 2nd ed. (New York: Routledge, 1994); Peggy Reeves Sanday, *Female Power and Male Dominance* (New York: Cambridge University Press, 1981); Joan Acker, *Class Questions, Feminist Answers* (Lanham, MD: Rowman and Littlefield, 2006); Barrett, *Women's Oppression*.

12. The point about males' greater size, strength, speed, and skill with weapons is sometimes misunderstood to mean that all males are bigger, stronger, faster, and more

skilled with weapons than all females. Obviously, this is not true. The physical differences are differences *on average*. Skill with weapons is also a difference on average, but it can be a sharp and substantial difference if training in the use of weapons is strictly sex-segregated.

13. In *Code of the Street* (New York: Norton, 1999), Elijah Anderson describes the importance of a convincing manhood act even on the part of males who are not bent on hurting or hustling anyone. The act is defensive, intended to forestall victimization. It is a protective adaptation in an environment where there is a good chance of encountering predatory males.

14. R. W. Connell, *Masculinities* (Berkeley: University of California Press, 1995), p. 79.

15. "The soldier realizes he should not act on empathy since empathy can be manipulated. But can he suppress this natural sentiment? It takes time." See Oded Na'aman, "The Checkpoint: Terror, Power, and Cruelty," *Boston Review* (July/August 2012): 39–45.

16. Robert Jackall examines this in terms of the bureaucratic ethos embraced by ambitious corporate managers. See *Moral Mazes: The World of Corporate Managers* (New York: Oxford University Press, 1988).

17. R. W. Connell and James W. Messerschmidt, "Hegemonic Masculinity: Rethinking the Concept," *Gender and Society* 19 (2005): 829–859.

18. Peter M. Hall, "Meta-Power, Social Organization, and the Shaping of Social Action," *Symbolic Interaction* 20 (1997): 397–418; and "Interactionism, Social Organization, and Social Processes: Looking Back There, Reflecting Now Here, and Moving Ahead Then," *Symbolic Interaction* 26 (2003): 33–55.

19. Michael Schwalbe, *Rigging the Game: How Inequality Is Reproduced in Everyday Life* (New York: Oxford University Press, 2008), pp. 170–182. See also M. Schwalbe and H. Shay, "Dramaturgy and Dominance," in J. McLeod, E. Lawler, and M. Schwalbe, eds., *Handbook of the Social Psychology of Inequality* (New York: Springer, 2014), in press.

20. Marvin B. Scott and Stanford M. Lyman, "Accounts," *American Sociological Review* 33 (1968): 46–62. On accountability, see Jocelyn A. Hollander, "'I Demand More of People': Accountability, Interaction, and Gender Change," *Gender and Society* 27: 5–29.

21. Terri L. Orbuch, "People's Accounts Count: The Sociology of Accounts," *Annual Review of Sociology* 23 (1997): 455–478.

22. Candace West and Don Zimmerman, "Accounting for Doing Gender," *Gender and Society* 23: 112–122. See also Hollander, "'I Demand More of People.'"

23. Anthony Giddens, *The Constitution of Society: Outline of the Theory of Structuration* (Cambridge, UK: Polity Press, 1984).

24. On side bets, see Howard S. Becker, "Notes on the Nature of Commitment," *American Journal of Sociology* 66 (1960): 32–42.

25. To be willing to use force against others, police and soldiers must accept the legitimacy of those who give them orders. Police and soldiers also have bills to pay and many side bets riding on keeping their jobs. Economic necessity thus enmeshes them in a net of accountability that compels *their* obedience to those through whom economic resources flow and from whom come orders to coerce others.

26. Joel Bakan, *The Corporation: The Pathological Pursuit of Profit and Power* (New York: Simon and Schuster, 2004).

27. Hans H. Gerth and C. Wright Mills, eds., *From Max Weber: Essays in Sociology* (New York: Oxford University Press, 1958), p. 82. See also Anthony Giddens, *Capitalism and Modern Social Theory* (New York: Cambridge University Press, 1971), pp. 234–235.

28. Young males from lower-class or working-class backgrounds often feel uncomfortable in entry-level service jobs that require submission to female bosses. For these young males, the feeling of social value that comes from putting on a compensatory manhood act may be canceled by having to take orders from a member of the lower-status gender group. Getting started on a path to a middle-class job may thus be difficult. See Philippe Bourgois, *In Search of Respect* (New York: Cambridge University Press, 1996); Jay MacLeod, *Ain't No Makin' It*, 3rd ed. (Boulder, CO: Westview, 2009).

29. Some of our most powerful feelings are those attached to images of ourselves. Social psychologists argue that a great deal of our behavior is motivated by a desire to protect these images and feelings. See Viktor Gecas, "The Self-Concept," *Annual Review of Sociology* 8 (1982): 1–33; and Roy Baumeister, "The Self," in R. F. Baumeister and Eli J. Finkel, eds., *Advanced Social Psychology: The State of the Science* (New York: Oxford University Press, 2010), pp. 139–175. Erving Goffman and subsequent dramaturgical social psychologists make the same argument. See Michael Schwalbe, "Situation and Structure in the Making of Selves," in C. Edgley, ed., *The Drama of Social Life: A Dramaturgical Handbook* (Burlington, VT: Ashgate, 2013), pp. 75–92.

30. The image of oneself as inadequate arises from the clash between the achievement ideology—which consists of the notions that everyone has an equal opportunity to get ahead, that merit is recognized and rewarded, and that all it takes to get ahead is effort and intelligence—and the limited opportunity structure offered by a capitalist society, an opportunity structure that guarantees failure for most. For males who construct themselves as men this clash between ideological promise and economic reality can be especially painful and evoke self-blame. For a classic study, see Richard Sennett and Jonathan Cobb, *The Hidden Injuries of Class* (New York: Vintage, 1972).

31. Or not so trivial. James Messerschmidt has analyzed criminal behaviors, from the petty to the monumental, as elements of (what I would call) manhood acts. See J. W. Messerschmidt, *Masculinities and Crime: Critique and Reconceptualization of Theory* (Lanham, MD: Rowman and Littlefield, 1993), and *Hegemonic Masculinities and Camouflaged Politics* (Boulder, CO: Paradigm, 2010).

32. Douglas Schrock and Michael Schwalbe, "Men, Masculinity, and Manhood Acts," *Annual Review of Sociology* 35 (2009): 277–295.

33. See Chapters 1 (Gender Theory after Auschwitz), 4 (Drone Morality), and 7 (Feminism or Barbarism).

34. Elsewhere my colleagues and I have called this "subordinate adaptation." See Michael Schwalbe, Sandra Godwin, Daphne Holden, Douglas Schrock, Shealy Thompson, and Michelle Wolkomir, "Generic Processes in the Reproduction of Inequality: An Interactionist Analysis," *Social Forces* 79 (2000): 419–452.

35. It is not that people have no awareness of what they're up to, or no insight into their motives. Yet there are a great many things about the childhood experiences that

shape us, about our habitual practices, about our desires, and about the effects of our actions that we simply cannot or will not see. Sometimes the celebration of "agency" or the reluctance to appear to condescend leads social analysts to forget that all people have blind spots, strong needs to rationalize and justify their behavior, and only a limited ability to see the social implications of that behavior. This is why we do social science at all. The point is to observe and analyze in disciplined ways the very things about us that we are least inclined to observe and analyze in disciplined ways—and thereby understand ourselves better than we otherwise could.

36.   Theodore Allen, *Invention*. See also Alexander Saxton, *The Rise and Fall of the White Republic: Class Politics and Mass Culture in America*, 2nd ed. (London: Verso, 2003); Noel Ignatiev, *How the Irish Became White* (New York: Routledge, 2008); David Roediger, *The Wages of Whiteness: Race and the Making of the American Working Class*, 2nd ed. (London: Verso, 2007); and George M. Fredrickson, *Racism: A Short History* (Princeton, NJ: Princeton University Press, 2003).

CHAPTER 6

1.   In *Femininity and Domination* (New York: Routledge, 1990), Sandra Bartky argues that feminist consciousness is *anguished* consciousness, because one constantly struggles with the internal contradictions between a feminist rejection of patriarchy and the habits of thought and behavior instilled by patriarchy. Feminist consciousness, in this view, is not something at which one comfortably arrives, but something one constantly struggles to maintain and develop.

2.   I am referring to being held accountable in the ethnomethodological/dramaturgical sense, as discussed in previous chapters. Even if male privilege and class privilege shielded me from many intrusive demands to explain my desire to become a woman, I would still feel compelled to make sense of this action to people with whom it was important to maintain relationships. For emotional and practical reasons, I would want to avoid being seen by friends, family members, and colleagues as nutty, unstable, or confused. Hence some kind of account would be necessary, and perhaps different accounts for different audiences.

3.   See, for example, Tre Wentling, Elroi Windsor, Kristen Schilt, and Betsy Lucal, "Teaching Transgender," *Teaching Sociology* 36 (2008): 49–57. The authors say nothing about how to approach the *analysis* of transgenderism as a social construction. The message, rather, is about how to create "trans-friendly syllabi, courses, and classrooms" and how to "positively integrate transgender communities into the classroom." Sociological analysis that is not explicitly trans-positive appears to be ruled out for its unfriendliness.

4.   The facts of male dominance and gender inequality throughout recorded human history are not in question. What is often thought to be less readily demonstrable is the degree to which the gender order is a cultural rather than biological construct. If cross-cultural differences and historical changes in gender norms and practices are not convincing, consider only the last fifty years in the Western world and the progress that has been made, at least in some quarters, toward eliminating the most blatant forms of

gender discrimination. Consider, too, the acceptance that transgenderism has achieved in just the last decade. If nothing else, these changes should attest to the fact that gender orders are human inventions potentially subject to reinvention. Or abolition.

5. See Bartky, *Femininity and Domination*, pp. 45–62. For an illustration of why it's important to subject sexual desire to political analysis, see Margot Weiss, *Techniques of Pleasure: BDSM and the Circuits of Sexuality* (Durham, NC: Duke University Press, 2011).

6. If most of the experiences that shape our erotic attachments occur when we are children and pass unnoticed—which is to say that we are not aware, at the time, that those experiences are shaping our sexuality—then it is understandable that sexual orientation does not seem to be a choice. If we have little or no insight into how we become erotically oriented to certain body types, body parts, or embodied practices, then it is likely to seem that we were "born this way," whatever "this way" might be. But this does not mean that sexuality is impervious to sociological analysis. It just means that it is hard for us to understand how we're being shaped by experiences while we're in the midst of those experiences. By the time the results are in, so to speak, it may be impossible to recall the experiences that produced those results.

7. On the concept of a gender order, see R. W. Connell, *Gender* (Malden, MA: Polity, 2002).

8. People who claim transgender identities can still suffer from discrimination and tremendous hostility. But many mainstream institutions (governments, universities, corporations) have readily accepted claims that trans people are a category of people whose rights should be protected by antidiscrimination laws and policies. Part of this ready acceptance—and no doubt some trans activists would disagree about how "ready" this acceptance has been—seems to me attributable to the fact that transgenderism poses no threat to capitalism's core economic and political hierarchies.

9. Although it is possible to signify a masculine self and claim manhood status in more or less destructive ways, all manhood acts and all claims to manhood status, it has been my point to establish, are inherently about domination. For discussions that consider the ethically problematic nature of masculinity in the context of transgender-ism, see Bernice L. Hausman, "Recent Transgender Theory," *Feminist Studies* 27 (2001): 465–490; Cressida J. Heyes, "Feminist Solidarity after Queer Theory: The Case of Transgender," *Signs* 28 (2003): 1093–1120; and Patricia Elliot, "Engaging Trans Debates on Gender Variance: A Feminist Analysis," *Sexualities* 12 (2009): 5–32.

10. See Michael Schwalbe, *The Sociologically Examined Life*, 4th ed. (New York: McGraw-Hill, 2008), pp. 56–78.

11. Based on what I've seen in the blogosphere, I'm not hopeful that a plea to avoid name-calling and focus on arguments will make much difference. People with impec-cable feminist credentials and serious, thoughtful views on gender politics have been vilified as transphobic bigots and "haters" for taking a critical, analytic stance toward transgenderism. This is, I think, a shame. Figuring out how to overcome gender as a system of inequality requires analysis of the various ways that people adapt to its oppres-sive aspects. If some of those adaptations—transgenderism, for example—are deemed off limits for analysis, the larger feminist project of social transformation is weakened.

Every adaptation should be examined for its liabilities as well as its liberatory potential. Every serious analysis should be seriously and civilly engaged, even if such an analysis discomfits people who are invested in a particular adaptation. The point, again, is not to blame or celebrate individuals for how they respond to oppressive social arrangements over which they have no control. The point is to find reasons for change and better ways forward. Of course, what constitutes "forward" is also a crucial matter for discussion.

12. Sheila Jeffreys, *Beauty and Misogyny* (New York: Routledge, 2005), pp. 46–66.

13. Transgender rights advocates have made the same point about the stories demanded by mainstream medical institutions that embrace a conventional gender ideology. See, for example, Dean Spade, "Resisting Medicine, Re/modeling Gender," *Berkeley Women's Law Journal* 18 (2003): 15–37.

14. In a 2012 radio interview, Jeffreys suggested another reason some young lesbians find it difficult to live in women's bodies today: "[it is] not simply that they find it difficult to be lesbians or to love women in the bodies of women.... I think they find it difficult to be women because of the way women are treated at this particular stage of male dominance—the pornification of young women, the way they are supposed to carry themselves, the contempt with which they are treated, the way the pornography industry has had an impact on the very concept of woman and the way women are able to think about themselves. That's been so very severe that I think that many young women—who wish to be self-respecting—find it difficult to picture themselves as women, or to inhabit the bodies of women, and I think we've got to recognize, very unfortunately, that for many young lesbians who transgender through surgery and drugs, [this] will have very harmful effects on their bodies—for instance, they have hysterectomies very, very young, and then have to take drugs all their lives, or they have premature menopause. Apart from all that, they are able to access some of the things that men have allocated to themselves, such as safety walking down the streets, promotion at work, being listened to and paid better attention—all very important social goods that are allocated to the class of men in male domination [and] which can seem very attractive to women who no longer wish to remain in the despised class of womanhood." See "'Anybody Can Be Absolutely Anything if They Simply Say They Are': An Interview with Sheila Jeffreys on Transgenderism and Feminism," *The F Word* (CFRO 102.7 FM, Vancouver, BC, May 7, 2012), available at http://feministcurrent.com/5039/anybody-can-be-absolutely-anything-if-they-simply-say-they-are-an-interview-with-sheila-jeffreys-on-transgenderism-and-feminism/.

15. The transracialist constructed in the teaching exercise seeks to enact a demeaning stereotype, though apparently without realizing it. The teaching exercise was written this way to highlight the issue of how dominant group members rarely grasp the experiential realities of subordinate group members. I do not mean to suggest that all transgender people—transitioning in either direction—seek to enact stereotypical versions of manhood or womanhood. There is in fact wide variation in aims and enactments.

16. I think most people are as smart as university professors, at least in terms of native intelligence. I also think that most thoughtful, well-informed adults can see through a lot of political bullshit. On the other hand, it is not only possible but routine for masses of people to be lied to, denied full and accurate information, fed false analyses, and generally propagandized by elites who seek to preserve the status quo. It's also common

to grow up imbibing the myths of one's own ethnic or national culture, and perhaps, because the need for self-justification is so strong, never seriously question those myths.

17. The idea that people are experts on their own experience is useful for bolstering the claims of people in oppressed groups who report discriminatory treatment and abuse. Too often members of privileged groups are oblivious to these realities, and so the credibility of reports from members of oppressed groups needs to be affirmed. But to extend this principle to include analysis of how the experiences of oppression are created, goes too far. This overextension forbids analysis by all except a select (and usually self-selected) group of insiders. For a classic statement on the insider/outsider problem in social research, see Robert Merton, "Insiders and Outsiders: A Chapter in the Sociology of Knowledge," *American Journal of Sociology* 78 (1972): 9–47.

18. On feminist therapy, see Chapter 2, note 11. Younger readers unfamiliar with the writings that came out of the women's consciousness-raising movement should see Robin Morgan's *Sisterhood Is Powerful* (New York: Random House, 1970) and the 1978 Redstockings compendium *Feminist Revolution* (see www.redstockings.org/).

19. Brian Fay, *Critical Social Science* (Ithaca, NY: Cornell University Press, 1987), pp. 143–164.

20. Knowledge of oneself or one's group always depends in part on being able to take the perspectives of others. The powerful have little incentive to do this vis-à-vis the powerless, whereas the powerless have great incentive to take the perspectives of the powerful—survival can depend on it. As a result, members of marginalized and oppressed groups often understand the powerful better than the powerful understand themselves. And so while all knowledge is created from some standpoint, some standpoints are better than others when it comes to seeing certain things about the social world. See Patricia Hill Collins's *Black Feminist Thought* (New York: Routledge, 1991) and Dorothy Smith's *The Everyday World as Problematic* (Boston: Northeastern University Press, 1987) for what have become the modern classic statements on feminist standpoint epistemology. As I argue in the text, however, the fact that an analysis comes from the margins does not guarantee that it is empirically correct or logically coherent.

21. On false empowerment and the denial of social harm, see Sherryl Kleinman and Martha Copp, "Denying Social Harm: Students' Resistance to Lessons about Inequality," *Teaching Sociology* 37 (2009): 283–293.

22. In addition to discussions by Hausman, Heyes, and Elliot cited in note 9, see Judith Halberstam, *Female Masculinity* (Durham, NC: Duke University Press, 1998), and R. W. Connell, "Transsexual Women and Feminist Thought: Toward New Understanding and New Politics," *Signs* 37 (2012): 857–881.

23. A libertarian perspective sees gender identity and expression as matters that should be subject to individual determination—without apology and without hindrance arising from conventional understandings—including feminist ones—of gender. Expressions of transsexual libertarianism can be found in Viviane Namaste, *Sex Change, Social Change: Reflections on Identity, Institutions, and Imperialism* (Toronto: Women's Press, 2005); Jay Prosser, *Second Skins: Body Narratives of Transsexuality* (New York: Columbia University Press, 1998); Henry Rubin, *Self-Made Men: Identity and Embodiment among Transsexual Men* (Nashville, TN: Vanderbilt University Press, 2003). A clear strain of

14, 2012); Michael Hastings, "The Rise of the Killer Drones: How America Goes to War in Secret," *Rolling Stone* (April 16, 2012).

11. Michael Schwalbe, "New Tobacco Image Masks Deadly Business as Usual," *Raleigh News and Observer* (August 2, 2004).

12. Matt Taibbi, "How Wall Street Is Using the Bailout to Stage a Revolution," *Rolling Stone* (April 2, 2009).

13. Maria Mies and Vandana Shiva, *Ecofeminism* (London: Zed Books, 1993); Val Plumwood, *Feminism and the Mastery of Nature* (New York: Routledge, 1994).

14. Ernest Callenbach, "Epistle to the Ecotopians: Last Words to an America in Decline," *TomDispatch.com* (May 7, 2012).

15. Sam Gindin reminds us that capitalism is inherently unjust in that it denies the vast majority of people the right to full and free development of their human potential. See his essay, "Anti-Capitalism and the Terrain of Social Justice," *Monthly Review* 53 (2002): 1–14.

16. Chris Hedges, *War Is a Force That Gives Us Meaning* (New York: Anchor, 2003).

17. Steven Pinker, *The Better Angels of Our Nature: Why Violence Has Declined* (New York: Viking, 2011).

18. Robert Kagan, *The World America Made* (New York: Knopf, 2012).

19. Andrew Bacevich, "Glory Days: A Pundit's Rosy View of the Pax Americana," *Harper's Magazine* (June 2012), pp. 70–72.

20. For critiques of Pinker's claims, see David Peterson, "Reality Denial: Steven Pinker's Apologetics for Western-Imperial Violence," *ZNet* (July 25, 2012); Edward S. Herman and David Peterson, "Steven Pinker on the Alleged Decline of Violence," *ZNet* (December 2, 2012); John Gray, "Delusions of Peace," *Prospect* (September 21, 2011).

21. Readers skeptical about the possibility of creating radically egalitarian social relations might wish to consider which course is likely to lead to a better human future: continuing to organize ourselves based on the exploitive social hierarchies to which manhood acts and contests for manhood status are endemic, or *striving* for equality and democracy—even if we never achieve perfection. The latter path seems likely to be longer and offer a journey worth making.

22. Ideologically narrow views of human nature keep us from seeing how alternative social arrangements could nurture human capacities other than those nurtured by capitalism. See Agustin Fuentes, *Race, Monogamy, and Other Lies They Told You: Busting Myths about Human Nature* (Berkeley: University of California Press, 2012).

23. C. Wright Mills, *The Power Elite* (New York: Oxford University Press, 1956), pp. 221–222. Crackpot realism arises when those who wield great economic, political, and military power embrace beliefs created in an echo chamber from which disruptive facts and dissenting voices are excluded. Crackpot realism is the mistaking of these self-serving delusions for accurate depictions of the world beyond elite enclaves. Were it not for the existence of a power elite capable of doing great damage to the rest of humanity, there would be no problem.